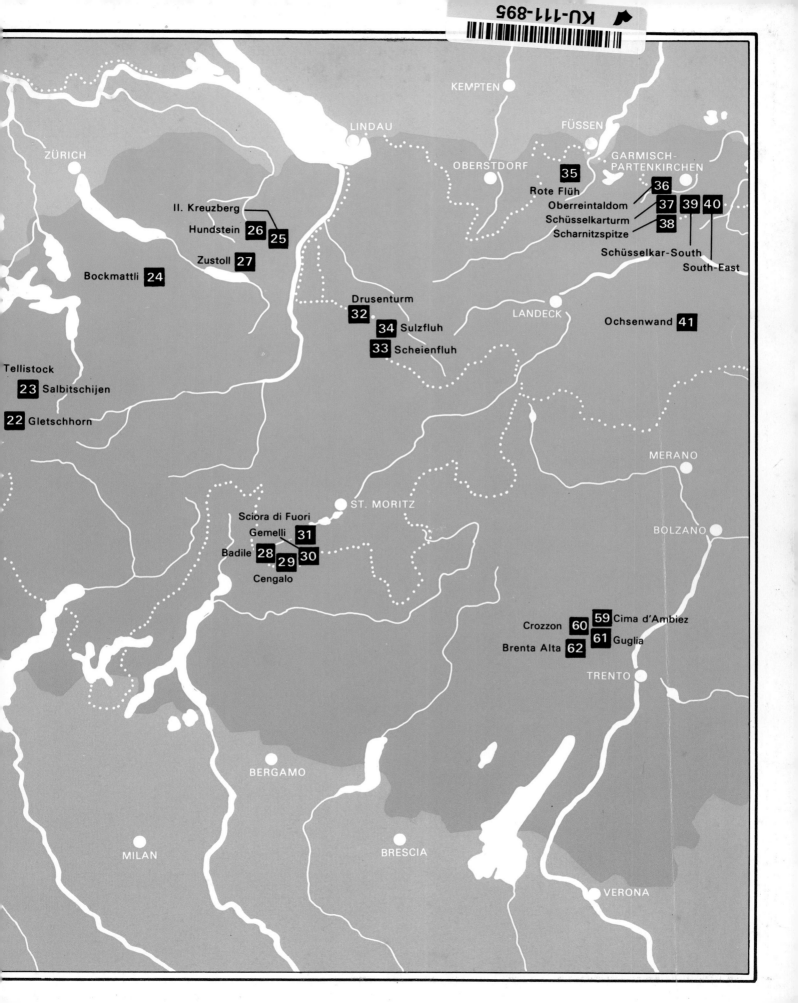

Extreme Alpine Rock

The 100 Greatest Alpine Rock Climbs

Extreme Alpine Rock

The 100 Greatest Alpine Rock Climbs

Walter Pause and Jürgen Winkler

Second revised edition
Translated by Hugh Merrick

GRANADA
London Toronto Sydney New York

Published by Granada Publishing 1979

Granada Publishing Limited
Frogmore, St Albans, Herts AL2 2NF
and
3 Upper James Street, London WIR 4BP
866 United Nations Plaza, New York, NY 10017, USA
117 York Street, Sydney, NSW 2000, Australia
100 Skyway Avenue, Rexdale, Ontario, Canada M9W 3A6
PO Box 84165, Greenside, 2034, Johannesburg, South Africa
CML Centre, Queen & Wyndham Streets, Auckland 1, New Zealand

First published in Germany under the title *Im Extremen Fels*
Copyright © BLV Verlagsgesellschaft mbH, München, 1977
Translation copyright © Granada Publishing Ltd 1979

ISBN 0 246 11056 2

Printed in Great Britain by
Fletcher & Son Ltd, Norwich

Granada ®

Granada Publishing ®

Contents

Acknowledgements

My respects and thanks are due to those mountaineers, Lucien Devies of Paris, Pit Schubert, Manfred Sturm, Klaus Werner and Dietmar Ohngemach of Munich. Their committed and at times passionate assistance has made it possible to reach a relatively positive decision as to the choice of our climbs and to guard the commentaries from haphazard ratings. My special gratitude is due to my Viennese friend Hubert Peterka, who died in the autumn of 1976, for his many contributions of Alpine history and dates. Also to my memorable assistant at the drawing-board Renate Maier-Rothe, whom death also claimed recently, who without any experience of rock, produced her route-sketches to the satisfaction not only of the most critical 'Sexogradists' but of the aesthete's eye. Pit Schubert checked them all for technical accuracy in the spring of 1976 and added many fresh details.

A remarkably lucky chance favoured this book of the 100 greatest extreme climbs in the Alps, in that the period of 'exploration' of the most difficult possibilities in Alpine climbing is finally at an end. As a result, this second edition of a highly specialised mountain-book is no longer exposed to the tide of critical vagaries. The book now stands on its own and I can only add that, for obvious reasons, the number of my collaborators, co-thinkers and co-critics rose to an unexpectedly vast total. And yet every 'tip' contributed was essential. My heartiest thanks, on the appearance of this new edition, to all those who have helped me, in the past and now. They are:

Max Nierdermann, Michel Vaucher, Othmar Stieger and Walter Belina from Switzerland; Hias Rebitsch, Ander Hörtnagl, Hannes Zechel, Fritz Sambra, Willi End and Wastl Mariner from Austria; René Desmaison, François Labande, Jacques Kelle, André Contamine, R. Jacob and Robert Paragot from France; Bruno Detassis, Reinhold Messner and Pepi Pellegrinon from Italy; Harry Rost, Peter Steiner, Reinhold Obster, Michael Schneider and Werner Schertle in Germany. All of whom helped me in the spitit of enthusiasm and friendship.

Walter Pause

For an explanation of the symbols used, see p. 202.

Both textual and pictorial presentations are in accordance with the best of the author's knowledge and belief. The climbing of any of the routes as a result of the information offered is entirely at the climber's own risk. Neither the author nor the translator can accept any responsibility.

The photos are by Jürgen Winkler, except for those by Willi End (Routes 96, 100), Jean Feuillie (Route 4), Ruedi Homberger (Routes 18, 33), Hans Schlüter (Route 24), Franz Thorbeke (Routes 25, 26, 27, 32, 34 and 35).

Granada Publishing wishes to thank West Col Productions for their help in checking the text and in listing the latest available guidebooks in English and other languages.

Preface to the Second Edition

'The most productive summit conferences are perhaps those between mountaineers'

The first edition of this book about the 'extreme' rock-climbing routes in the Alps was slanted towards an intentionally small elite of climbers; it was none the less sold out by the end of 1976. This second edition appeared in German in 1977. Many besides Munich climbers have declared that this collection of rock-climbs of extreme difficulty has long been a household article in modern Alpine literature and is now a 'classic'.

That may sound a considerable boast. But I am in a position to say that Klaus Werner, one of the supreme rock-climbing aces, who met with a fatal accident two years ago on the Aiguille du Plan, left me a copy of the first edition, in which he had 'bagged' 98 of the 100 extreme routes it describes, occasionally marking in pencil the names of his climbing-partners. That precious volume, enriched by additional corrections from the hand of my friend and first-edition collaborator Pit Schubert, lies before me now. He and my one-time co-worker Manfred Sturm read this book through and related the difficulty-ratings to the new UIAA standards. The separation of 'free' and 'artificial' climbing has been effected by the introduction of the grade AO, which certainly facilitates the down-grading of almost every route. Here it should be noted that, owing to the general 'nailing' of all the routes fashionable among 'Extremists', it is hardly possible to find a

genuine 'VI' any more, with the possible exception of the Torre Trieste, on which the pitons have been removed. On the last pages of this edition I have, with Pit Schubert's concurrence, set out the chief formulae for the new assessments of difficulty on Alpine rock.

The contents of the first edition have hardly been altered. Only the Grosse Ochsenwand (41) offers its arête in place of the North-East Face – on the Grundschärtner (48) the Felskopf (Zsigmondy) arête has given way to the North Ridge – on the Marmolada (67) the 'Vinatzer' has ceded pride of place to the 'Gogna' – and naturally, the Schiara Pillar has yielded to the South-West Face of the Cima Scotoni. All the 100 sketches once again received the unrivalled expertise of my collaborators Manfred Sturm and Pit Schubert; only seven of them needed any alterations, and these resulted from the regrading of their difficulties.

My thanks to everyone who helped me with the first edition, who have already received mention there. I thank them again for the good fortune which has fashioned out of an originally ice-cold climbing guide to the extreme routes an unexpectedly readable and responsible piece of mountaineering literature.

Walter Pause

Haut Dauphiné

Ailefroide Occidentale 3954 m

North-West Face (Coste-Rouge Wall)

Grade VI−/1050 m

As evidence of the attractions of this high Alpine rock-climbing route of 1050 metres and finishing close to the 4000-metre level, the men who made the second and third ascents dubbed it the 'Walker Spur of the Dauphiné'. Both climbs demand discipline but, while there are greater difficulties on the Walker Spur, there are greater objective dangers on the face of the Ailefroide. While the Ailefroide summits, the eastern half of the mountain's two-kilometre-long rock-ridge, falling towards the Glacier Noir, are decorated high up with big hanging glaciers, the North-West Face which plunges towards the small Coste-Rouge glacier, presents a naked wall of granite, no less daunting for that. It is only in its deepest gullies that one finds the occasional ice-bulge. Consider our photograph. Lucien Devies, the first to climb the face, described this gigantic undertaking, which has long been numbered among the great classic Dauphiné routes, as one of the finest but also one of the hardest high climbs in the French Alps. In that description he must surely have meant to include the immensity of its scenic setting. Seen from close-to, it is of course of such alarming size and difficulty that even the most experienced climber feels very small indeed in face of the manifold dangers surrounding him; and will continue to do so till, gaining height rope's length on rope's length, he has behind him the entry-pitches and the dangerous passage of the Coste-Rouge couloir. If he follows, no doubt with a growing sense of tension, the original route up the crest of the pillar, he will want to take a breather at the very latest on the top of the middle pillar and survey not only the lower part of the route up which he has come, as from a military observation-post, but also the huge rampart of grey slabs overhead, with a snow-rib leading up to it. The very first gigantic slab, fully 100 metres high, is planed smooth by falling stones. Above it looms the menace of more red cliffs, giving food for further thought. As you gain height the granite gets worse, and snow and ice show up. You can almost count on iced rock in

the difficult (V) chimneys and on the traverses leading to the summit-ridge, close to the 4000-metre line. Guidebooks describe a number of variants, some avoiding the pillar (though that is where the finest pitches are), others offering another exit-route, heading more directly for the summit and mostly even more iced-over. If you avoid the pillar, you will have difficulties in a couloir of rock at an angle of 50°, usually iced, and brittle into the bargain. As always, it is essential to get as much vital information from the climbers' guides as you do at the foot of the face itself. And if, as frequently happens, you cannot depend on reliable weather conditions, don't start the climb. The Dauphiné has a great many less exposed routes to offer all around the basins of the Noir and Coste-Rouge glaciers, many of them on sun-warmed southern flanks.

Valley Resorts La Bérarde, 1711 m. Ailefroide, 1506 m.
Bases Refuge Temple-Ecrins, 2410 m, CAF, 2½ hours from La Bérarde. Descent to Refuge de la Pilatte, 2572 m, CAF, serviced; or to Refuge du Sélé, 2710 m.
Starting Point At about 2900 m at the foot of the wall, where the snow-cone below the great gully descending from the Coste-Rouge couloir rises above the Coste-Rouge glacier, a good 2 hours from the Temple-Ecrins hut. Climbing-time for a strong party of two, say 10 hours.
Descent By the normal route down the South-West Ridge (II) to the Brèche des Frères Chamois, 3545 m, down a couloir to the Glacier Gris and in 3–4 hours to the Pilatte Hut. The quickest descent is down the South-East Spur (II) to the glaciers of Ailefroide and Sélé. From the summit to the Sélé Hut 2–3 hours. The crossing from the Sélé Hut to the Pilatte Hut requires 5–6 hours.
First Ascent L. Devies and G. Gervasutti, 23/24.7.1936. Variant (circumventing the pillar) J. Franco and K. Gurékian 17.8.1943.
Guides/Maps AHD *Massif des Ecrins*, vol III (French). AC *Selected Climbs in the Dauphiné Alps and Vercors*. IGN 25M.(T) Sh. 241 – Massif des Ecrins, Meije – Pelvoux.
Plate Top left, appearing as a shoulder, the summit of the Ailefroide Centrale, 3928 m; top right, the Ailefroide Occidentale (West Summit) 3954 m. The left side of the photo shows the mighty Coste-Rouge Couloir, up which we start, at the left-hand bottom of the picture.

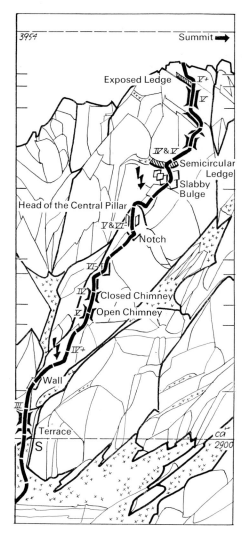

Haut Dauphiné
Pic Sans Nom 3914 m
North Face
Grade V (2 rope lengths V+ and VI)/1000 m

The upper basin of the Glacier Noir resembles an icy stage, above which rise the granite wings of some world-drama: a setting of gigantic walls, shattered, scored, but still retaining their full majesty. Opposite this colossal ring, swinging round from the Pelroux massif through our own Pic Sans Nom to the Ailefroide summits, all of whose crests are knocking on the 4000-metre line, stands the high black mass of the most southerly 4000-metre peak – the Barre des Ecrins, which, seen from the north, presents a steep fortress of gleaming ice. Everything here is savage, frightening, lonely, but never silent, for the ice- and snow-avalanches thunder and detonate by day and by night. A bivouac on the Glacier Blanc is one of the great mountaineering experiences. The North Face Route pioneered by George and Russenberger would be one of the most attractive in this book were it not for the great danger from falling stones. One look at the picture reveals that the ramps and cliffs to the right of the deeply-carved couloir, in themselves not the easiest of free-climbing passages, act as a reception-zone for the stones that fall from the topmost summit regions, with their indifferent quality of rock – in the picture they are seen under snow. It is, however, impossible either to avoid or to hurry over this zone; the angle and exposure hereabouts are considerable. The stances are very small and one would always hope for dry rock, so as to be able to friction-climb; nor is it easy to fix belaying pitons. These drawbacks apart, this route, from its first pitch to the summit, is a fabulous, attractive mixed climb, the granite of whose ridges and slabs is splendid. Every experienced climber knows that the rock under the summit is rotten, brittle and, naturally, often coated with ice. Lucien Devies postulated dry rock on the lower part of the Face as a 'must', if his North Face Route is to be embarked on at all. The descent after completing the climb is relatively free from problems for an experienced Alpinist. In good visibility it is possible to be at the Pelvoux hut in two hours; and from there, taking a short-cut to the east, down at Ailefroide

village in another two. It is possible, but what a pity to hurry so. The summit view is a triumphal realisation of the promise offered to the eyes all the way up the long ascent. For here, the whole of the Haut Dauphiné is on show, one mass of granite after another, and all of them rising to such an altitude that glacier scenes like that on the very left of our photograph (below the Col du Pelvoux) are numerous. Whoever penetrates this high-mountain tract, savagely picturesque in the highest degree, and magically lit by the stronger colouring of southern Alpine light, will find himself welcomed like the prodigal son.

Valley Resorts Ailefroide, 1506 m (by motor-transport from Briançon). La Bérarde. 1711 m.
Bases For the approach: Refuge Cézanne, 1874 m, inn accommodation; at the head of the valley, below the tongues of the Glacier Blanc and the Glacier Noir (accessible by motor). Or, the bivouac-box below the Col de la Temple, 3250 m, a wooden hut to sleep six, then down again to the foot of the climb. For the descent: Refuge du Pelvoux, 2704 m, CAF, on the south flank of Mont Pelvoux.
Starting Point At 2920 m from the upper southern basin of the Glacier Noir, at the foot of the wall, to the right close below the opening of the great gorge-like gully, near a prominent 10-m-high block. Time of the ascent for a rope of two, about 20 hours. Beware of falling stones.
Descent South-eastwards from the summit over steep snow-slopes and poor rock (Glacier de Sialouze) to the Pelvoux Hut about 2½ hours.
First Ascent L. George and V. Russenberger, 22/24.8.1950.
Guides/Maps AHD *Massif des Ecrins*, vol. III (French). AC *Selected Climbs in the Dauphiné Alps and Vercors*. IGN 25M.(T) Sh. 241 – Massif des Ecrins Meije - Pelvoux.
Plate The bulk of the Pic Sans Nom rising from the Glacier Noir. Upper part, from left to right: the Col du Pelvoux, the summit mass, consisting of the main summit and its two shoulders (the east shoulder, to the left of the broad main summit is in fact much lower), the deep gash of the Coup de Sabre (Sabre-Cut) and the Pic du Coup de Sabre. In the centre of the picture, the deeply-carved couloir, whose right-hand (western) rim the route follows.

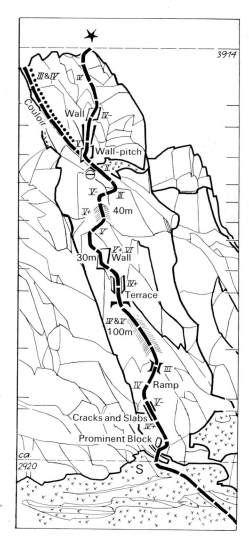

4

Haut Dauphiné

Barre des Ecrins 4101 m

South Pillar

Grade IV and V– (1 rope length V+)/1100 m

The prospect of climbing the Dauphiné's highest peak and southernmost four-thousander in the Alps by a long route, then down over a huge bergschrund and steeply on among the crevasses, to reach the valley-level safe and sound, is one to entice every strong and tried Alpinist. Two days are about right for the 1100 metres of up and down, the bivouac close above the entry-pitches being enforced by the unhelpful heights of the available huts. Dietmar Ohngemach writes: 'The climber descending the Glacier Noir from the Col de la Temple feels shattered, scared, very small and solitary as he looks round the corner to the left and suddenly sees that immense mountain-mass, dark in spite of being lit by the sun.' Later, he says: 'the bergschrund is already on a Cyclopean scale . . . but one is soon happy, the whole mountain vibrates with life and presents a prodigious Alpine thrill. The climbing is not particularly difficult, but when you get back to your tent at La Bérarde after two days you know you have accomplished a great Alpine undertaking.'

Another Munich climber Georg Gruber, makes an interesting comment: 'though the technical difficulties are not very great, the climb can only be recommended to the experienced Alpinist. Weekend climbers (coming from the Eastern Alps) like to talk of a "rubble-heap", but . . . it calls for finger-tip sensitivity. It all starts with an icefield, which is usually polished, where you also have to cross the dangerous debris-chute from the Col des Avalanches (as quickly as possible). Only then does one get onto rock (I and II) so one should put the first left-hand loop upwards (to the bivouac-spot) behind one as soon as possible, for the danger from falling stones is considerable here. The bivouac-spot is good, but only takes two. The lower part of the climb presents few difficulties, but any ascent of 1100 metres is quite an assignment. The middle section offers some fine grade IV climbing on reasonably firm rock, in spite of which caution must always be observed. Then the Bastion, a 300-metre cliff with difficulties up to V– and some

friable rock, bars the way, a time-consuming operation. The old pitons met with here and there are not always confidence-inspiring and it would be nice to have a few kilos of cement along with one hereabouts. It is essential to study the climbers' guide meticulously beforehand, as there are ample opportunities for going astray. It is comforting to find the occasional old piton, even if the huge blocks next to it are waiting to topple over. And it would be folly to start at all except in the most settled weather conditions. Even the long descent can present its problems.' The view from the 4101-metre summit is indescribably beautiful, if that be the right adjective for the shattered condition of the Earth's upflung surface, caught between dim and distant valley-trenches and the circular sweep of a deep blue horizon.

Valley Resorts To the west, La Bérarde, 1711 m; to the east Ailefroide, 1506 m.
Bases Refuge Temple-Ecrins, 2410 m, CAF, serviced, 2¼ hours. Bivouac-box on the Col de la Temple, 3250 m. Refuge Cézanne, 1874 m, inn accommodation (accessible by motor).
Starting Point At about 3000 m to the right of the exit of the East Gully descending from the Col des Avalanches, 3 hours from the Refuge Cézanne or 4 from the Refuge Temple-Ecrins by way of the Col de la Temple, 3322 m. The use of the two-man bivouac (see sketch), about 50 m from the Great Couloir, is recommended, in view of the 7–10 hours still needed for the ascent from the bergschrund (to say nothing of the long descent). There are other bivouac-sites in the upper sector.
Descent By the very icy, steep ordinary route down to Brèche Lory (bergschrund) and the Col des Ecrins (4–6 hours) to La Bérarde, or by way of the Refuge des Ecrins, 3170 m, and Refuge du Glacier Blanc, 2550 m, down to the Refuge Cézanne in the valley (5–6½ hours).
First Ascent J. Franco and his wife, 15.8.1944.
Guides/Maps AHD Massif des Ecrins, vol. II (French). AC Selected Climbs in the Dauphiné Alps and Vercors. IGN 25M.(T) Sh. 241 – Massif des Ecrins, Meije – Pelvoux.
Plate The picture was taken from the east, not the south. To the left is Le Fifre, 3698 m, followed by the notch of the Col des Avalanches, 3479 m, finally still just hidden by the South Buttress, the South and South-East Flanks of the Barre des Ecrins. To the right, the huge North-East Ridge, flanked on every side by the Glacier Noir, sweeps down from below the summit.

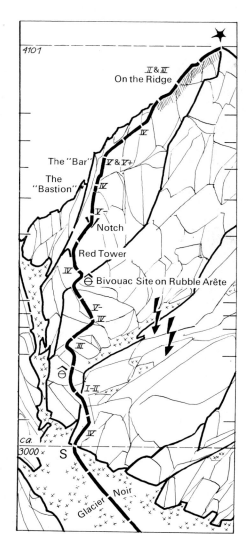

Haut Dauphiné
L'Olan 3564 m
North-West Face

Grade IV/V (1 rope length, VI) or V+, A2/1050 m

Not to include the 'Dru of the Dauphiné', as the great French climber Lucien Devies calls the Olan, would be a crime. No, worse. To revise Talleyrand's famous joke: '*Les alpinistes sont entêtés. Ne pas figurer l'Olan, c'est plus qu'un crime, c'est une faute.*' This Olan (means Summit) stands in the south-west of the Dauphiné, far from the Meije, Grande Ruine, Barre des Ecrins and Pelvoux, but still on the southern level of the Sommets des Bans and a little further west than the fabulous spring-skiing peak of Les Rouies, accessible from La Bérarde. The Valjouffrey, housing the waters of the Bonne, runs south-westwards, almost parallel with that once notorious horrid little thread of a road from Bourg d'Oisans to La Bérarde, under the huge naked North-West Face of the Olan, through which slashes an enormous couloir. The valley is remote, recondite, sparsely populated and poor in hostelries, but rich in that primitive, savagely-romantic, heavenly innocence of the great shapes of primaeval peaks which fills the mountaineer with peace and deep well-being. High above the head of the valley soars that fearsome wall with a small glacier at its feet and another in the couloir half-way up the steep face, while the cloud-banners blaze above the twin summits, 3564 m high. The wall height, as on the North-West Face of the Civetta, is 1050 m and there is no doubt about the seriousness of either proposition. As shown in the sketch, we offer two routes: first, the classic one opened up by Devies and Gervasutti, running all the way up the right-hand side of the couloir, coming out on the West Ridge of the main summit; secondly, the Direct North-West Face climb to the North Summit, which Couzy and Desmaison climbed for the first time in 1956, staying on the left side of the huge couloir and going straight up the vertical granite face of the North Summit, the upper part being mastered by way of two great grooves. The sketch explains all the details not only of the old route, then and now an outstanding example of the old-style classic climb, but also of the technically super-modern 'Direttissima',

the real difficulties of which only start high above the tiny hanging-Glacier de la Maye. This route, linking the classic with the most advanced style, with its 500-metre-high, vertical upper section, took those two pioneers three days, and their successors still require one or two bivouacs. The grading of its difficulties as marked in our sketch, as in all our other Dauphiné routes, is supplied by French climbers. We are quite unable to judge how far the grading of the artificial pitches on the 'Direct' route corresponds to today's most exacting valuations. We have as usual adopted what is probably the most recent assessment available, of V+ and A2. Between ourselves, it is not the mountains which change, but man's judgement of them.

Valley Resorts For the approach: La Chapelle-en-Valjouffrey, 956 m, in the west of Haut Dauphiné. By road from Gap or Bourg d'Oisans. After the descent, La Chapelle-en-Valgaudemar.
Bases For the approach: Refuge de Fond Turbat, 2194 m, CAF, at the head of the valley under the North-West Face of the Olan. Drive possible to Valjouffrey-le-Désert, 1255 m, thence 3 hours. For the descent: Refuge de l'Olan, 2345 m, CAF, over 300 m below the Pas d'Olan at the foot of South Ridge. Both huts are open but not serviced, 12–16 sleeping-places, water close-by.
Starting Point Both the routes shown start at about 2450 m at the snow fan below the outlet of the enormous rift. Just an hour from the hut. A two-man rope needs from 9–16 hours for each of the routes.
Descent Down the normal route on the south-east side, and across the small Glacier de l'Olan. 2–3 hours from the summit to the hut. Then a path to the valley – after studying the French guidebook.
First Ascent The classic route: L. Devies and G. Gervasutti, 23/24.8.1934. The 'North-West Face Direct': J. Couzy and R. Desmaison, 1956.
Guides/Maps AHD *Massif des Ecrins*, vol. IV (French). AC *Selected Climbs in the Dauphiné Alps and Vercors*. IGN 25M.(T) Sh. 242 – Massif des Ecrins, Olan – Muzelle.
Plate Shows the 1100 m North-West Face of the Olan. 3564 m, in the western part of Haut Dauphiné. At the top left is the North Summit, on the right the Main Summit. Both routes are recognisable when the photograph is compared with the sketch.

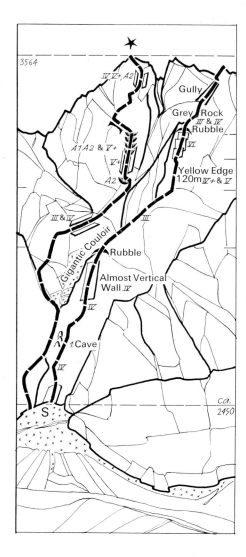

Haut Dauphiné

Grande Pic de la Meije 3983 m
South Face Direct

Grades IV and V (1 rope length, V+, A0)/800 m

It is impossible to find a comparison by which to measure the impression made by the first sight of the granite wall of the Meije's South Face. This face boasts a marvellous architecture: to the left is the towerlike upthrust of the Promontoire Ridge, which houses the new aluminium hut; close to its right, the perpendicular wall dominating the head of the valley and, perched high up on that wall as if kept in reserve, the little Glacier Carré, a clean four-cornered cloth of snow, with a fascination all its own. The Grand Pic lords it over the scene, isolated between two deep notches, its South Ridge winging like an arrow above the valley-bed. The sketch acts as a guide to the photograph so clearly that we can identify almost every detail, as well as the escape-route to the left, crossing the Glacier Carré to reach the normal route. This Southern Face is, in contrast to the ice-plastered Northern Flank, of good solid rock. The official description says: 'One of the finest and most rewarding free-climbing routes in the Western Alps.' Dietmar Ohngemach is more outspoken. 'Exceptionally lovely to look at,' he writes, 'but rich in hidden, unexpected attack by stone, icy chimneys, crippling heat as often as not, on very steep granite and to cap everything, route-finding difficulties. Which, of course, adds up to a "must" if only for the joy, after the endless descent of the Promontoire, of loitering on through the fields of Alpine-roses in the Vallée des Etançons, at peace with oneself and the world.' This is what his friend Manfred Sturm says: '800 metres of the firmest reddish-brown rock. No shadow of worry even for the owner of small biceps, no need to use force, lovely free-climbing, but you do want a good sense of direction.'

A third voice from Munich, that of Willi Schroettle, says: 'The translation of the French route-description is misleading in places. Some of the pitches are exactly described, others, unexpectedly, too freely. My own impression: approach and descent excepted, this is a pure rock-climb. In the lower sections there is some very fine free-climbing at places. Higher up, the rock is often

brittle and the climbing is strenuous. The problem of the face itself is beautifully solved. My opinions of the upper part is not shared by others who have done the climb: probably because there are a number of variants up there.'

So we have three conflicting commentaries, but that seems to me to carry more weight than the customary consensus of opinion. It is important for East-Alpine climbers to realise that great West-Alpine climbs up to the 4000-metre line are all, very naturally, menaced by objective dangers. The finest feature of this route is the continual view back to the south over the pride and might of the Dauphiné's peaks, glittering with many a glacier; and, finally, the first tremendous glance from the summit ridge northwards, the eye plunging abysmally to La Grave, down and down across the great world of cascading ice-fields. Emil Zsigmondy who, with his brother and his friend Purtscheller, accomplished the first end-to-end traverse of all the Meije's summits, was to die on that ridge. Many a Viennese climber followed in his footsteps, many a German and a Swiss; and, needless to say, when in 1912 the Mayer brothers climbed the South Face for the first time by a diagonal route, Angelo Dibona was also a member of the party.

Valley Resorts La Bérarde, 1711 m (bus from Grenoble/Bourg d'Oisans/La Bérarde, camping site).
Bases Refuge du Châtelleret, 2225 m, CAF, serviced in the Vallée des Etançons, 2 hours from La Bérarde. Refuge du Promontoire, 3093 m, CAF, 3 hours from Refuge du Châtelleret.
Starting Point At about 3150 m on the base of the South Face, to the right below the snow-gully which runs eastwards behind the Promontoire-Hut rocks, where a rock-pulpit with a small terrace juts out. In the direct fall-line from the Glacier Carré's eastern end, 1 hour from the hut, downhill. Three waterfalls and a bergschrund at the pulpit. The start is at the small waterfall. Time for the ascent by a two-man rope, 9–12 hours.
Descent By the classic (ordinary) route down the south side and the Promontoire Ridge (III), 3 to 4 hours.
First Ascent P. Allain, J. Leininger and J. Vernet, 12.9.1934.
Guide/Maps AHD *Massif des Ecrins*, vol. I (French). AC *Selected Climbs in the Dauphiné Alps and Vercors*. IGN 25M.(T) Sh. 241 – Massif des Ecrins, Meije – Pelvoux.
Plate The magnificent South Face of the Meije, seen from the Vallée des Etançons. From the left: Brèche de la Meije (just off the picture), Grand Doigt (left of the snowfield), Pic du Glacier Carré (above it), Brèche du Glacier Carré, Grand Pic de la Meije.

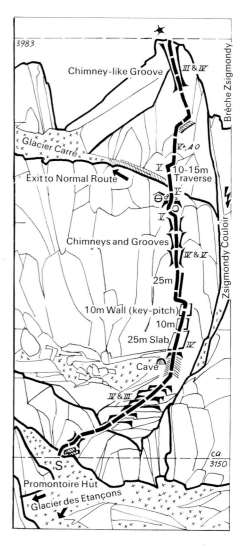

Mt Blanc Group
Aiguille Noire de Peuterey 3772 m
South Ridge

Grades IV and V (1 rope length, V+, A0)/1050 m

The Aiguille Noire, sweeping up almost to the 4000-metre line in two savage granite ridges is the second outlying subsidiary summit in the colossal Peuterey Ridge, which leads on over the Aiguille Blanche to Mt Blanc itself. This ridge, greatly respected by mountaineers of all ranks, supports, with the parallel Innominata and Brouillard Ridges, the massif of the highest mountain in the Alps. At the summit of the Noire it divides like a fork into two ridges, which enclose the cwm of the Fauteuil des Allemands. We propose to deal with both. The very difficult South Ridge provides one of the outstanding Alpine rock-climbs, sought after from the earliest days of climbing: Paul Preuss got as far as the Pointe Gamba in 1913. After the First World War the Munich climbers, Willo Welzenbach and Eugen Allwein, reached the third tower (Pointe Welzenbach) and it was as early as 1930 that Schaller and Brendel fought their way through to the summit. The climb is a laborious example of free-climbing on steep, good granite. The difficulties are extraneous. Hermann Froidl writes: 'This extreme ridge of primitive rock is pitiless if the weather breaks. For more than 1000 metres one revels in granite tough as ice, with plenty of pitons at some points. The East Ridge, too, is not to be despised, because of the difficulties of route-finding. The continual detonations in the ice-falls of the Frêney Glacier and the sight of the West Face as smooth as a wall are awesomely impressive.' The Swiss, Willy Auf der Maur, writes differently: 'This is a bride truly worth wooing, but she is obstinate and has a horrid mother-in-law (the descent). All the way up its long height the dismal question is: "Who is going to get me back onto terra firma if I come unstuck?" It is a *recherché* dish for the insatiable and the fanatic for heights.' Again, Kurt Kettner says: 'In these days the South Ridge presents few technically difficult pitches. It is a pure rock-climb on good red granite, offering plenty of holds. You can dispense with a bivouac only if you are in top form, and you have to count on one. The descent, which takes at least 4 hours, is in itself a serious proposition and it can take as long as 8. In all, this is one of the finest and most varied routes in the Mt Blanc group.'

In our photograph illustrating the next route (7), the West Face of the Noire, you have a 'close-up' of the details in the area of the upper part of the South Ridge, above the Pointe Bich. Seeing the Aiguille Noire for the first time, one is disconcerted by the immensity of this gigantic ladder of rock, pitch-black against the white of the streaming glaciers, as it soars mightily to heaven. You have to stare upwards again and again in disbelief. It is not till you come down to the Noire Hut among the bilberry-thickets of the Val Veni that you can relax. The hut-path, too, is a 'superlative'; you will have to search a long way to find a more difficult one. But, of course, it is natural that the penetration of that huge cwm with the rare name of the Fauteuil des Allemands should be a great experience in itself and that, yet again, the impression of that gigantic granite staircase overhead should grow even greater – for the how-manieth time?

Valley Resorts Courmayeur, 1226 m. Entrèves, 1306 m.
Bases The Noire Hut, 2316 m, CAI, in the lower basin of the Fauteuil des Allemands, 10 beds, unserviced; approach-path from the Val Veni, 2 hours from the Purtud Inn, 1489 m.
Starting Point At about 2700 m at the rocky base of the needle-sharp Pointe Gamba. You climb up a rocky spur projecting from the East Face of the Gamba. Half-way up, you cross the couloir between the Gamba and Tower II, traversing to the right. Time for a top-class Alpine team of two, 8-12 hours.
Descent Down the normal East Ridge Route (II and III) very difficult to see ahead at places (follow the cairns). If in doubt always keep to the left. At the notch before the Mont Noir, down to the right into the cwm 4-5 hours in good weather. When traversing the whole Peuterey Ridge* as far as Mt Blanc the descent is by the North-West Arête. Height 500 m, mostly by tricky abseiling.
* NOTE: the route is not always easy to find. Every time you think you have reached the summit, it turns out to be another of the many subsidiary summits. No belaying-pitons, plenty of good bivouac-sites. The old Noire Hut was renovated in 1969.
First Ascent K. Brendel and H. Schaller, 26/27.8.1930.
Guides/Maps AHD *La Chaîne du Mont Blanc*, vol. I (French). AC *Mont Blanc Range*, vol. I. IGN 25M.(T) Sh. 232 – Massif du Mont Blanc – Mont Blanc, Trélatête.
Plate Looking from the south-east into the remote cwm of the Fauteuil de Allemands, between the South Ridge, to the left, and the East Ridge. Top right, main summit of the Aiguille Noire de Peuterey with the subsidiary summit next to it, left. At the very bottom left, the Col des Chasseurs and the Pointe Gamba, then (moving right) Tower II, Pointe Welzenbach, Pointe Brendel, Pointe Ottoz, Pointe Bich. Top right, parts of the descent route.

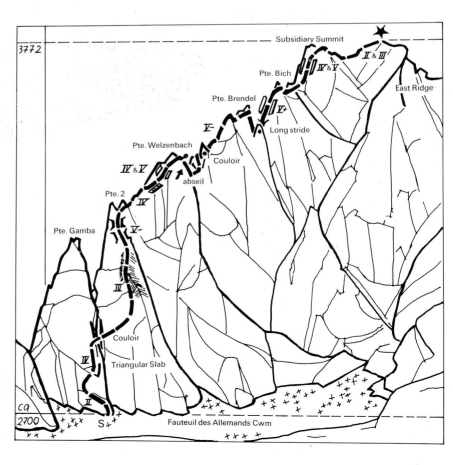

Mt Blanc Group
Aiguille Noire de Peuterey 3772 m
West Face Direct
Grade VI–, A1/650 m

There are good reasons for our more than once presenting two routes on the same peak: for the Aiguille Noire, Marmolada, Dru, Schüsselkarspitze, Fleischbank and Civetta do rank as an elite among mountains in the world of the 'extreme' climber. The South Ridge and the 'Direct' West Face while differing widely in character and history are each in their own way classic high climbs on one of the mightiest and finest mountains in the Western Alps. The ranking of our second route can be judged by the names of those who followed the pioneers: Pierre and Rébuffat made the second ascent; Bonatti and Oggione took part in the third, Cassin and Mauri in the fourth, Schliessler, Martini, Hechtel and Feuchtel in the fifth; Terray shared in the sixth, Hiebeler and Uli Wyss in the seventh. Dietmar Ohngemach called this route the 'Badile' of the Mt Blanc group. He wrote: 'Rope length upon rope length of sheer delight till you come to the slightly overhanging groove 27 metres long. It is in a class of its own . . . but over there on the Capucin it wouldn't create much of a stir among the "also rans". There is a problem too: either you hump with you, all the way up the route, and simply because of that groove, all the otherwise unnecessary equipment required for such places – or the groove becomes a damned struggle.' It is a sound remark, for the climber already has an ice-axe, crampons and his bivouac-gear with him.

This rock-climb, at an elevation of between 3100 and 3772 metres, is subject to serious risks from the weather, safe-retreat and route-finding, and certainly deserves a special category of its own. It should be planned as a two-day tour, with the descent down the East Ridge, which, because it is difficult to see the route ahead, several times forced even Cassin to bivouac. And yet it is only a typical Western Alps climb, a rather special Mt Blanc enterprise. No one who climbs that route to the summit of the Noire can leave his heart at home. According to some, that organ is only a blood-pump, but here, high above the Frêney Glacier or on the summit with

the view up the Peuterey Ridge to the Aiguille Blanche, the Frêney Pillar, the ice-cap of Mt Blanc and the riven ice-cauldron of the Brenva – it remains the core of our emotions, reflecting our joys and sorrows.

In the *Oesterreichische Alpenzeitung* (1953 March/April) Toni Hiebeler wrote a valuable account of the climb, well worth studying.

Valley Centres Courmayeur, 1226 m. Entrèves, 1306 m.
Bases Ascent: Monzino Hut 2590 m, serviced, 60 places, on the North Ridge of the Aiguille du Châtelet between the Brouillard and Frêney Glaciers; accessible from Châlet de Miage, 1540 m, in the Val Veni (thus far by motor) by path with fixed ropes on some slabs, in 3 hours.
Starting Point At about 3100 m on the far side of the Frêney Glacier, 50–60 m to the right of the bergschrund under the mouth of the ice-gully coming down from the saddle between the Dames Anglaises and the Noire, 3–5 hours from the hut to this point. Bivouac-sites are marked on the sketch preferably the lower one with its very suitable terrace before the great difficulties start. It is earnestly recommended that any approach from the Monzino Hut be made over the Col de l'Innominata, 3205 on to the upper part of the Frêney Glacier, so as to avoid the exhausting and dangerous ice-passages from below. Time for the climb 10–12 hours from the starting point, for a rope of two.
Descent By the normal route (II and III) down the East Ridge of the Noire, 4–5 hours of it (see also route 6).
First Ascent V. Ratti and G. Vitali, 18/20.8.1939.
Guides/Maps AHD *La Chaîne du Mont Blanc*, vol. I (French). AC *Mont Blanc Range*, vol. I, IGN 25M Sh. 232–Massif du Mont Blanc – Mont Blanc, Trélatête.
Plate The West Face of the Aiguille Noire de Peuterey. Shown (top left) is the main summit, with the subsidiary summit close to its right. By comparing the plate with the sketch, the whole course of the route can be followed exactly, except for the lowest, easier pitches coming up from the left. At the top left is the col of the Dames Anglaises, and top right the Pointe Bich on the South Ridge, against the background sky.

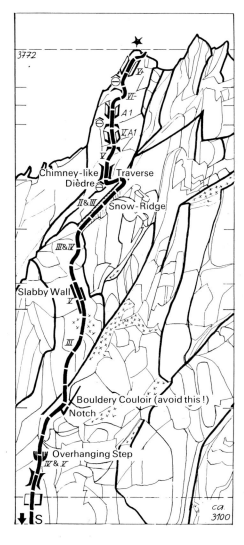

Mt Blanc Group
Mt Blanc 4807 m
East Face (Central Pillar of Frêney)
Grade VI−, A2/700 m

Our plate shows Mt Blanc's Frêney flank with the three prominent pillars bunched together between 4000 and 4700 metres. Our sketch shows the middle one, the 'Central Pillar'. The Frêney Glacier's wildly-shattered upper basin, often impossible of access, has often set the stage for high Alpine errors and dramas; only a few years ago the 'Central Pillar' became the scene of one which reached a truly tragic level. We refer to the tragedy of 1961, when outstandingly brilliant Alpine rock-climbers of the two countries which share Mt Blanc joined in an effort to solve the 'last great problem of the Alps' – the direct route up the Central Pillar of Frêney. In 1959 the Italians Bonatti, Oggione and Gallieni had already made attempts, as had the Frenchmen Desmaison, Payot, Audibert, Lagesse, Laffon and Mazeaud a year later. None of these attempts was successful, but all those who had taken part remained committed to their target, while avoiding all publicity.

And so followed that remarkable meeting at the tiny bivouac-box on the Col de la Fourche on the night of 8 July 1961. The Frenchmen, Kohlmann, Guillaume, Vieille and Mazeaud, all set for their attempt, were asleep when the Italians, Bonatti, Gallieni and Oggione – equally astonished – burst in on them. The weather deteriorated, but on the 10th the united party went forward to one of the most appalling high-Alpine disasters of the century. They had already reached the base of the 80-metre-high cliff next day, the 11th, with Pierre Mazeaud in the lead. At this point the bad weather became a hurricane. Yet, for two more days these seven experienced men fought the raging high-altitude gale standing anchored to the ropes, day and night, on that vertical wall of granite, long plastered with ice. On the 12th all Hell broke loose, with gales and thunderstorms. On the morning of the 13th the sun broke through, eliciting shouts of joy from frozen lips; but before long the storm was raging again with hurricane force and the snow was winding a shroud. They started to retreat on the 14th, by a series of abseils, none less than 40

metres. They crossed the bergschrund seven men at the last gasp, staggered across the glacier and bivouacked in a crevasse on the Col de Peuterey. Next day, four men died, one after the other, fighting their way through the tempest. You can read it all in the book written by Mazeaud, that superlative climber and writer . . . Even in good weather the route up the Frêney Pillar remains the *crème de la crème* of vintage high-Alpine rock-climbs, a preserve for ace climbers fully familiar with Mt Blanc's special conditions. From start to finish it demands the highest of standards and then, perhaps, even more.

Valley Resorts Courmayeur, 1226 m. Entrèves, 1306 m. Chamonix, 1040 m.
Bases Monzino Hut, 2590 m, 60 places, serviced, 3 hours. Bivouac-box on the Col de la Fourche (Fourche Bivouac, 3680 m, or Trident Hut, 3690 m) approachable from the Torino Hut, 2–3 hours.
Starting Point At about 4000 m at the foot of the Pillar, where the rock comes down furthest (see sketch). It is reached from the Monzino Hut across the Col de l'Innominata, Frêney Glacier, and the Gruber Rocks (III) to the upper ice-terrace; better from the bivouac-hut on the Col de la Fourche, or from Trident Hut over the Col Moore and up the North-East Couloir of the Col de Peuterey. Both approaches are serious mountaineering expeditions on their own. Time for ropes of two, 1–2 days depending entirely on the conditions.
Descent Quickest by way of the Vallot Hut (no warden) to the Gouter Hut (3817 m). 2–3 hours.
First Ascent The first complete ascent by the British–Polish party of Chris Bonington, I. Clough, J. Djuglosz, D. Whillans, 27/29.8.1961, with the French–Italian rope of R. Desmaison, P. Julien, I. Piussi and Y. Pollet-Villard, 1961.
Guides/Maps AHD *La Chaîne du Mont Blanc*, vol. I (French). AC *Mont Blanc Range*, vol. I. IGN 25M.(T) Sh. 232 – Massif du Mont Blanc – Mont Blanc, Trélatête.
Plate Looking into the Upper Frêney bowl from south-east (lower centre) with the sharp granite rib of the Gruber Rocks, which facilitate the approach to the uppermost ice-terrace. Above, the three Frêney Pillars, jammed close against each other, like a façade of columns.

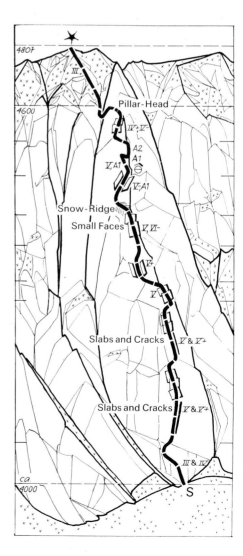

Mt Blanc Group
Grand Capucin 3838 m
East Face
Grade A2, V+/400 m

This, is the most imposing of several buttresses near the base of Mt Blanc du Tacul's Arête du Diable, its summit crowned by a hood-like roof, soars up out of the ice-bowl of the Géant Glacier like some magic sentinel, guarding the ridge. This terrifying 400-metre high column would be a giant peak if it stood in the Kaisergebirge; in the context of Mt Blanc's Brenva flank it is just another small pinnacle in a world of pinnacles. All the same, it has exerted a spell-like effect. When its East Face yielded, Walter Bonatti and Luciano Ghigo shared with Magnone the 'Turning-point in Alpinism', as the ascent of the Dru's West Face in the following year was to confirm. Instead of re-hashing Alpine history, we bring you the observations of modern climbers, so as to give an idea of the impression made now. Writing some years ago, Manfred Sturm describes it as follows: 'Chiefly crack and groove climbing, practically a piton route, at least so it has become over the years. The direct start, so rarely done, is highly to be recommended on account of its ideal line for the leader. Now, only a third or so of the pitons remain in place.' Reinhold Messner writes: 'This is Mt Blanc's training-ground; its granite is red and the pitons are safe. This is a remarkable Western Alps climb, short and sweet – dwarfed by the neighbouring Brenva. Should the weather break, even this short face can exact the utmost of the climber's resources.'

Dietmar Ohngemach says: 'This is an artificial climb on a reddish-yellow obelisk, demanding strength and stamina. In spite of the immediate magnificence of the surroundings, the climb leaves a joyful and proud memory. Of course, the Capucin is a modern-style "practice-ground" – the comic "ski-addicts" on the Géant piste and the gaily-coloured gondalas of the ropeway across the glacier fit in beautifully – it is rather like being on Munich's Dult. At times one forgets that one is a tough, dour North Face climber, on nodding terms with death.' Well said, and with a nice ironic 'personal dig'. But at Filippo's Bar in Entrèves, while compil-

ing this book, I have talked to Capucin men who carried away anything but proud memories: they got caught by a break in the weather and for two days had to fight and freeze pitifully before they could extricate themselves and force a way back to the Torino Hut through the driving mists. Experienced 'Extremists' know what it took to climb it that first time: 160 ordinary pitons, 20 wooden pegs and one bolt, which were all left on the Face. That first climb of the Capucin took the party four days for the 400 metres of its wall; the second party, from Cortina, apparently got through without a bivouac on the Face. Our sketch, 'read' in conjunction with the photograph, should act as a stimulus to those who contemplate the East Face of the Capucin . . . Those who come back in one piece from that Face and its abseil-piste have something to celebrate . . . Our considered expert advice is to do so by visiting 'Filippo's' in Entrèves and dining there at a bargain price; which can be comfortably done in 2–4 hours.

Valley Resorts Courmayeur, 1226 m. Chamonix, 1040 m
Bases Rifugio Torinò, CAI, 3322 m, below the Col du Géant, serviced all the year round, reached by cablecar from Entrèves or across from Aiguille du Midi to Pointe Helbronner, or else, Col du Midi Hut, 3613 m, 20 minutes from the cablecar terminus of the Aiguille du Midi.
Starting Point At about 3450 m to the right, next to the first rocks of the base above the big bergschrund ('Direct' Route), or climb about 100 m up the left-hand couloir until you can traverse on good rock-bands like steps. To this point a bare 2 hours from both bases. Time for the ascent for a rope of two, 8–12 hours. Ideal bivouac-sites a third of the way up the Face.
Descent Numerous abseils northwards down the rock- and ice-couloir visible in the photograph to the right of the East Face. Danger from falls of stones and ice. Abseil pitons available.
First Ascent W. Bonatti and L. Ghigo. 20/23.7.1951.
Guide/Maps AHD *La Chaîne du Mont Blanc*, vol. I (French). AC *Mont Blanc Range*, vol. I. IGN 25M. (T) Sh. 232 – Massif du Mont Blanc – Mont Blanc, Trélatête.
Plate The Grand Capucin soars up from the Géant Glacier's ice-fields in a vertical granite column, whose East Face can be seen to overhang frequently. The rock, with scarcely a break in it, has a steely quality. To the right the abseil descent-route (pitons in position) is visible. Left bottom is the start of the original route, with that of the 'Direct' clearly visible in the bottom middle of the picture.

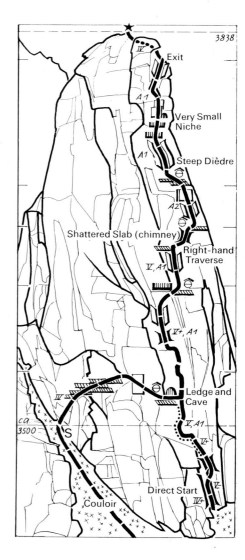

FRANCE 10 Mt Blanc du Tacul 4248 m
South-East Ridge (Arête du Diable)
Grade IV (1 rope length, V)/700 m

It is necessary to look at the previous picture of the Capucin as well as at the photograph opposite to appreciate the lofty surroundings into which we are ushered by this characteristic Mt Blanc climb. Civilisation is wiped out, but the harmony of the permanent and the ephemeral is complete. Here we finally find ourselves in an oasis in the negation of all order, which confronts the townsman of today, satiated by small pleasures, with the big simple things in life: with strenuous exertions and danger. There will be protests at that description, but we will refute them. Admittedly, this 'Devil's Ridge' (IV) is not an extreme climb and only the inclusion of the Isolée pinnacle justifies its nickname. But why belittle ourselves? To climb a granite ridge of this kind, its approach and finish on steep ice, the ascent lying at an altitude of from 3500 to 4200 metres, enormously exposed and rich in stultifying abseil pitches, ringed by the crowning glories of the Mt Blanc range, from the enormous Brenva face to the Grandes Jorasses, the Aiguilles, the Dent du Géant and the Mer de Glace, would be a first-class undertaking, let alone the objective dangers involved. And that goes for the 'Extremist' too. Kurt Kettner ranks it, not surprisingly, among the greatest Alpine climbs. This is what he writes: 'With or without the Isolée, this route remains a rewarding and magnificent experience. Ice and rock, wonderfully exposed climbing, and airy abseils succeed one another all the way. Naturally this consumes a great deal of time, especially for climbers less experienced in such routes. So darkness can catch one unawares, and any bivouac at 4000 metres is a severe test. In no way should this climb be compared with Grade IV climbs in the Eastern Alps. The rock is mostly firm and exhibits the marvellous profusion of holds common to all Mt Blanc's granite.'

Anyone can study the texture of this 'young' primitive rock on the photograph of the Grand Capucin. The Arête du Diable could become very fashionable as technical progress and its paraphernalia draw nearer to Mt Blanc. High as it stands among superlative climbs, on account of its altitude and magnificent rock-quality, its attractions will be continually enhanced by the ropeways to the Aiguille du Midi and the Torino Hut. It is now in close touch with the world; you can fly in from Paris or Munich, be wafted up in a cabin and off you go. If the weather turns out bad you can – faithful to the motto of all Mt Blanc climbers: 'see you at Filippo's' – enjoy a marvellous welcome at Entrèves, first by sitting at the cleanest table in the world and then by just raising your eyes to the great sweep of the Peuterey ridge above it . . . Visions of this kind are no longer pipe-dreams: developments which once took years break on us nowadays like summer-storms – in the Alps as elsewhere. Even then, arrive as you may in garish gondolas or huge cabins, Mt Blanc's Arête du Diable will certainly never become a climb to be 'just taken in on the way', nor the sort, like the South Face of the Aiguille du Midi hard-by, visited as a 'practice-ground'. That is out of the question, even for an ace 'Extremist'. Say what you will, here we are on the highest mountain in the Alps, and the ice glacis from which we start is our companion, to right and to left of the route all the way up the ridge to the 4000-metre line. Cloud at midday or an afternoon thunderstorm can turn the sunlit beauty of the scene instantly and painfully into a Hell, which one must be equipped to combat. But every reader of this book must be well aware of that. For, be it on the North Face of the Wetterhorn, the towers of the Salbitschijen, the Civetta, the Marmolada, the Pelmo or on the Brenta's sheer wall, the 'perils of the Alps' remain constant; and in the Mt Blanc group is added the phenomenon of the greatest altitude – a phenomenon, respect for which is learnt by bitter experience or by reading Pierre Mazeaud's book (see the text for route 8).

Valley Resorts Courmayeur, 1226 m. Entrèves. 1306 m. Chamonix.
Bases Torino Hut, 3322 m, CAI, below the Col du Géant, serviced all year round, 70 places, by ropeway from Entrèves. Additional 110 places at inn/hut on Col itself.
Starting Point At about 3570 m, 1½ hours from the Torino Hut. At the bergschrund of the second couloir falling from the Cirque Maudit through the South-West Flank (counting from the Clocher du Tacul) to the Col du Diable, 3955 m. The actual start of the rock-climb is slightly above the Col du Diable, so the whole of it lies between c. 3900 and 4200 m, as does the abseiling. Time for the whole climb for a rope of two, 8–12 hours.
Descent Over the glaciated North-West Flank (avalanche danger after fresh snow) to the Col du Midi and the Aiguille du Midi. Tracks of the complete Mt Blanc traverse often visible. 2 hours to the Col.
First Ascent Miss M. E. O'Brien, R. M. Underhill, G. Cachat and A. Charlet, 4.8.1928.
Guide/Maps AHD *La Chaîne du Mont Blanc*, vol. I (French). AC *Mont Blanc Range*, vol. I. IGN 25M.(T) Sh. 232 – Massif du Mont Blanc – Mont Blanc, Trélatête.
Plate The whole 'Arête du Diable' to Mont Blanc du Tacul (top left) taken from the bivouac-box on the Col de la Fourche. From (right) Corne du Diable and Pointe Chaubert to (left) the highest point 4248 m, all the towers of the ridge are shown and (left centre) the Isolée as well.

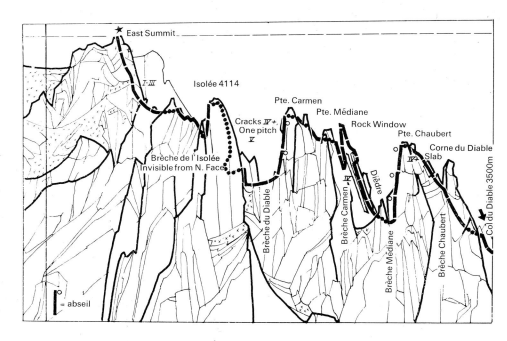

Mt Blanc Group
Grandes Jorasses 4208 m
North Face (Walker Spur)
Grade VI−, A1/1200 m

There can no longer be any doubt about it: the Walker Spur remains the most sought-after prize for all 'Extremist' climbers. Our picture explains why: for here is a true pillar of primitive rock which soars, a gigantic broadly-based column, from the ice-blankets of the Leschaux Glacier, to shoot up in absolute verticality, growing ever more slender, to the highest point in the enormous black wall of the Grandes Jorasses. It is a marvellous sight. Even though it radiates nothing but dire hostility to life, we recognize it as beautiful. More than any other in the Alps, the Spur goes winging upwards, overwhelming and alluring, huge, menacing – and, straight up its back, there runs a clearly defined route with no detours all the way up to the summit-cornice. It is the supreme, classic granite-and-ice route of the 'Moderns'.

Thirty-nine years ago, the Walker Spur ranked among the last three 'problems of the Alps'; today its fame outstrips that of all the Welzenbach face-climbs in the Bernese Alps and even that of the Eiger. Compared with the Eiger's, the fame of the Walker Spur shines out with an unusual aura of seriousness – which in no way detracts from the courage of those who first attempted, or those who eventually climbed, the Eiger: Kurz and Hinterstoisser, Heckmair, Harrer, Vörg and Kasparek. (The first two named perished in opening an important section of the route; the last four made the first ascent together.) One should not really try to compare the two climbs. On the Walker Spur, relatively free from objective dangers, it is not a question of the most extreme difficulties. The 'Extremist' of today finds few of them, albeit the climb is far from being an easy one; but it brings out the true mettle of an Alpinist in the climber for whom the highest vision of an ideal mountain-climb here becomes a reality, and for whom there is no less drive because he remains unimpressed by the absence of even greater difficulties to master.

Dietmar Ohngemach writes: 'To climb the Grandes Jorasses by the Walker Spur is beyond all doubt the

fulfilment, rather the Grand Finale to a love-affair with the Alps.' He is quite right, and what he says is confirmed by the considerable volume, almost all of it highly readable and often gripping, of literature which has grown up around the Spur. Among it is the report by Ricardo Cassin, who led the first successful ascent, and also Walter Bonatti's account of the first ascent in winter. Cassin gives a report (*Oesterreichische Alpenzeitung*, May 1949), epic in breadth, of the terrible but immensely brave earlier attempts; while Bonatti, a brilliant journalist, arrays the dry facts, step by step, but still achieves a shattering effect which holds one fascinated. This material should all be read, if only to sharpen one's own conception of mountaineering. Afterwards, the meadows in the valley will be greener, the wine more tasty and Filippo's fare at Entrèves even better.

Valley Resorts Chamonix, 1040 m. Entrèves, 1306 m.
Bases Refuge de Leschaux, 2431 m, CAF, permanently open, unserviced, on the right bank of the Leschaux Glacier (3 hours from the rail-terminus at Montenvers, 1909 m, cogwheel railway). Grandes Jorasses Hut, CAI, 2804 m on the South Flank (descent thence to Entrèves 2½ hours).
Starting Point At the foot of the spur at 3010 m, 2 hours from the Refuge des Leschaux, across the upper Leschaux Glacier.
Descent Normal route down from the South Flank by way of the Grandes Jorasses Hut (from Entrèves by the Mt Blanc Tunnel to Chamonix, motor-road). Time, summit to valley, 5–6 hours.
Special Note Time for a two-man rope, 18–22 hours in good conditions. Mainly free-climbing on good rock with fairly good stances. Hardly any objective dangers except breaks in the weather. Equipment needed: 2 40-m ropes, 10 pitons (the route is pitoned), 20 karabiners, toe-loops, crampons, ice-axe or, better still, ice-hammer.
First Ascent R. Cassin, G. Esposito, U. Tizzoni, 4/6.8.1938.
Guides/Maps AHD *La Chaîne du Mont Blanc*, vol. IIa and IV (French). AC *Mont Blanc Range*, vol. II. IGN 25M. (T) Sh. 231 – Massif du Mont Blanc – Argentière – Jorasses.
Plate The Massif of the Grandes Jorasses, seen from the north. From the left, Col des Hirondelles, 3480 m (almost out of the picture); Pointe Walker, 4208 m; Pointe Whymper, 4184 m; Pointe Croz, 4110 m; far right, the Col des Grandes Jorasses.

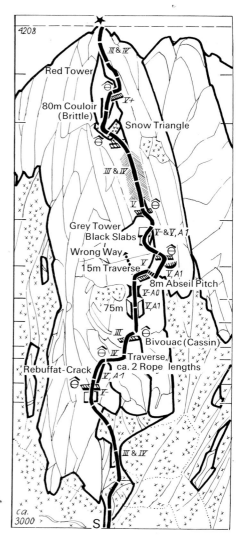

Mt Blanc Group
Grandes Jorasses/Pointe Croz 4110 m
North Pillar (Croz Spur)
Grade VI, A1/1000 m

As you stand outside the Leschaux Hut you realise the monumental proportions of the face of the Grandes Jorasses. Its three difficult columns, reduced by altitude and weathering to a lightweight elegance, form one of Nature's masterpieces, eloquent of primaeval artistry as much as the symmetry of a veined leaf, a flower or a sea-shell. Here, in the face of this gigantic wall of granite and ice, fear is tempered by its compact harmony. So perfect are its proportions that human nature responds to them, transforming terror into admiration . . . Naturally, so captivating a wall was doomed to fall. Many a European climber, after the First World War, attacked its difficulties with insufficient means, in the absence as yet of artificial aids. At that time the aim was to climb the face, not one of its buttresses. The rock of those pillars was too unhelpful, too smooth, too dangerous, and you had to switch from it to ice and back again. Rope traction and the kind of traverse undertaken nowadays were unheard of. Not a few chanced their luck. Those plucky men of Munich, Haringer, Rittler and Brehm, paid for it with their lives. Anderl Heckmair, Rudolf Peters and Martin Meier worked their way up, first to the left of the buttress, then, higher up, to its right and at last, in June 1935, Peters and Meier got to the top. Their success sparked off a number of fierce controversies. But only three more attempts on the new route were successful for a time; the second party were Chabod, Gervasutti, Mlle Boulaz and Lambert; the third, Messner and Steinauer; the fourth, devotees of such routes, Rébuffat, Lachenal, Bréchu, Michel, Muller, Revel and Vergez.

Then a new era dawned and with it came the route on this other pillar, shown in our sketch. It is one which always depends on an element of luck, for it is hardly ever in good condition. Today the climb starts straight at the base of the pillar and – following the pattern of the Walker Spur – never deviates from its face, taking towering walls and high towers in its stride, whether dry or plastered in ice; and even the final exit simply prolongs the

direct line. The smoke-screen of danger which for a long time obscured this 1000-metre face has been dissipated. This Croz Spur lies somewhat in the shade of its neighbour, which leads to the true summit and is definitely more difficult, but the climber who is not obsessed by names and popular ratings will find just as much satisfaction on it as on the 'Walker'. It certainly ranks among the very difficult combined granite-and-ice high climbs in the Alps. It has hardly a parallel outside the Mt Blanc group and challenges the courage, stamina, high-Alpine technique and basic character of the climber with a supreme test. Guidebooks unravel, in minute description, the details of the Croz Route, and our sketch extends these descriptions by showing it in its latest state.

Valley Resorts Chamonix. 1040 m.
Bases For the approach: Refuge de Leschaux, 2431 m, CAF, unserviced, always open (see previous route). For the descent: Grandes Jorasses Hut, 2804 m, on the left bank of the Glacier de Planpincieux (on the normal approach from the Val Ferret to the south).
Starting Point At about 3100 m to the right of the big protruding pillar where it and a second smaller pillar form a groove in the base, 2 hours from the hut. Bergschrund here. Time for the climb for a rope of two in settled weather, 14–18 hours. Plenty of free-climbing. Not many pitons.
Descent By the normal route down the South Flank to the Val Ferret (see previous route).
First Ascent R. Peters and M. Meier, 28/29.6.1935. Direct straight up the pillar Helmut Kiene and Klaus Werner, 5/6.8.1974.
Guides/Maps AHD *La Chaîne du Mont Blanc*, vol. IIa and IV (French). AC *Mont Blanc Range*, vol. II. IGN 25M.(T) Sh. 231 – Massif du Mont Blanc – Argentière – Jorasses.
Plate The North Face of the Grandes Jorasses with the Walker Spur, left, and the 'Croz' just to right of centre. The new start of the 'Direct' is bottom right next to the centre of the picture in the groove between the big tower (left) and a smaller tower. At the top, from the left: Pointe Walker, 4208 m, Pointe Whymper, 4184 m, Pointe Croz, 4110 m, Pointe Hélène, 4045 m, Pointe Margherita, 4065 m. In the left-hand part of the Face, the huge couloir, in which Rittler and Brehm fell to their deaths on their courageous attempt.

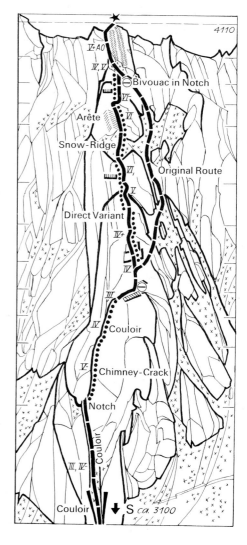

Mt Blanc Group
Petites Jorasses 3650 m
West Face
Grade VI−, A1/650 m

The way up to the West Face of the Petites Jorasses, across the ice-desert of the Leschaux Glacier, leads past the foot of the Walker Spur, the greatest of all Alpine targets. That may be the reason why this West Face climb was discovered so late in the day. It lies in the gigantic comb of granite which wings its way from the Aiguille de Talêfre over the Aiguille de Leschaux, then over the crowning bastion of the Grandes Jorasses to the distant Dent du Géant, high above the Charpoua Glacier's cauldron, through which the climbers pass, full of high enthusiasm on the way up, worn out and weary for the shelter and comfort of a hut on the return. Hosts of them have trudged their way through its white, apparently limitless hell, shrouded by the mists . . . Our picture confirms what Michel Vaucher and his wife Yvette declare so firmly in a letter from Geneva: 'We found this climb amazingly impressive. Beyond any doubt it is one of the finest in the Mt Blanc group.' Interesting, too, is Vaucher's assurance that it offers almost without exception magnificent free-climbing on excellent granite, whose compact composition is, however, such as to make the fixing of pitons difficult.

The climbing is very exposed, but there is only one pitch, on the roof above the top of the crack in the middle of the Face, which can only be overcome by artificial means. Its feature is the number of airy traverses on huge, smooth slabs. Stances are small, and few and far between . . . Hardly ever repeated till the 1960s, the climb, like several other worthwhile rock-climbs, has since gained an increasing repute; climbers are enthusiastic about it. Today the difficulties are assessed at VI− and A1. Should it perhaps be rated higher? The repetition of a route is of course always definitely easier than the pioneering of it. This West Face forms a kind of recess, facing almost due west, in the great North Wall. The terrific overhangs dominating the first big 200-metre rock-groove are characteristic of this slabby face, on which there are no ice-gullies. The first party to climb it used 45 pitons, including belaying-pitons; today all the essential ones are in position. After bad weather an ice-hammer and crampons may prove necessary even on this face, especially on the triangular firn-patch (visible in the picture), which has to be crossed to gain access, by an airy right-hand traverse, to the upper part of the face, rounded-off to the shape of an arête. Once on the summit, the descent through the Frébouze basin, where there are two old bivouac-huts, awaits the tired climber, before continuing steeply into the Val Ferret.

Valley Resort Chamonix 1040 m.
Bases Refuge du Couvercle, 2687 m. CAF (rebuilt), 3–4 hours from Montenvers (railway from Chamonix). Nearer to the start: Refuge de Leschaux, on the right bank of the Leschaux Glacier, unserviced, 3–4 hours from Montenvers. For the descent: Refugé Gervasutti, 2833 m. wooden hut, 12 places, or below it, bivouac-hut of Frébouze, 2363 m, 5 places, in poor state of repair, thence 1 hour into the Val Ferret.
Starting Point At about 3000 m, left of the fall-line of the huge, frequently-overhung West Face Gully. 1½ hours from the Leschaux Hut, towards the end very steeply to the bergschrund. This is usually easy to cross and places one immediately in the groove. Time for the climb, for a rope of two, 8–11 hours.
Descent From the summit first northwards, then southeastwards to the Gervasutti bivouac-hut, or to the Frébouze bivouac; thence down to the Val Ferret and back through the tunnel to Chamonix. Using this road-tunnel, fast parties can be back in Chamonix the same evening.
First Ascent M. Bron, P. Labrunie and A. Contamine. 20/21.8.1955.
Guides/Maps AHD *La Chaîne du Mont Blanc*, vol. IIa and IV (French). AC *Mont Blanc Range*, vol. II. IGN 25M.(T) Sh. 231 – Massif du Mont Blanc – Argentière – Jorasses.
Plate The West Face of the Petites Jorasses is effectively separated from the North-West Face by a broad, partly glaciated substructure. Extreme left, the Col des Petites Jorasses with the rocks sweeping up to the Aiguille de Leschaux, just out of the picture.

Mt Blanc Group
Aiguille de Blaitière 3522 m
West Face (British Route)
Grade VI, A2/750 m

The Aiguille de Blaitière is one of the grotesquely-clustered chain of the Chamonix Aiguilles – a three-pronged pyramid of granite. Three ice-basins rise to lick its feet on every side: the Nantillons, Blaitière and Envers de Blaitière. On the West Face of this steeply-thrusting peak – our picture shows its abrupt surge – accomplished French climbers have lived through hell. On 10 September 1947, a 'modern' route, called the 'Allain-Fix', was opened up on it. Ten days after the first ascent, the terrifying mass of two face-fractures roared down the face, just as a second French party was attempting a repeat. They escaped with their lives, but not without a crippling shock. A year later, another such rock-fall wiped out the most difficult part of the first route. In 1951 G. Herzog and Lionel Terray ventured onto the fearsome face, skirted the dead zone and actually discovered a new route, which has, however, never been repeated. In 1954 two Englishmen, Joe Brown and Don Whillans, opened up the British Route. This climb has become famous, since it was reported that its (few) artificial pitches invited comparison with those on the West Face of the Dru. The most exciting pitch is the 'Fissure Brown', in the second rope length. Here the route runs close to the shattered zone, whose right-hand rim it follows.

The Munich climber, Michael Schneider, whom we have to thank for the preliminary sketch, writes about this great face: 'In contrast with the first impression, the climbing is only particularly extreme at one or two places. The "Fissure Brown" is no longer the hardest pitch. Its legendary fame dates from the first (and second) ascents, when it was said to have been mastered in free-climbing with the help of a stone jammed in the crack. Today it is provided with thick wooden wedges, though the pitons are occasionally missing. Except for two, the stances are excellent. Contrary to other opinions, I do not consider the face particularly dangerous. The possibilities for a retreat or, alternatively, an escape-route across the Fontaine Ledges are very good, and there are relatively few falling stones. The only possible, and very serious, danger comes from further disintegration of the rock-face . . . My general impression is of a splendid free-climbing route with [in 1964] only two artificial pitches, highly enjoyable if in good condition, varied and almost entirely on good rock.' . . .

His is an informed commentary for this route, which lies between 2700 and 3500 metres. The descent is relatively simple and even if resort to the escape route across the Fontaine Ledges becomes necessary, the traverse brings you out onto the ridge, from which it is possible to go down eastwards onto the Nantillons Glacier (abseil pitons are available).

Valley Resort Chamonix, 1040 m.
Base Plan de l'Aiguille Inn, 2202 m, close below the half-way station of the Midi ropeway, private, simple fare, 3 hours on foot from Chamonix, or by ropeway.
Starting Point At about 2700 m in the upper basin of the Blaitière Glacier, 100 m to the left of the broad, dark couloir, 1½–2 hours from the hut. Time for the climb, for a two-man rope, according to the conditions, 8–10 hours.
Descent Down the Central Summit's East Ridge (III) to the first snowy hollow in the Nantillons Glacier and down to Montenvers or back to the Plan de l'Aiguille Inn, about 3 hours.
First Ascent J. Brown and D. Whillans, 25.7.1954.
Guides/Maps AHD *La Chaîne du Mont Blanc*, vol. II (French). AC *Mont Blanc Range*, vol. II. IGN 25M.(T) Sh. 231 – Massif du Mont Blanc – Argentière – Jorasses.
Plate Looking from the rock-spur between the lower and upper Blaitière Glacier to the West Face of the Aiguille de Blaitière. At the top, the North Summit (Pointe de Chamonix), 3507 m, the Central Summit, 3522 m, and the South Summit, 3521 m. Close to the vertical centre of the picture, our 'British Route'.

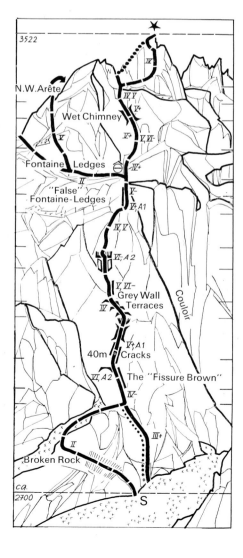

Mt Blanc Group
Petit Dru 3733 m
South-West Pillar (Bonatti Pillar)
Grade A2, VI−/1100 m (combined with approach from the west)

Of all the Alpine epics, the most heroic must surely be that of the Italian climber Walter Bonatti's courage and endurance when, between 16 and 22 August 1955, he completed the solo climb of this, his own Dru Pillar. The only other fully comparable feat, though achieved in the entirely different ambience of the high Himalaya, was Hermann Buhl's solo ascent of Nanga Parbat. Of course, Bonatti had at his disposal the most refined techniques and the most modern of artificial climbing aids, but why mention that? Anyone standing on the Flammes de Pierre and looking at the profile of the South-West Arête must experience a twinge of fear. Only here does one become aware of the true perpendicular, which in this instance doubles the perils, taking into account the sheer structure, the incomparably smooth and unbroken texture of those granite walls and an altitude approaching 4000 metres. And to master all this without rope-mates and over a stretch of seven lonely days, what an achievement! ... A study of the photograph of the arête on p. 80 of Bonatti's book will help you to appreciate its immensity. At the first sight of the Pillar, every climber wants more than anything to climb this compelling route. But when some day, he arrives, heavily-laden, at the foot of that grim ice-couloir, seen from below in all its pitiless and revolting peril, let him not be 'sicklied o'er with the pale cast of thought' – he has a job on his hands.

In his expert commentary, Pit Schubert warns: 'The free-climbing is never worse than V+, the rest is sheer piton-technique. To sum up: an immense climb which never seems to want to finish. When your nose has been gradually blocked by the granite-dust chipped over and over again from the face, there are still innumerable rope lengths before you can at last cast-off on the summit. It might be possible to retreat by climbing down or abseiling, but it would be a dicey undertaking, against which I cannot sufficiently warn. Route-finding presents no problems; all the pitons are there on the face. A bivouac is always necessary; first-class climbers have bivouacked as much as four times in bad weather.'

Peter Bednar, the Oberland specialist, writes, with expert experience: 'The rock is absolutely firm; foot- and hand-holds exceptionally clear-cut. The long stretches of vertical granite demand the acme of technical climbing and top-class condition. There are plenty of good stances, some of them suitable for bivouacs. It is impossible to lose the route, but a descent in bad weather would be a problem. All the same, the many and varied demands set by this pillar make it the fulfilment of every ace-climber's dream.' As Pit Schubert's sketch demonstrates, the height of the Ice-couloir alone is 300 metres; its sombre menaces matching up to that length. The Couloir can be avoided by coming over from the Charpoua hut, roping down from the Flammes de Pierre, thereby without any doubt setting at risk any parties at work in the Couloir. The well-informed will be aware of the shorter and more comfortable approach to the foot of the face from the Grands Montets by ropeway.

Valley Resort Chamonix, 1040 m (railway to Montenvers, 1909 m).
Base Only for the descent: Charpoua Hut, 2841 m. CAF, open, unserviced, no wood, no blankets; down to Montenvers in 2 hours. Otherwise, bivouac-sites on the Rognon between the two glaciers (see route 16).
Starting Point On the Pillar itself at about 3000 m from the basin at the top of the ice-couloir at the edge of the Pillar. The actual start is at the bottom of the couloir at about 2700 m. Here already difficult rock- and ice-work, serious danger from falling stones and ice, especially when there are several parties climbing. At least one bivouac needed – numerous good sites shown in the sketch. In unfavourable conditions you must count on several bivouacs. The start up into the couloir is not actually direct from its mouth, but 20–30 m to its right, then up into the couloir itself.
Descent As in route 16.
First Ascent Walter Bonatti, solo, 16/22.8.1955.
Guides/Maps AHD *La Chaîne du Mont Blanc*, vol. III (French). AC *Mont Blanc Range*, vol. III. IGN 25M.(T) Sh. 231 – Massif du Mont Blanc – Argentière – Jorasses.
Plate The Petit Dru's rampart of granite, magically lit. To the right, the South-West Pillar rising out of the ice-couloir. To its left the vertical West Face, further over, the North-West Ridge and the North Face in profile. In the background at the top, the Aiguille Verte.

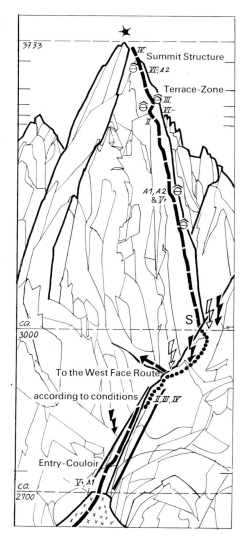

Mt Blanc Group
Petit Dru 3733 m
North Face
Grade V, A1/850 m

Seen from close by, a sharp obelisk of rock 1000 metres high, as regularly proportioned as a cathedral; seen from a distance, an out-thrust granite shoulder of the Aiguille Verte. Such is the appearance of this gigantic mountain, on whose faces and ridges the last problems of modern mountaineering were resolved. History has been made on the Petit Dru: in 1935 this epoch-making North Face was climbed by Allain and Leininger, in 1952 the 'turning-point in Alpinism' came with Magnone's expedition up the vertical West Face, in 1955 Bonatti achieved his hare-brained solo ascent of the South-West Pillar. The next generation, too, kept on breaking new ground on the Dru. In 1962 Hemming and Robins opened up a direct approach to the Magnone Route, a great piece of rock-climbing. Three years later Harlin and Robbins achieved the 'Direttissima'. In 1967 Y. Seigneur and three friends found a direct route up the North Face. The last epoch-making first ascent, even putting Bonnatti's exploit in the shade, was the solo-ascent by the 'Swiss' Czech Tomas Gross on a sky-raking direct line between the Bonatti Pillar and the 'Direttissima' which occupied him from 20 April to 8 May 1975.

There is not much new ground left to break on the Dru!... Modern technical aids first came into the reckoning on the first climb of our North Face. The guidebooks and all the available literature should be studied. This climb demands great toughness, endurance and a high degree of Alpine training at altitude. It is not safe to count on an enjoyable climb unless there has been at least a fortnight's settled weather. If you start up it in 'normal' Mt Blanc conditions you will find it icy and therefore very exhausting, at least from the Niche onwards. Just because the rock is so splendid when dry, it becomes incomparably more difficult when iced over. Yet Gaston Rébuffat did the whole face in half a day...There are good bivouac-sites, one above the other, at the rim of the Niche, where Magnone traversed out onto the West Face (his bolts and rope hand-rail are still in posi-

tion); and further possibilities on the terrace in the West Face above the major difficulties and finally, partly overhung, on the Quartz-Band. The classic approach is from Montenvers across the Mer de Glace, its moraine and the Rognon. Connoisseurs prefer the shorter, easier way to the foot of the face by the cablecar from Les Montets. There is a note below on the easiest descent-route. 'It is an indescribable experience,' Hans Muller writes. 'My enthusiasm for this face is such that I would do it again, time and weather permitting.' The lateral views from its upper section onto the marble-smooth slabs of the Western Face are enough to daunt all but the stoutest hearts.

Valley Resort Chamonix, 1040 m.
Base None for the ascent. Only bivouac-possibilities (usually) at the foot of the wall or on the rocky crest of the Rognon, or below it (several small caves) coming from Montenvers, a large block-cave on the left. For the descent: Charpoua Hut, 2841 m, CAF, open, unserviced. Down to Montenvers in 2 hours.
Starting Point At 2900 m at the first gully to the right of the glacier-fall (between the Drus and Pic Sans Nom) as you come from the Rognon: called the 'Ryan-Lochmatter Couloir'. Time for the climb, for a two-man rope, 9–12 hours in good conditions.
Descent You climb directly southwards from the Quartz-Band with many abseils (40 m abseil pitons always available) till you reach easier ground (recognisable tracks) before the cliff breaks away. Care necessary here: not straight down, but in a wide loop to the left across ledges to the upper glacier, then straight across to the hut.
First Ascent After R. Gréloz and A. Roch had abseiled down the face in 1932, the first ascent was made by P. Allain and R. Leininger, 31.7/1.8.1935.
Guides/Maps AHD *La Chaîne du Mont Blanc*, vol. III (French). AC *Mont Blanc Range*, vol. III. IGN 25M.(T) Sh. 231 – Massif du Mont Blanc – Argentière – Jorasses.
Plate The twin summits of the Drus, seen rising from the upper ice-basin of the Glacier du Nant Blanc. Left top, the Grand Dru 3754 m, to the right the Petit Dru, with its prominent ice-niche, which has to be crossed at its lower rim, from left to right.

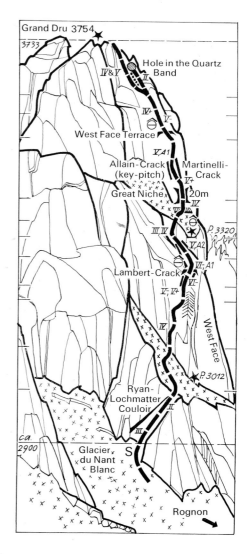

Mt Blanc Group
Les Droites 4000 m
North-East Pillar Direct
Grade VI/1200 m

No aspirant to the North-East Pillar of the Droites can deny the mighty and incredible impression made on him during the two hours' walk to the Argentière hut, that lonely trail through an unrivalled arena of ice. The Koncordiaplatz, the Morteratsch circle, the Mer de Glace and the Charpoua Cauldron or the Glacier Noir are all forgotten in face of the closely-ranged 1200-metre walls of sand-grey, red and black slabs, which sweep up from the level glacier, streaked by ramps and rifts of ice. One is speechless with that sense of awe which the new age of 'the masses' tries so hard to eradicate. Lucien Devies classified this pillar as a great and glorious undertaking, though one of the hardest and weightiest. Climbed for the first time in 1937, only ten parties were seen on its summit in the next thirty years. The second consisted of Frendo and Fourastier, the third, in 1942, of Raymond Lambert and André Roch with Mme S. d'Albertas; then, in 1946, the fourth: André Contamine, Louis Lachenal, Paul Leroux and Lionel Terray. There were equally good names among those who made numerous subsequent attempts and survived perilous retreats. There were climbers from the Eastern Alps and also Poles, who in the end succeeded in making the first winter-ascent in 1963 and, later, in 1967, the 'Polish (Eastern) Pillar'.

Jürgen Winkler, to whom we owe the photograph and sketch of the 'North-East Pillar Direct' route, had to turn back at the 'Castle', as did other parties likewise. The 'Castle' is a prominent tower marking the halfway stage, beyond which the route follows an almost level snow-crest leading to the next perpendicular cliff. Beyond it there is for the greater part either iced rock or frozen snow. A picture worth studying is that of the sloping profile of the North-East Pillar (also from Winkler's camera) in *Alpinismus*, vol. 4, 1970: in it the 'Castle's' tower rises as the central feature. Another picture of importance in preparing for the climb is that in the December 1969 issue of *La Montagne*, as it shows the true angle of inclination and also illustrates the Alpine history of the

North Face: to the left is the 1967 East Pillar Route, then the left-hand North-East Pillar Route of 1969 (Reinhold Messner and Erich Lackner), which keeps to the right of the couloir all the way; next, the original Pillar-Route of 1937, starting further to the left near the Pillar's base, then our route (1962) directly up the North-East Pillar itself, and finally, to the left again, below the 'Castle', the other 1946 variant, circumventing the lower part of the base. Klaus Werner, acquainted with 98 of the 100 routes in this book – among them the North-East Pillar Direct, here under discussion – said: 'Although predominantly only V or easier (with 2 pitches of VI), this is one of the greatest climbs in the whole of the Alps.'

Valley Resorts Chamonix, 1040 m. Argentière, 1257 m.
Bases For the ascent: Refuge d'Argentière, 2771 m. CAF, opposite the base of the North-East Pillar, 80 persons, serviced, 5–6 hours from Argentière; or from the Croix de Lognan, 1975 m. 3 hours: or from the Grands Montets, 3297 m. 1½ hours. For the descent: Refuge du Couvercle 2687 m. CAF, at the Glacier de Talèfre, serviced: then 3 hours to Montenvers.
Starting Point At 2800 m at the lowest point in the Pillar's broad base above the Glacier, see sketch and photograph, 1 hour from the hut. Time for the climb, for a two-man rope, 14–20 hours.
Descent By the normal route down the South Flank: the West Ridge, to the Talèfre Glacier.
First Ascent Ch. Authenac and F. Tournier, 20/21.7.1937, second, with variant, E. Frendo and M. Fourastier (1937). Later variation on the upper section by A. Contamine, L. Lachenal, P. Leroux and L. Terray.
Guides/Maps AHD *La Chaîne du Mont Blanc*, vol. III (French). AC *Mont Blanc Range*, vol. III. IGN 25M.(T) Sh. 231 – Massif du Mont Blanc – Argentière – Jorasses.
Plate The North Flank of the Droites above the Argentière Glacier. In the vertical centre, precisely, the North-East Pillar, rising straight to the main summit, 4000 m. Top right, the West Summit, 3984 m. Top left, the Col des Droites, 3733 m, top right, the Col de l'Aiguille Verte. Right centre, the North Face, with its 50° inclination. To the left of the North-East Pillar, the North-East Face, with its 'Bergland Pillar', climbed by Reinhold Messner and Erich Lackner, 25.7.1969.

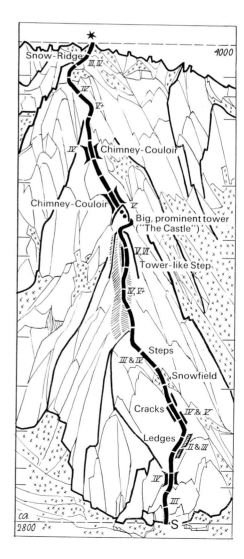

Bernese Alps
Stockhorn-Bietschhorn 3934 m
South and South-East Ridges
Grade IV (2 pitches V)/1300 m, climbing distance at least half again

Soaring solitary, a tower surrounded by ice, the Bietschhorn, only just short of 4000 metres, lords it above the beautifully withdrawn age-old idyll of the Lötschental and the Rhône Valley, overflowing with people and vineyards. It is always the first peak to don a cloud-cap when a break in the weather threatens. The two sketches by Willi Auf der Maur, who has done the complete traverse, leave out the greater part of the 1.5 km-long connecting ridge between the Stockhorn summit, over P.3138 and P.3301, to the angle-point 3535 (where an approach-route comes up from the Baltschiederklause) and the start of the Bietschhorn's South Ridge at P.3588. We present an extraordinary, and even by Swiss standards, unique climb of great dimension, every metre of which has to be solved by free-climbing. We include it in this book not as an exception to a possibly one-track list of 'Extremes', but more as a signal for a reconsideration of the highest targets, a kind of 'Grade VII' for high-Alpine rock-climbers ... Here we have two days at least of Grade IV, a few pitches of Grade V; the total vertical interval to be overcome by climbing, not counting descents, is fully 1800 metres: but the granite is of the best, often of a gritty structure, and with a few old pitons on the way.

There is now a new bivouac hut at the foot of the South Ridge. Auf der Maur says: 'The South Ridge of the Stockhorn

is a firework-display of first-class, prime rock-pitches, including the Fifth Tower with its Grade V key-pitch. It is a tit-bit for the free climber. Still remains enjoyable, though easier, after the 5th Tower.' There are many towers on the connecting ridge, some rock, some ice, and good facilities for bivouacs. Ruedi Homberger writes: 'You don't really need a description, it is simply a question of climbing the ridge for two days, over a multitude of towers and teeth.' Erich Friedli's comment is simply: 'Shorter than the North Face of the Eiger and less exhausting!' However, the connecting ridge along to Point 3588 is composed of rotten rock, out of keeping with the rest of this tremendous traverse, and some of the rickety towers must be descended by abseils.

After this section you reach the South-East Ridge proper of the Bietschhorn, with its two massive steps and associated gendarmes in good gneiss. It is an outstanding rock climb in its own right. Access to this key section is quite easy for those who do not contemplate doing the complete traverse over the Stockhorn, and you start from the Baltschieder hut. The first party to scale this ridge, Stösser and Kast, were among the most daredevil rock climbers of the early 1930s. During their 2½-day ordeal they lost a rucksack containing all their money down the side of the ridge. So from half-way up the mountain they calmly climbed down 500 metres of very diffi-

cult ground to the glacier below to retrieve it and fought their way back to the ridge after dark to continue the ascent – as if nothing had happened – but at the cost of another bivouac and the loss of 12 hours. Climbers are not made like that anymore!

This ridge is now fully described in the new English guidebook *Bernese Alps Central* published in 1978.

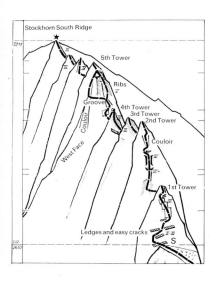

Valley Resorts Visp, 651 m, Ausserberg Station, 932 m, Lötschberg railway.
Bases For the ascent: Stockhorn bivouac hut 2598 m, 12 places, self-catering, a long way up the Baltschieder Valley, about 6 hours from Ausserberg. For the descent: Bietschhorn Hut, AAC Berne, 2565 m, below the Bietschjoch.
Starting Point For the South Ridge of the Stockhorn at the foot of the ridge, 2650 m, a few minutes from new bivouac hut. Time 8–9 hours. Then the traverse over ice and rock, crossing P.3138, P.3301 and Red Towers to P.3535 (+4–6 hours); here you start up, at 3588 m, the South-East Ridge of the Bietschhorn (+5 hours).
Descent By the ordinary West Ridge Route, 6–7 hours to the Bietschhorn Hut, in the absence of ice and snow. Otherwise, the North Ridge, same time.
Note This is a huge two-day trip. Rock and ice, two 40-m ropes essential, a small selection of pitons, ice- and bivouac-equipment.
First Ascent (of the combined traverse): Erich Friedli and Ruedi Homberger, 1964 (2 days).
Guides/Maps SAC *Berner Alpen*, vol. III (German). AC *Bernése Alps Central*. LK 25M. Sh. 1268 – Lötschental.
Plate The picture, taken from the Stockhorn Summit, shows the huge Bietschhorn towering overhead, with the West Ridge, top left. In the foreground, the connecting-ridge from Stockhorn to Bietschhorn, with the Red Towers, above which, to the right, the South-East Ridge of the Bietschhorn starts with the 'Great Step'. Top right, part of the North Ridge.

Scheideggwetterhorn 3361 m

North Wall Direct

Grade VI, A2/1300 m

The Scheideggwetterhorn, high above the Great Scheidegg, is the Wetterhorn's northern buttress, projecting far from the main mass of the group, which consists of Wetterhorn, Mittelhorn and Rosenhorn. It is at the same time the huge eastern pillar of the gigantic Oberland chain stretching from the Eiger, Mönch and Jungfrau to the Ebnefluh and Breithorn. The fearsomely steep face, with its considerable horizontal stratifications consists mostly of good, firm sedimentary rock, not of granite. The direct ascent of the North Wall is one of the longest, hardest climbs described in this book and therefore entirely dependent on good weather conditions. Quite unfairly, it is overshadowed by the Eiger and its dangerous North Face. Maybe that of the Wetterhorn is less highly prized because it is less greatly feared. How many have climbed that famous and feared face on the Eiger simply because it excites publicity? In difficulty, the North Face of the Wetterhorn yields nothing to that of the Eiger. On the contrary, it is technically more difficult. Admittedly, dangerous ice-fields of the extent of those on the Eiger are absent here; but any summit of 3361 metres involves snow and ice . . .

Both picture and sketch show clearly the three divisions of its enormous wall. After the start near the two leaning rock-buttresses – a long stride from the top of the left-hand one, where there is a piton, lodges you on the face – you have to surmount two huge slabby bands. Above them, in the second 'third' of the wall, you meet with a theatrical screen of towers and cliffs, up which two chimney-cracks of unusual severity offer progress. On the final part, after a slight breather on easier pitches, you come again to very difficult cracks and chimneys, finishing with Grade VI, A3 climbing – and that, at an altitude of more than 3000 metres. Those plentiful chimney-cracks between leaning buttresses afford progress from ledge to ledge between successive bands. The last one leads out onto the sloping roof of the summit, which is usually snow-covered. The first party to make the ascent met

bad conditions in the final chimney and had to cope with bulges of polished ice with the aid of ice-pitons, as so often happens on the Eiger's 'Ramp'. Max Niedermann, who was the first to complete this climb with Seth Abderhalden (later killed on another climb) advises every aspirant to take along half-a-dozen wooden wedges of various sizes and a few ice-screws over and above the normal equipment, which is sufficient in other respects. In favourable conditions the climb takes 10–14 hours, followed by a descent requiring 3–4 hours. A bivouac is usually compulsory. This route up the Wall is not especially dangerous, as it is possible to traverse the great ledges fairly quickly and the cliffs are so steep that they are relatively safe from falling ice or stones. But there is that long descent in store for you!

Valley Resorts Grindelwald, 1034 m. Grindelwald-Mühlebach, 1223 m (Hotel Wetterhorn). Rosenlaui, 1328 m.
Bases Gasthof Gr. Scheidegg, 1961 m, 3 hours from Grindelwald, 2 hours from Rosenlaui.
Starting Point At the upper end of the grassy ridge leading from the Great Scheidegg to the rocks of the North Wall, at about 2060 m.
Descent Over the (difficult) towers of the South-East Ridge to the north at 3370 m, then south-westwards along a tottering pinnacled ridge and down a gully to the Hühnergutz Glacier, to reach ridge gap near point 3053 m, then along ridge and down to the Krinnen Glacier and the Gleckstein Hut, SAC. According to conditions 4–5 hours.
Special Note 5 rope lengths VI, long stretches IV and V, short I–III. Time of the first ascent, 25 hours.
First Ascent M. Niedermann and S. Abderhalden, 12/13.8.1954.
Guides/Maps SAC *Berner Alpen*, vol. V (German). The route described is not included in English guidebook, cf route 20. LK 25M. Sh. 1229 – Grindelwald.
Plate The North Wall (North-West Wall in the SAC-guide) of the Scheideggwetterhorn, taken from the Great Scheidegg. The start is 4 cm above the lower rim of the picture. Centre: the two huge slanting-bands are at 2300 and 2700 m. In the central part, the Wall, riven by three massive pillars to its left: to the right of the pillars the crack-chimney, which leads up to a series of cliffs 50 to 100-m high, above which towers the prominent triangular summit wall.

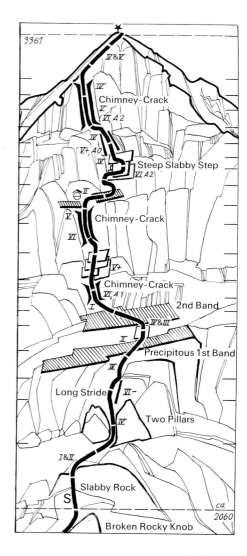

Bernese Alps
Kingspitz 2621 m
North-East Face
Grade V+, A0/520 m

The Kingspitz, as the Swiss call it, is the most prominent feature in the Engelhörner Group, and its North-East Face Direct is the most attractive and 'extreme' of the climbs in this outlying limestone range abutting on the Bernese Alps. The entry into the idyllic Alpine setting of the Rosenlauital is as impressive as that into the Ochsental above the Engelhorn Hut, yet there could be no sharper contrast anywhere. Down below there is the harmony of a green world against a backcloth of rock and ice; up above, a grim narrow re-entrant surrounded by huge vertical walls. A climber from the Eastern Alps is immediately reminded of the Oberreinthal – but for the appeal of the summits, a world of monstrous ruins. As our picture shows, the North-East Face of the Kingspitz is a huge wall of slabs, often as solid as granite, but again riven by cracks and smooth into the bargain, very smooth indeed. In fact, here is a smoothness rarely to be found in a limestone formation. The climbing is in keeping – you grope and feel your way up the steep rock on slender holds; there is little to be done by frictioning.

Max Niedermann, the reliability of whose judgments is underlined by his great experience, thinks that the wall does not present any difficulties which call for pitons. Those which once seemed necessary have been there for years and are now employed more as hand- and foot-holds, useful for belaying but also as a means of progress. A bonus-point of this very high face – which is not quite so sheer as our picture would have you believe – is that the start of the climb can be reached from the Engelhorn Hut in half an hour. The first rock-hollow (shadowed at the bottom right of the photograph) is fairly easy of access (II) and therefore reached relatively quickly. The exit is by climbing the diagonal slabby groove up its floor and then to the left. From then on, all the way up to the summit-wall, except for the little ridge (III) leading to the vertical cliff and on to the great shallow upper-hollow, the difficulties are ever-present. Nowadays the pendulum-traverse of earlier times is dispensed with and the

troublesome pitch is climbed 'free'. Dietmar Ohngemach writes: 'The pitch can be climbed and there is no real need for a pendulum-traverse!' The finish marked on our route-sketch is preferable to the so-called direct exit, which is crumbly and dangerous. Up on the summit the icy breeze of the Bernese Alps blows and the eye never tires of taking in great Alpine landscapes. Quite close by it is possible to trace the gigantic downhill run on the Wetterhorn ('Abseits der Piste') and in the same direction we discover the marvellously sheer East Face of the Wellhorn, which ought by rights to have been Route 101 in this book, but isn't . . .

Valley Resort Meiringen, 595 m, in the Haslital (the meeting-point of the Brünig, Susten and Grimsel passes).
Base Engelhorn Hut, 1901 m, Akad. Alpenklub Bern, in the Ochsental, 60 places, hut-keeper not always in residence, from Rosenlaui, 1328 m (by bus from Meiringen) then 1½ hours to the hut.
Starting Point In the Ochsental at about 1970 m, to the right of a fall-line from the summit, below a huge funnel-like basin visible 80 to 100 m above the foot of the wall. 20 minutes from the Hut. Time for the climb, for a rope of two, 4–7 hours.
Descent Down the couloir on the west flank till you can traverse the west flanks of Kastor and Pollux, northwards to the left, towards the Ochsensattel. Then head towards the grassy terrace of the 'Schönbidemli', which is soon visible, and there pick up traces of a track to the Engelhorn Hut (I and II). 1½–2 hours.
First Ascent M. Lüthy, H. Steuri and H. Haidegger, 26.9.1937.
Guides/Maps KF *Engelhornführer* (German). WCP *Engelhörner and Salbitschijen*. LK 25M. Sh. 1210 – Innertkirchen. Sh. 1230 – Guttannen.
Plate The Kingspitz (top centre) with its 'granite-wall of limestone'. Top left, the Teufelsjoch, to the right, the Kastorsattel, the twin summit of Kastor and Pollux and the Ochsensattel (outside the right-hand edge of the picture).

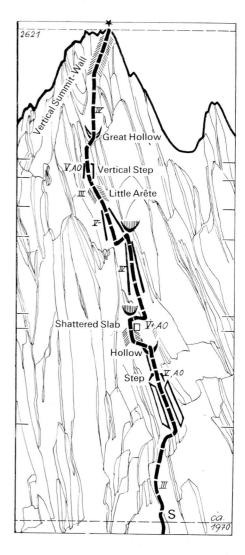

SWITZERLAND 21
Tellistock (Tällistock) 2579 m
South Face
Grade VI, A1/400 m

As you drive up the western side of the Susten Pass road, you find, southwards to your right, the ice-covered rock of the Western Uri Alps, on the left the Tellistock in the limestone fretwork of the Gadmenfluh. The South Face of that mountain offers the severest type of free-climbing on its limestone. The almost vertical wall rising from its base was climbed for the first time at its left-hand end (the South-West Face) in 1959 by Max Niedermann and Dietmar Ohngemach. It is a climb containing four Grade VI pitches as well as easy and moderate climbing . . . A year later, S. Inwyler and W. Richard climbed the east part of the wall close to the left (west) of the prominent buttress so highly lit in our photograph. They took 15 hours, but today the 400-metre face is climbed in 5–7 hours. All the necessary 35 pitons and belaying-pitons are still in place, as is customary. This route runs, with only a few divergences, straight as a plumbline up the yellow South Face.

Here is Max Niedermann's description of this extreme route he knows so well: 'This face, which reminds the climber of Dolomite bastions, offers him an extremely varied climb on good, mostly vertical and frequently overhanging rock.' We quote this brief commentary by that great Eastern-Swiss mountaineer to facilitate identification of this face by type. Max Niedermann crops up as the pioneer of many climbs in this book and whenever he does so it is a question of a highly modern, extremely difficult route, whose line does not have to be searched for, but is the logical one already *in situ*. Examples are the North Face of the Scheideggwetterhorn, the South Gully of the Second Kreuzberg, the Grosser Drusenturm, Scheienfluh, Graue Wand, the Bockmattliturm's North Face Direct and the Hundstein Gully . . . Up on the Gadmenfluh, between the Gadmertal and the Gental, one is perched on the long limestone ridge running straight as a die south-westwards, with the Reissend Nollen, Wendenstöcke and Tellistock rising from it as its main culminations. To the right there is a tantalising glimpse of the great Bernese peaks – but who wants to talk about nothing but

those mighty mountains? Why, even the journey here from Zürich is a voyage of exploration fit for a Columbus, rich in incomparable treasure-trove – Lake Zug, the hills rising straight out of Lake Lucerne's trench, the fresh green of the meadows under a dark-blue sky, then the Rigi, Pilatus, the Urirotstock, Titlis itself, all conveniently assembled as if by chance – in fact exquisitely arranged by a talented Swiss Tourism promoter. Such riches make even a proud denizen of Upper Bavaria feel small indeed.

Valley Resort Gadmen, 1205 m, on the western ascent to the Susten Pass.
Bases Telli Hut, serviced, 1 hour from Gadmen, or Alp Birchlaui, 1597 m, about 1 hour above the Susten road.
Starting Point At about 2150 m (¾ hour from the Telli Hut, 1¼ hours from Alp Birchlaui), after crossing the vegetated ramp above the cwm and up its deeply embedded middle to the left below the prominent pillar in the right (eastern) part of the wall. Time for the climb, for a two-man rope, 5–7 hours.
Descent From the exit about 20 minutes down to the right (eastwards) to the big cairn, then south down a gully (I) to the abseil pitons. Several 40-m abseils (abseil chute) to reach easier terrain. Summit to Telli Hut, 1–1½ hours.
First Ascent S. Inwyler and W. Richard, 24/25 September, 1960.
Guides/Maps SAC *Urner Alpen*, vol. I (German). (No English guide.) LK 25M. Sh. 1210 – Innertkirchen.
Plate South Face (to the right) and South-West Face of the Tellistock in the Gadmenfluh close above the Susten road. To the right of the exact vertical centre of the picture, still in strong sunlight, the pillar up whose left side our route runs vertically to the summit ridge.

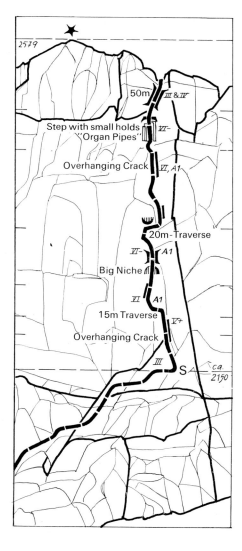

42

Alps of Western Uri
Graue Wand 3172 m
South Face

Grade V+, A1/300 m

Among the Alps of Western Uri – above the Göschenental, not far from the Furka Pass – this book is able to feature two extremely difficult rock-climbs on beautifully rough, mainly very solid granite. One of them runs over the huge towers of the Salbitschijen's West Ridge, the other up the South Face of the Graue Wand. The latter is (on the Swiss Federal map) Point 3172 in the 900-metre-long connecting-ridge between the Gletschhorn and Winterstock, above the comfortable Albert Heim Hut of the SAC. These two granite climbs in the heart of Switzerland form a nicely contrasting programme to the superfluity of our Eastern Alps limestone routes in the Kaisergebirge, the Wetterstein and the Dolomites. As shown in the photograph, the strikingly vertical wall of granite rises, with the mirror-smooth sweep of slabs bordering it, sheer from a side-basin of the Tiefengletscher. Comparison with the sketch will allow you to make the route out quite clearly. It starts at the minor crack rising from the glacier to the right of the dominating series of longer diagonal cracks. The problem is mastering cracks – the little gullies which continually invade the neighbourhood – slabby pitches and the frequent out-thrust of overhangs and roofs, one by one, in severe free-climbing.

The first party to make the ascent, Max Niedermann, Werner Sieber and Heinz Stähli needed two days' and exactly 20 hours of climbing time. Their bivouac-site, next to a grassy gully, is marked on the sketch. The 'rough-polish' of the primitive rock, which is unusually solid, demands a special technique, based on friction. Almost all the 50 to 55 pitons and the five wooden wedges used by the pioneer party are still there on the face. Exact descriptions are to be found in *Alpinismus*, vol. 4, 1965, and *Bergkamerad*, vol. 10, 1965. The summit of the Graue Wand, at 3172 metres, is on the great Eastern Ridge running up to the main south-to-north ridge of the Furkahorn-Tiefenstock-Dammastock chain. Here you take your rest at Switzerland's most beautiful core, before hastening down eastwards to the

deepest notch in the ridge, just before the Winterstock – the Untere Gletschjoch – whence you climb southwards down the gully to the Albert Heim Hut. Max Niedermann, to whom we are indebted for this difficult but lovely granite-climb, has to his credit – among 'extreme' climbers – an exciting list of modern-type first ascents, mainly in Eastern Switzerland. Finally, a serious word of warning: when it is wet in this Gotthard area, beware! Owing to the relatively low altitude of these peaks there is often a strong growth of lichen on the rocks. And while in dry conditions you can rely 100 per cent on the most exaggerated friction technique, when it is wet, even on the less steep pitches of that solid, ancient rock, it can take your legs from under you. Don't be caught unawares – you have been warned!

Valley Resorts Realp, 1540 m, better still Tiefenbach, 2106 m, both on the eastern approach of the Furka Pass road (railway station 250 m below Tiefenbach).
Base Albert Heim Hut, 2541 m, SAC on a rock-spur below the Tiefen Glacier (2½ hours from Realp, 1 hour from Tiefenbach, red marks, along the east bank of the Tiefenbach upwards).
Starting Point At about 2750 m, 40 minutes from the Hut, to the right of the wedge-shaped projecting buttress, surrounded by glacier. Time for the climb, for a rope of two, 4–6 hours.
Descent The summit of the South Face at 3172 m marks the middle of the connecting-ridge between the Gletschhorn (to the west) and the massif of the Winterstock. We go eastwards towards the Winterstock to the Untere-Gletschjoch, the deepest saddle in the ridge, before the ridge rises again to the Winterstock. Then down the gully falling away to the south.
First Ascent M. Neidermann, W. Sieber and H. Stähli, 13/14.9.1964.
Guides/Maps SAC *Urner Alpen*, vol. I (German). WCP *Central Switzerland*. LK 25M. Sh. 1231 – Urseren.
Plate The South Wall of the ridge connecting Gletschhorn (top left) and Winterstock (top right), with Point 3172 m in the centre top, is known as the Graue Wand (Grey Wall).

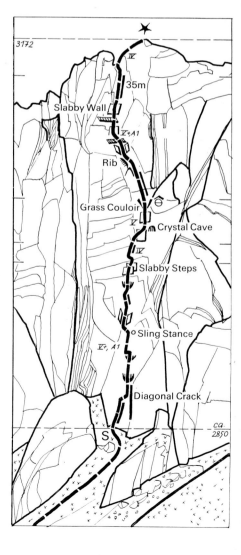

44

SWITZERLAND 23 Salbitschijen 2981 m
Traverse of the West Ridge Towers
Grade V+, A (2 pitches VI—)/600 m

This 12-hour granite climb in the Salbitschijen Massif is one of the greatest climbs in this book. The two enthusiastic experts, Willy and Franz Auf der Maur (not related, just rope-mates), who have also provided the new bivouac-box, have given us their basic notes for this finest of fine ventures . . . *First tower*, 2699 m: from the northern sub-structure three-quarters of the way up the South-West Face, then straight up to the left to the red section of rock (visible from the valley), then up the sloping roof to the top. *Second tower*, 2800 m: abseil into notch between towers I and II and then 80 m further down into the couloir. Then grooves, cracks, ledges and pulpits, on the north flank, to the top. (Better still, a marvellous traverse on the extremely severe South-West Flank Direct from the notch.) *Third tower*, 2750 m: approach along the ridge. There is an interesting but exposed piece of climbing round the Northern Arête on the first grooved part of the Summit's base. Abseil from the last block of the Summit 40 m directly into the notch between towers III and

IV, where there are good facilities for a bivouac on the north side. At this point, too, it is feasible to get off the ridge. *Fourth tower*, 2850 m: whereas the previous towers offer various possibilities, there is only the one compulsory route after the third tower. The difficulties of the second section now begin. Before reaching the foot of the 'Flamme', which demands 35 metres of piton-climbing, three shoulders interrupt the ridge. From the triple-headed Fourth tower the West Summit is left untouched, standing as it does aside from the ridge. *Fifth tower*, 2900 m: there are two prominent shoulders in the West Ridge. The direct crests of the ridge consist of unclimbable overhanging rocks. Move out southwards with the assistance of pitons on to the smooth faces sweeping up from below. The last rope length then leads straight up from the Fifth tower along the crest of the ridge between the two prominent 'Ears' of the summit. *The Summit-structure* of Salbitschijen, 2981 m: this belongs to the West Ridge Traverse and is the crowning glory of the whole climb. A flat sec-

tion of the ridge beyond the Fifth tower forces one, after a step, to 'pendulum' over to the south side. The Summit-structure itself starts with a 15-metre piton-crack below the overhanging crest . . . and as the evening sun goes down you achieve the summit – and fulfilment.

Valley Resort Göschenen (North entrance of the Gotthard tunnel), 1106 m. One can go by car as far as the 'Voralphütte' turning (1404 m). Good view here of the whole West Ridge.
Bases For the ascent: Horefelli Alp, 1786 m, night quarters. Better: bivouac-box, SAC (Mythen) at the foot of the West Ridge at 2400 m, 15 persons, water at 100 m. Best of all, over the Horefelli Alp, from the parking-place, 2½ hours. From the bivouac-box to the start, 15 minutes. Salbit Hut, 2105 m, SAC, 2½ hours from Göschenen.
Starting Point At the western corner of Tower I's north side, at about 2450 m. Time for the climb, for a two-man rope, 10–12 hours.
Descent By the ordinary route down the North Flank to the Salbit Hut (1 hour).
Note On the ascent to the bivouac-box or the start avoid using the Horefelli Couloir, but go up the next to the left, as seen from the Alp. Red marks on the path from the hut on the Alp. Then cross the Horefelli Couloir quickly and never try to escape into it, on account of the great danger from falling stones. Several good bivouac-sites on the route.
First Complete Traverse 25/26.6.1962 by Artur Oswald of Rottweil and Manfred Vögtle of Chur.
Guides/Maps SAC *Urner Alpen*, vol. II (German). WCP *Engelhörner and Salbitschijen*. LK 25M. Sh. 1211 – Meiental, Sh. 1231 – Urseren.
Plate The West Ridge towers, II, to the left, III, to the right below it, and IV (West Summit, 'Flamme', Main Summit) of the Salbitschijen. Seen from the south and in the opposite direction to the sketch.

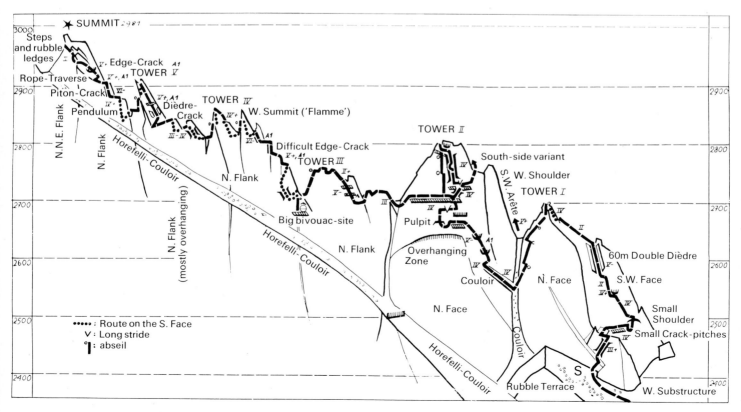

Alps of Glarus
Grosser Bockmattliturm 1835 m
North Face Direct
Grade V+, A1/400 m

The two Bockmattli Towers, rising above the Wägitaler See, are the prime features in the much-frequented climbing-grounds of Zürich mountaineers. Little more than an hour from Zürich's famous Bahnhofstrasse, with its splendid tea-shops and fashionable stores, huge rocky slabs stab the sky above the little lake near Innerthal. These are the North Faces, with their inviting gullies and plentiful cracks. There is no doubt about the grading of these climbs: V+, A1 are no false claims on the North Face Direct Route, and others on the 400-metre-high wall qualify for the same assessment. In spite of their northern aspect, these faces are fit for climbing once April is over. From then on, the climber temporarily inhabiting the little town of Bockmattli can dream his dreams. He can see those walls from the lake shore as he sits under the Chinese lanterns at 'Bellevue' savouring his ice-cream and the smiles of pretty girls – and thinks of the difficulties of 'extreme' rock. It is simply a question of fitness. Any of these climbs – the splendid old North Face Route on the Great Tower, the fine West Face Direct, the enjoyable Western Arête Direct and the elegant Bockmattli West Buttress – is a single day's outing (if you get up early enough) from Zürich. The rock is as firm and rich in holds as the climbs in the Kaisergebirge and the Gesäuse, and it is only an hour from the lakeside hostelries to the starting-points.

Our chosen Direct Route on the North Face of the Great Tower demands top-class free-climbing. Impressive straddles on the left-hand edge of this enormous vertical dièdre, above the unbroken smoothness of the great limestone slab (seen in the left of our picture) emphasise the feeling of an abysmal void ... Even the first pitch is a joy, for it entails an 8-metre abseil or a rope-manipulated descent. After that, one enjoys the rarest of climbing delights on the left-hand rim of the dièdre; but be sure you stay on the rim and not in the dièdre itself or you will go badly astray. If there is anyone who believes that rope-traverses are only to be found in the Kaisergebirge, he had better do the old

North Face (Hauser-Kost) Route where, immediately after branching off from the 'Direct' at the huge piton-ring, a rope-traverse of nerve-racking exposure leads across to an amusing stance – a totally unexpected barrel-like hole in the rock. There is nothing like that in the Kaisergebirge! The gigantic slab bordering our dièdre is as smooth (I boggle at the description) as the famous one on the Argentine across there in the Rhône Valley ... And when the climber finally sits on the summit, he rediscovers his – in local parlance – 'Zürisee' – and in a trice he sees himself sitting once again under those lanterns, enjoying his ice-cream and the smiles of the pretty girls. And so the wheel comes full circle for a youngster whom 400 metres of V+, A1 are far from having turned into an old dodderer. So, doubly reassured, he starts to slog his way down the scree.

Valley Resort Wägital-Innerthal, 906 m (bus Siebnen-Innerthal).
Bases Kletterhüttli, private, below the Bockmattli; other possibility, Alp Gwürz or hay-barn on the Alp Schwarzenegg. Also inns at Lake Wägitaler, 906 m; adequate, Gasthoff Oberhof; 1½ hours to the starting point.
Starting Point At about 1500 m on the vegetated substructure, at the eastern edge of the Little Tower's base, i.e. to the west of the deep gorge separating the two towers. Time of the climb for a two-man rope, 3 hours.
Descent Down the ordinary route southwards into the saddle between the Grosser Bockmattliturm and the Schiberg, where you have to climb over two small towers (III) then up again out of the saddle towards the north, 40 m up a gully (III) and on to a grassy crest, which you follow till you are able to traverse to the right on to the normal route (tracks, 45 minutes). Then down in 1 hour to Lake Wägitaler.
First Ascent M. Niedermann and P. Diener 16.9.1956 (11 hours).
Guides/Maps SAC *Glarner Alpen* (German). (No English guide.) LK 25M. Sh. 1133 – Linthebene, Sh. 1153 – Klöntal.
Plate Left, the Grosser and, right, the Kleiner Bockmattliturm. Between them the deep North Gorge, which is crossed from right to left soon after the start. The huge polished slab is easily identified in the middle of the Great Tower's North Face: our route goes up to the summit by way of the gullies and cracks bordering it to its left.

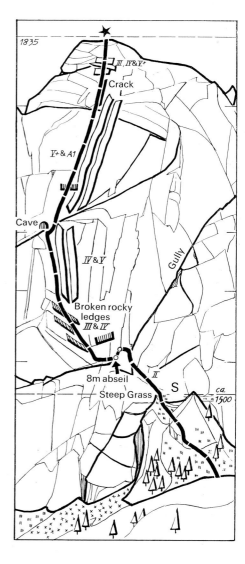

48

Alpstein Group
Zweiter (Second) Kreuzberg 1970 m
South Face Dièdre
Grade VI−, A1/300 m

The map of Switzerland shows us that the Alpstein Group boasts three sharply chiselled limestone ranges running strictly parallel from south-west to north-east. The serried row of the eight Kreuzberge, forming a sharp-toothed comb, rise in the southernmost range, facing the Freiheit and Hundstein, those delectable climbing grounds over in the central range. The Säntis region climbing guide lists 82 routes and variants in this rocky paradise, famous far beyond the borders of Switzerland. The limestone is mostly compact and firm. One source of danger is the occasional appearance of grass, especially at the base of the range, introducing an element of risk during damp and rainy periods. Our South Face Dièdre, 400 metres if you include the plinth, a bare 300 metres from the actual start of the climb, ranks as one of the most splendid modern routes in the Alpstein, for which we have to thank those who first made it in 1954, Max Niedermann and Seth Abderhalden. The climbing makes great demands on the aspirant's fitness; the time taken for the climb varies widely between $4\frac{1}{2}$ and 7 hours.

As shown in our photograph, the gigantic dièdre sets its stamp on the whole character of the South Face. Our sketch shows clearly that the route does not lie up it in its entirety. It is only after a third of the climb – after the stances in the cave-like niche, over the slabs barring the way and above the open crack and the overhanging ones which succeed it – that we get into the gully itself and climb up it to the steep turfy ledge, the bivouac-site on the first ascent. Almost immediately we leave the branch which veers off to the left and keep to the right by climbing 60 metres in the right-hand of the two available cracks, continuing all the way to the big overhanging roof which is such a prominent feature. Here an overhang takes us up to the right on to the big ramp, so splendidly defined in the photograph. We continue up it in a crack running up to the right and a further series of cracks above it, which land us on the East Ridge after fully 100 m of stiff climbing, half a rope's length to the right (east) of the summit.

A typical feature of this limestone climb on the rock of the lesser Alps is the grassy entry pitches of broken rock and the interesting fungus-like clumps of turf on the traverse into the bottom of the gully. To cap everything, at the most difficult pitch in the whole climb, climbing out of the bed of the dièdre, we come upon a shrub with chough's nests in it. To quote Dietmar Ohngemach: 'The nests were occupied. We couldn't decide which was worse, the actual climbing or the attacks by a furious chough, thrashing about like a Lämmergeier!' As usual, all the essential pitons are still in position. The clumps referred to – and they are dangerous – are like firm tree-growths which in some peculiar way support themselves and withstand the weight put upon them by a climber. Which seems to call for explanation from a botanist!

Valley Resorts Brülisau, 922 m. Sax im Rheintal, 480 m.
Bases Bollenwees, 1470 m. on the Fälensee (inn), $2\frac{1}{2}$ hours from Brülisau. Next to it, the new SAC Hundstein Hut (1551 m). Unteralp, 1393 m, unserviced, 2 hours.
Starting Point At about 1670 m at the bottom lower edge of the huge gully which splits the wall in the middle, at a bush just above the pine tree (*Pinus mugo*).
Descent By easy ridge and chimney climbing westwards into the saddle between Kreuzberg II and III. After the chimney a narrow arête, red markings, a slabby step in the wall, then broken rock and a steep funnel down to the base of the rock (Chimney Grade II).
Special Note The South Face climb dries out early. Never attempt the face after rain. The rock is good, the stances poor. Nowadays the climb takes $4\frac{1}{2}$–7 hours. Few objective dangers, except wet (grassy) broken rock. When the rock is wet the difficulties are 'grim', according to those who have climbed it 'wet'.
First Ascent Max Niedermann and Seth Abderhalden, 27/28.5.1954.
Guides/Maps FB St. G *Säntisführer* (German). LK 25M. Sh. 1175 – Vättis, 25M.(T) Sh. 2506 – Säntisgebiet.
Plate The South Face of Kreuzberg II, taken from the south-west. The whole of the enormous dièdre in the middle of the wall is visible, only the vegetated rocks at the start being cut off. Top left, the West Ridge leading to the saddle between Kreuzberg II and III.

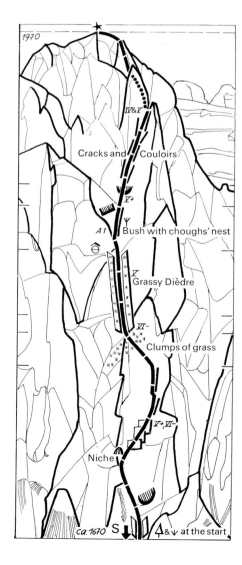

Alpstein Group
Roter Turm (Red Tower)/Hundstein 2156 m (combined)
South Face and South Dièdre
Grade VI−, A0/150 m + 200 m

The rocky comb diverging north-eastwards from the Altmann in the Alpstein contains two summits of interest to 'Extremists' – the Freiheit, 2140 m, and the Hundstein, 2156 m. At their southern base, as shown in the photograph, stands the 2002-metre Roter Turm, rising from the grassy slopes above the Fälenalp. It is possible to combine the South Face of the Red Tower and the South Dièdre in the Hundstein's face in a total time of 4–6 hours, yielding climbing of 150 + 200 metres for the day's work. Both routes are on sunny south faces, free of snow early in the year and scenically attractive into the bargain. The vista deep down to the Fälensee and the interesting glimpse across to the teeth of the Kreuzberge rising behind the Roslen- and Saxer- plateaux must appeal even to one hooked on extreme rock-climbing routes. The South Face of the Red Tower, almost as difficult as the Hundstein South Dièdre which follows it, provides the connoisseur with marvellous free-climbing; it is distinguished by three overhangs. The third forms a roof over a vast slab, slashed by a crack which grows ever narrower towards the top.

The start, at the actual foot of the face, where the grass reaches its highest point, at once presents two difficult rope's lengths up to the first overhang; but before getting to the start, the lover of flowers will find himself going up through a veritable Alpine garden. All the way from Fälensee up the broken rock there are auricula and gentians in such a profusion of colour and growth that one forgets all about overhangs . . . The exact route in the guidebook should be carefully studied. On the abseil from the little 'Aiguille' of the Red Tower one swings airily for 40 m clear above the abyss: it is important to know that beforehand. If you are combining the Hundstein with the Red Tower, the first thing you meet is a Grade IV corner as a sufficient prelude to the magnificent Main Dièdre, which is such a feature of our photograph. There are splendid hand-holds like jug handles, your legs straddle wide apart as

you go vertically upwards all the way to the ridge, and the overhang which has to be mastered on the left half-way up is nothing but a proof of courage for a man of parts. The whole thing is a delight, provided you come to it in the right condition . . . You will soon know that this Alpstein area of Eastern Switzerland is no mere buttress of the Alps, but an interesting high target in its own right, to set beside the Bregaglia, the Rätikon and the Engelhörner. For the descent, you stroll happily down the West Ridge till you reach the start of 'Hell', as the abseil-gorge southwards towards Fälensee is known. Down there, we shall be greeted again by flowers, and further down still by brimming tankards like those whose handles we gripped in the rift. Incidentally the linking of these successive climbs is a practical proposition even in doubtful weather, for you can, if necessary, abandon living dangerously after the 'Aiguille Rouge' and practise *dolce far niente*.

Valley Resorts Brülisau, 922 m. Sax im Rheintal, 480 m.
Bases Bollenwees, 1470 m (inn) and Hundstein Hut, SAC, both 2½ hours from Brülisau. Unteralp, 1393 m, unserviced, 2½ hours from Sax.
Starting Points For the Red Tower at 1850 m at the southern foot of the middle of the face, 1½ hours from Bollenwees or Fälenalp. For the Hundstein from the saddle between the two mountains at about 1950 m. The direct approach from Fälenalp follows tracks and partly a climbers' path. Times: Red Tower 2–3 hours, Hundstein, plus 2–3 hours.
Descent Path, red-markings from the Hundstein Summit down the eastern flank, 1 hour; or, if a depot left at the start, down 'Hell', a gorge between Hundstein and Freiheit. There, from the overhang (abseil piton), a free abseil of 28 m (take care, risk of a 'pendulum', and only feasible with two ropes).
First Ascents Red Tower South Face, A. Baumann and F. Bürkle, 27.6.1947. Hundstein Gully, W. Fleischmann and M. Niedermann, 1.5.1955.
Guides/Maps FB St. G *Säntisführer* (German). LK 25M. Sh. 1175 – Vättis, 25M.(T) Sh. 2506 – Säntisgebiet.
Plate Aerial shot from the south. Left below, Roter Turm, right top, Hundstein with the great dièdre, in shadow, in the left-hand half of the face. Top left, in conjunction, Feiheit, 2140 m (on which there is a fine Grade IV South Face Route)

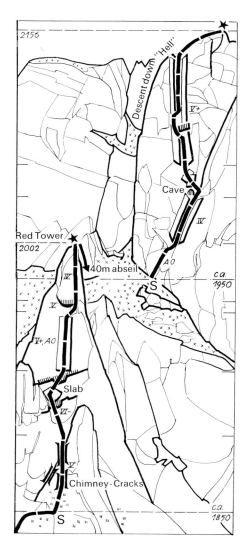

SWITZERLAND 27

Churfirsten Group
Zuestoll 2235 m
South Face

Grade VI−, A1/300 m

Our aerial photograph gives no idea where this Zuestoll, with its sheer South Face, is situated or that it belongs to that stark regiment of the seven Churfirsten which present geological as well as scenic phenomena between the deep basin of the Walensee and the Obertoggenburg country in the shadow of the Säntis. From the north, from the Säntis side that is, they look like seven slightly presumptuous green pulpit roofs, arranged in single file, and really rather a comical sight. Looking from the Walensee side, however, that is from the Zürich–Chur motorway, at those same Churfirsten, you see the precipitous outlines of seven peaks which testify to their late-Alpine origin in the last era of the folding of old seabeds. Here, a thousand stratified slabs, thrust up by the upheaval of this limestone range, broke away – and what they left was a geological museum. Climbers can observe this sharp scenic contrast from stance upon stance for 4 to 6 hours in a wall of truly Dolomitic character while their rope-mates are climbing, and in doing so discover this magnificent world of steps forming a staircase from the lake to the summits of the range.

We are lucky to have the adjoining aerial photograph. On it, it is easy to follow the difficult, and in wet conditions extremely risky, approach to the actual start of the climb at an altitude of 1950 metres (seen in the middle of the picture). You traverse westwards out of the gorge falling from the saddle between the Zuestoll and Schibenstoll at the first green terrace, to reach the first pine-trees in a corner and then after traversing a tricky groove, the second clump of pines. The ascent from here to the second prominent green terrace goes straight up, forcing you into a dièdre leading to a very dicey cliff; then straight up again – an uncomfortable section on grass-grown slabby rock – to the last of these prominent green terraces. You traverse along this outward-sloping ledge to that flat buttress in the face (exactly in the centre of the picture, horizontally and vertically), which is seen to have a pyramid-like overhanging roof. This is the actual start, up the roof

of the buttress (40 m, IV), after which there is little difficult climbing before arriving at the Eastern Arête, outlined by sunlight and shadow, at the top. The text of the Churfirsten guidebook provides detailed information. From the start at the flat buttress, the climb takes 4 to 6 hours. Once on the summit, remember what we have written above: drink it in, marvel at it, recognise its message and, at the same time, realise that the citizen of Zürich, no less than the man of Munich, has a glorious climber's paradise right at his front door.

Valley Resorts Walenstadt, 426 m. Walenstadt-Berg (Sanitorium), 967 m (Postauto). Thence by a road to Hochrugg and Schrina, 1290 m.
Base Possible accommodation at Alp Tschingel, 1527 m, 1½ hours by marked path, by way of Grund and the Palis shoulder.
Starting Point At about 1950 m on the green rock-terrace in the middle of the Zuestoll's South Face (see the direct centre of our photograph). Approach, out of the gorge between Zuestoll and Schibenstoll.
Descent First northwards, then to the left (westwards) back to the Palisnideri, 2010 m, the saddle between Zuestoll and Brisi; thence to the south on traces of a path to the high-level path, Tschingel–Palis–Grund–Hochrugg, 2 hours.
Special Note The approach to the starting point is exceptionally dangerous in wet conditions owing to the outward-sloping stratification of the steep grassy terraces.
First Ascent Ferdy Bürkle and Hans Frommenwiler, 16/17.9.1948.
Guides/Maps FB St. G *Churfirstenführer* (German). LK 25M. Sh. 1134 – Walensee.
Plate Aerial shot taken from the south, of the South Face of the Zuestoll, one of the seven Churfirsten above the Walensee in Eastern Switzerland. With the aid of the photograph and sketch there is no difficulty in following the route, especially the far from danger-free and somewhat tortuous approach to the starting point.

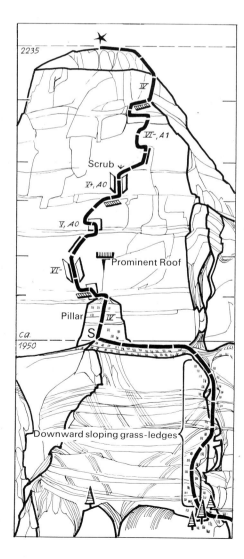

54

Bregaglia Group
Piz Badile 3308 m
North-East Face
Grade V+, A1/800 m

The mountaineer, whom the severest form of climbing has in thrall, dreams at an early stage – time and financial worries permitting – of the grandest targets: the Bonatti Pillar of the Dru, the North-East Face of the Badile, the North-East Gully of the Brenta Alta, the South Face of the Marmolada, the Torre Trieste – but the Badile's 'North-East' is always in the forefront of his dreaming. The mountain's North Ridge, sweeping up sheer and clean, exerts its lure from far away, whether the approach is over the Julier Pass or from the Lower Engadine. Even from Bondo down in the Bregaglia Valley, seen in worm's-eye view, it is a breathtaking vision, sheer and smooth as a giant tooth. If you have time, first drive up to Soglio and, from behind a heap of gleaming spaghetti, with a glass of good Valtellina wine next to you, look across to the most beautiful *cirque* of climbs between Mt Blanc and the Civetta. What marvellous proportions grace this overwhelming row of north ridges almost 1000 metres high, set close to one another! This prospect will always remain at the core of your Alpine memories. Don't make any mistake at Bondo: one can mostly drive up to Laret, 1377 m, and so save two hours of unnecessary uphill slogging. Up in the Bondasca bowl, all around the Sciora Hut, only rain or fog can deny the delights of long hours of staring and wondering at the terrific prow of the Badile's North Ridge, the massive Cengalo Pillar, the smooth 'Flat Iron' Arête of Pizzi Gemelli – all two or three times bigger than anything in the Kaisergebirge or Wetterstein; and all in the icy air of high altitude and in face of the terror of glaciers shattered into savage ice-falls . . .

It was in 1937 that the North-East Face was first climbed in a sensational venture lasting four days, on which rivalry between dissimilar and almost competitive parties tragically led to loss of life. The first to reach the top, Riccardo Cassin and his companions Esposito and Ratti, cannot have had any pleasure from their achievement, seeing that the courageous partners in their success had to die on the mountain . . . The rock of the apparently unapproachable North-East Face is a light-grey 'young' granite, only superficially weathered; it is compact and the often tile-like stratification of its slabby walls confronts the climber with exceedingly smooth cracks and corners. The fine-roughness of the rock, rather like porphyric granite, admits of progress by pressure and friction. The route is not always easy to find in its lower sections and a look-out has to be kept for stone-fall dangers from the funnel above, which often sends down blocks as big as a table. Speed and care are essential on the less steeply-inclined rope lengths up to the patch of snow, and especial alertness is called for at that spot. There is a safe variant for escape, leading to the North Ridge without climbing the funnel (as shown in the sketch): at the belaying piton (abseil piton into the funnel) avoid the abseil and climb straight on, even though it doesn't look possible – it will 'go' all right. The proof that so much 'goes', and that this feared and famous face has grown easier as the standard of climbing techniques has developed, lies in the first solo climb, accomplished by Hermann Buhl.

Valley Resorts Promontogno, 821 m. Bondo, 823 m (both on the north side, bus from Chiavenna or Maloja). Laret, 1377 m (motorable from Bondo to bridge at 1247 m). Bagni del Masino, 1172 m.
Bases Sasc-Furä Hut, SAC, 1904 m, at the foot of Badile's North Ridge, serviced, 3½ hours from Bondo, 2½ hours from Laret. Sciora Hut, SAC, 2118 m, serviced. Times as for the Sasc-Furä Hut. Bivouac-box close to Badile's summit-ridge, 3300 m. To the south, Rifugio Gianetti, CAI, 2534 m, serviced.
Starting Point At about 2420, at the base, 100 m to the right of the fall-line of the funnel. Approach from the Sasc-Furä Hut, shortly before the start of the ridges, down to the left to the glacier and thence to the face. Time for the climb, for a two-man rope, 8–10 hours. Much strenuous free-climbing. Falling stones.
Descent By the normal route (II) on the south side, 2–3 hours to the Rifugio Gianetti or by abseil and climbing down the North Ridge (IV) 4–6 hours – difficult but safe and direct and avoids the long return to the Sciora Hut over the Passo di Bondo.
First Ascent R. Cassin, G. Esposito, V. Ratti, M. Molteni, G. Valsecchi, 14–16 July 1937.
Guides/Maps CAI *Masino, Bregaglia, Disgrazia*, vol. I (Italian). SAC *Bündner Alpen*, vol. IV (German). WCP *Bregaglia West*. LK 25M. Sh. 1276 – Val Bregaglia, Sh. 1296 – Sciora. ATP 35M. Bregaglia Area.
Plate The North-East Flank of Piz Badile with the North Ridge, right. Above the middle of the picture, in the upper part of the North-East Face, the deep score of the giant funnel, which is always dangerous. The patch of snow in mid-face (see sketch) disappears in hot summers.

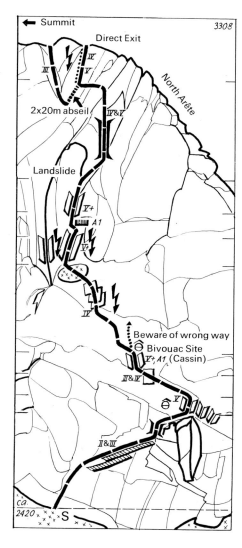

Bregaglia Group
Piz Cengalo 3370 m
North-West Pillar
Grade VI–, A0/900 m

Your first sight of it should be from Soglio, 'the prettiest village in Switzerland', which sits on a terrace of green meadows high above the Bregaglia Valley, huddled close round the old castle of the Salis family. From there the Cengalo Pillar, one of three granite ridges, stands between the 'Flat-Iron' Arête of the Gemelli and the North Ridge of Piz Badile. The prospect is as daunting as it is attractive. Only two generations ago nobody would have dreamed of the possibility of climbing those monstrous primitive wedges. Yes, you should first drive up to Soglio . . . or do as Dietmar Ohngemach did: climb the famous Badile North Ridge and, waiting on a stance, look around you at what he describes in these words: 'Away out there, the Engadine Lakes, mirrors glistening in the shadowy blue depths, while opposite, near enough to touch, soars the North-West Arête of the Cengalo. I caught my breath, clung more tightly to my holds, deep in trouble, peering down between my legs to the glacier . . . What had happened? I had spotted climbers on the Cengalo Arête, but it looked so horrifyingly smooth that I felt unnerved . . . in the evening, at the Badile Hut, those same climbers waxed enthusiastic about this marvellous climb and told us they were just as scared for us on our Badile face!' . . .

It would be a good idea to bivouac at the base of the Cengalo just to study the Badile Face stuck up there like a blackboard. The climb of the Cengalo's 900-metre pillar of granite shooting up to 3370 m is without any doubt one of the really big examples of a high-Alpine route bordering on the limits of the extreme described in this book. It ranks a degree higher than the Badile's North-East Face in that it offers more free-climbing and therefore a higher degree of skill. You will find nothing given away here. Be careful not to start too low down, and make sure you are to the right of the arête (at the very bottom of the picture), for it is there that you will find the only way up: a couloir to be climbed till a practicable gully leads up on to the ridge itself. The route always

remains to the right of the snow-sprinkled steps and ledges showing up white in our photograph till, after the grassy gully, you reach the key-pitch, bang-on the arête itself. Then, like a donkey on an ice-rink, you start up that mirror-smooth, rounded slab of granite, which only seems to yield to friction methods and whose angle only eases off very gradually a long way further up . . . While the Baden climbers, Fred Gaiser and Bertel Lehmann were making the first ascent, Riccardo Cassin and his party were fighting their way up the great Badile Face, close at hand – a venture on which two of the Italians lost their lives. The lovely South Ridge of the Cengalo is also worth noting as a big tough target for a 'pleasure climb'. You will need an ice-axe and crampons on the descent, if you haven't needed them before. A glance, on the photograph, at the fiercely-jutting cornices on the Cengalo will serve as a reminder of the altitude of this route.

Valley Resorts Promontogno, 821 m. Bondo, 823 m (bus from Maloja or Chiavenna). Bagni del Masino, 1172 m (bus from Ardenno/Valtellina).
Bases On the north side, Sciora Hut, SAC, 2118 m. below the Fuori Arête, serviced; 3½ hours from Bondo, 2¼ hours from Laret, 1377 m, motorable. To the south, Rifugio Gianetti (Badile Hut), CAI, 2534 m, serviced; 2 hours down to Bagni del Masino.
Starting Point At about 2420 m. Coming from the Sciora Hut, you pass the projecting rock, then climb to the western foot of the pillar. Avoid traversing too far down on to partly rotten rock. Only start up from the right. Ice-hammer or axe often of great importance for the crossing of the crevassed Cengalo glacier. Time for the climb, for a two-man rope, 7–9 hours.
Descent By the normal route on the south side, first down the South-West Ridge, then at the second-deepest notch, down the chimney-couloir over snow and boulders to the Gianetti Hut, 2½ hours.
First Ascent F. Gaiser and B. Lehmann, 15 July 1937.
Guides/Maps CAI *Masino, Bregaglia, Disgrazia*, vol. I (Italian). SAC *Bündner Alpen*, vol. IV (German). WCP *Bregaglia West*. LK 25M. Sh. 1276 – Val Bregaglia, Sh. 1296 – Sciora. ATP 35M. Bregaglia Area.
Plate Piz Cengalo from the north, photographed from the moraine. The powdering of snow shows up the rock-structures of this huge granite pillar to great advantage.

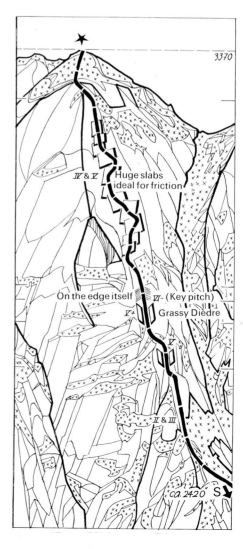

Bregaglia Group
Pizzi Gemelli ('The Twins') 3262 m
North Ridge (Flat-Iron)
Grade V, A1/850 m

Three of the finest and toughest granite ridges in the Alps rise above the Bondasca re-entrant in the Bregaglia: those of the Gemelli, Cengalo and Badile, all about 900 metres high and reaching an altitude of about 3300 metres. Their high-Alpine exposure is extreme, and the midday thunderstorms working up from Lake Como, not far away, are an additional source of danger. To the right and left of these polished ridges fall ice-couloirs shattered to an amazing degree and rich in every kind of crevasse. The famous granite is firm beyond compare, light in colour and compact; it is porphyric, smooth as skin and yet rough, solid and apparently devoid of hand- or foot-holds, but the fine gritty texture allows friction. The lower part of the North Ridge of the Gemelli ('The Twins') could hardly have attracted any other nickname than the Flat-Iron. Climbed for the first time in 1935, today it has become a sought-after, fashionable route, starting from the Sciora Hut. Its sharp crest, in texture reminiscent of elephant-hide, is rounded, as you will discover when you first get on to it and test its reaction to adhesion. The experience is a 'must'! Most people are puzzled by the speed with which this exposure can be overcome. Suddenly you realise that this elephant's-hide grips your soles and, seen in close-up, even provides finger-holds as large as hazel-nuts and foot-holds as big as fingertips. Where flakes, cracks and narrow grooves are met with, the edges of the granite are sharp as razor-blades — and many a rope has been cut by them — even a brand-new one. On this granite a 9 mm rope is a hostage to fortune; only an 11 mm provides enough chance of survival.

Every belaying-piton on the Flat-Iron carries its abseil-slings: a reminder that these speed-merchants, bless them, cheerfully come up the Flat-Iron, then go down again the same way, roping-down where they can . . . Naturally both the time required and the high-altitude risks are redoubled if the second half, on the North Ridge, is added to the first half on the Flat Iron. 2–4 hours escalate into 7–12, at least. The Flat-Iron is

only 2680 metres, the Gemelli another 600 metres higher. Manfred Sturm writes: 'Though longer, the upper half is easier, but noticeably more high-Alpine in character, and the route is not easy to find.' The Flat-Iron's last cliff is usually turned by its flank, as stated in guide-books. Beware of any attempt to find an escape-route down from the ridge, either to the east or to the west: just study the photograph with a magnifying-glass and note the smoothness of its rock-armour. The climber who has the mettle for the whole climb must think beforehand about the descent. The one to the Badile Hut is relatively short, that over the Bondasca Pass (bivouac-box) is very long. Both lead down to the glacier level after a couple of abseils. If you are going down to the Sciora Hut, you keep to the right on the Bondasca Glacier, sticking to the trail and trusting to a good 'nose'.

Valley Resorts Promontogno, 821 m. Bondo, 823 m (bus from Maloja and Chiavenna). Bagni del Masino, 1172 m (bus from Ardenno/Val Tellina).
Bases Sciora Hut, SAC, 2118 m, serviced, 3½ hours from Bondo, 2½ hours from Laret (motorable). To the south: Rifugio Gianetti (Badile Hut) CAI 2534 m, serviced, 2 hours to Bagni Bivouac-box of the CAI, 3160 m, on the Bondo Pass, open, no blankets.
Starting Point At 2350 m, to the right of the arête, 1 hour from the Hut (at first horizontally across the crevassed Bondasca Glacier on to the broad terrace above the lower rock-wedge).
Descent To the south: over the South-East Summit, then the normal way down (II) the South-West Ridge into the moraine-cwm between the Gemelli and the Cengalo's South Ridge, then further down to the Rifugio Gianetti, about 2½ hours descent to the north: after two abseils of 20 m each, up and down in a south-easterly direction to the Bondo Pass (bivouac-box), then with ice-axe and crampons (bergschrund and crevasses) down the glacier, keeping to the right, to the Sciora Hut. At least 4 hours.
First Ascent H. Frei and J. Weiss, 27/28.7.1935 ('Flat-Iron'). G. Hentschel and H. Mathies, 12.8.1934 (Gemelli North Ridge).
Guide/Maps CAI *Masino, Bregaglia, Disgrazia*, vol. I (Italian). SAC *Bündner Alpen*, vol. IV (German). WCP *Bregaglia West*. LK 25M. Sh. 1276 – Val Bregaglia, Sh. 1296 – Sciora. ATP 35M. Bregaglia Area.
Plate The Flat-iron and the adjoining Gemelli North Ridge run diagonally to the twin summits of the Gemelli. Right top, the massif of the Cengalo with a long crown of cornices on its flat summit-ridge. To the left, below, the Bondasca Glacier, our descent-route.

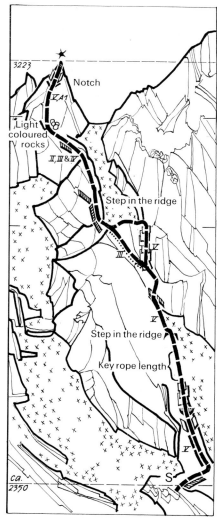

Bregaglia Group
Sciora di Fuori 3169 m
North-West Ridge (Fuorikante)
Grade VI−, A1/600 m

The Sciora's rocky comb between the Albigna and Bondasca basins, so richly endowed with famous 'pleasure climbs' on its 'young', light-coloured, almost unbroken granite, also has its snags, and these have brought the celebrated Fuorikante into ill-repute. A well-known Swiss cragsman wrote this about it, having climbed it after the great rock-slide of 1961: 'This is a route through a landslide, brutal and uncomfortable – a route for the crack specialist and would-be suicide. Once, but never again!' The guide and author of climbing-guides, Paul Nigg, gives a contrary opinion, having done the climb three times, after the landslide and, in 1968, even in winter, saying it remains a truly great climb. The cause of all the trouble is this: the compact mass of a granite slab to the west of the arête, where there used to be a chimney with a wobbly block, has disappeared for about 20 metres . . . there remain not even the smallest stances. At this point it became necessary to traverse out on to a very brittle ledge on the right (the West Face). This once so famous ridge can be climbed even after the landslide and everything has become much easier since the introduction of bolts. Today the landslide is turned to the left of the arête by the employment of this technique.

Our sketch shows the vital points on the climb. Unfortunately the Fuorikante does not slope back as amiably as it would appear in the photograph, taken from its foot. However, the picture does show the confusing rock-formation of this very 'recent' primitive rock, whose origin is the subject of conflicting explanations in various guidebooks; for while the extremely similar granite of Mt Blanc arose out of the folding of the Alps, that of the Bregaglia rose out of the depths at the end of the shaping of the mountains when the raw structure of the Alps was already complete. Today this granite, fresh as the morning dew, is still compact, unbroken and only surface-weathered, rough, gloriously rough for the rock-enthusiast. Its components are felspar, quartz and mica, and lately a new ingredient – wooden wedges.

Valley Resorts Promontogno, 821 m, or Bondo, 823 m, on the south side of the Maloja pass (bus from St Moritz or Chiavenna).
Base Sciora Hut, 2118 m, SAC, in the upper Val Bondasca, serviced, close under our Fuori Arête, 3½ hours from the valley, or by motor to near Laret, 1377 m, then only 2¼ hours.
Starting Point You climb up across the snowfield between the towers projecting in front of the ridge and the Pioda Arête, then from the foot of the West Face to the left over slabs up to the starting point, which is easily recognisable at the foot of the Fuorikante, at about 2500 m.
Descent First you climb down northwards to the Colle della Scioretta (II), 3000 m (seen on the left-hand edge of the photograph), then down snow-couloirs and a rubble-basin westwards into the cwm on snow or boulders. Just 3 hours to the hut.
Special Note Heavy rock-slides on the upper sector of the arête in 1961 and subsequently have altered this fine route to a marked degree at key-point. Our text relies on the comments of the guide Paul Nigg, who has climbed the arête since the landslide. Time for the climb, for a rope of two, 6–8 hours.
First Ascent W. Weippert and K. Simon, 17.9.1933.
Guides/Maps CAI *Masino, Bregaglia, Disgrazia*, vol. I (Italian). SAC *Bündner Alpen*, vol. IV (German). WCP *Bregaglia West*. LK 25M. Sh. 1276 – Val Bregaglia, Sh. 1296 – Sciora. ATP 35M. Bregaglia Area.
Plate The North-West Arête of the Sciora di Fuori. Right top, the Punta Pioda with its splendid North Ridge, top left, the Scioretta Saddle, by which the descent is effected.

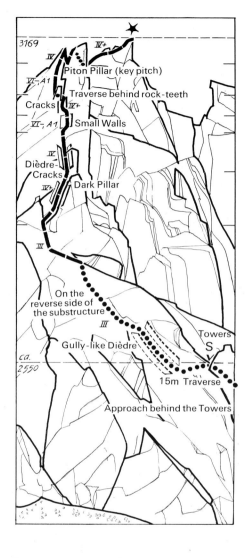

Rätikon

Grosser Drusenturm 2827 m

South Pillar ('Swiss Route')

Grade VI, A1/500 m

As you come to Partnun over the Garschinafurka or from the Gauertal over the Drusentor, a little way to the west you find yourself at the foot of the Drusenturm, looking very much as it does in our picture. It is a matter for surprise and wonder that the earth's old crust in decay can show such architecture. The vertical wall of limestone with its beautifully proportioned summit-sweep stands as if supported by immense columns of rock, while the face and its pillars go soaring up for 500 metres above the bottom of the cwm. Not even the Marmolada can match this impression. The Laliderer Wall is more gloomy, that of the Civetta wider and larger, but what our aerial photograph, taken seconds before the plane banked away, shows is a nobility of architecture, overwhelming and uplifting at the same time, which matches up to the proportions of Leonardo's Ideal. This limestone castle with its three towers offers a multitude of fine climbs, on its southern as well as its northern side, and at the beginning of May it is also possible to ski down from the summit through the Sporertobel to the Lindauer Hut on splendidly steep, hard snow. Our pillar was long considered 'unclimbable by fair means' on account of the critical slab-pitch after the two first rope lengths, which simply have to be climbed 'free'. A modern, Wagner-conscious climber has written: 'One longs for some kind of magic formula for producing greater friction against the monolithic smoothness of the rock. On the slabs at the start of the pillar it is easy to "learn what fear means".' The rock is good, smooth and firm, but not exactly rich in holds, and the crux of the climb lies in mastering the exciting exposure of the free-climbing.

It was in 1954 that the two ace-climbers from Eastern Switzerland, Max Niedermann and Wisi Fleischmann first did the climb, taking ten hours over it, late in the summer, when they were at the peak of their form. Route-finding is relatively easy, as the main line of the climb is logical. The pioneers used 75 pitons, of which they left 25 to their successors – but the number has since increased again considerably... The first 100 metres do not require the rope. Max Niedermann, that sympathetic member of the Alpstein Climbing Club, has written a short but vivid description of the climb in the Flaig guidebook. He still maintains that the route, so rewarding from start to finish, is easy to find. All the same today's normal time of 6–8 hours is frequently exceeded. The photograph shows that the 1933 Burger route (IV and V, one pitch VI−), the Seth Abderhalden Memorial route (VI, A2) of 1957 and the KCA route (V–VI/A1) of 1958 all adjoin that on the South Pillar. There is also, over on the North Face, a very fine extreme route, although there are only 250 metres of it. The descents to the Lindauer and Garschina Huts are simple. The South Pillar should never be attempted too early in the year, lest icing be encountered during the last very difficult rope length. Finally, whoever approaches or leaves this impressive South Wall and has a good pair of eyes should not miss the walk between the Schweitzertor and the Drusentor – it is a deeply stirring experience, and very good for the soul.

Valley Resorts Tschagguns/Montafon, 684 m. St Antönien, 1420 m (bus from Küblis).
Bases Lindauer Hut, 1744 m, DAV, serviced; 2½ hours from Latschau (bus from station), otherwise 4 hours from Tschagguns. Garschina Hut, 2201 m, SAC, adjoining the Garschinafurka between the Suizflun and Schafberg, unserviced; 3 hours from St Antönien, 1½ hours from Partnun (accessible by motor).
Starting Point At 2300 m to the right of the projection in the wall (bottom right of the picture). Reached in 2 hours from the Lindauer Hut over the Drusentor, 2342 m. Only ¾ hour from the Garschina Hut. Time for the climb for a good rope of two, 6–8 hours, often more.
Descent By the normal route on the east flank down the Sporertobel to the Lindauer Hut, or over the Drusentor back to the Garschina Hut. 1½ hours and 2½ hours respectively.
First Ascent M. Niedermann and W. Fleischmann, 6.9.1954.
Guides/Maps RR *Rätikonführer* (AV series, German). LK 50M. Sh. 238 – Montafon (25M. scale map falls short).
Plate The Grosser Drusenturm of the Rätikon, from the south, to its left the Stockzahn. The South Pillar, above its broad triangular ramp, is identifiable to the right of the vertical centre of the picture.

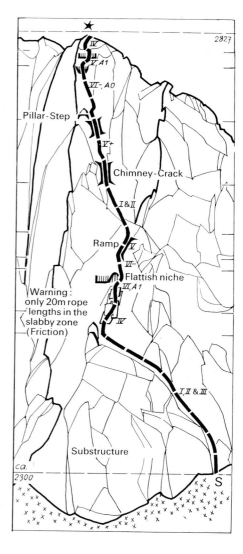

Rätikon
Scheienfluh 2625 m
West Face (Scheienwand)
Grade VI, A2/300 m

At the point where the Rätikon range, running from Falknis and Naafkopf over the Schesaplana, Drusenfluh and Sulzfluh, ceases to be pure limestone and starts to rise as a primitive rock-formation into the Silvretta Group, stands the last limestone bastion of the Scheienfluh. It was for a long time over-shadowed by the fame of its neighbours; but there were always ambitious 'Extremists', coming from their high adventures to rest among the beds of 'Alpenrosen' around the little lake of Partnun, whether alone or not, who were bewitched by the silent, beautiful, lofty chaos they found there. High above them soared the walls of the Sulzfluh and Scheienfluh, often winging to the illimitable and invisible like the settings for some *Götterdämmerung* while, below, everything which had once been a mountain ran together into a forgotten green funnel. It was from here that the Scheien Face was discovered, slashed for two-thirds of its height by a vast angular rift which often overhangs, but below which a long, almost vertical pillar stands away from the marble smoothness of the wall. It is shown in our picture to the left of the lower dièdre, and the sketch shows that the top of the pillar is reached not from the right but up its left-hand side by a series of difficult cracks, separating the Marmorwand and the pillar.

The dièdre always used to look impossible, but what a change there has been – it is now hailed as the most important extreme route in the Rätikon. For a long time it was rated at VI+ and a bivouac was definitely thought essential; but by the summer of 1959 there had been at least 55 ascents. It was Max Niedermann and Peter Diener who made the impossible possible. In 1956 they got up a quarter of the Face before turning back; the next year, in 26 hours of actual climbing time and with two bivouacs, they got to its top. Naturally, it had to fall a victim to the most modern techniques, though even then some exhausting free-climbing could not be dispensed with. The second party to succeed compared the climb with the Livanos Dièdre. Today no one ever

bivouacs on this West Face. A search was made for the direct exit shown in our sketch and it was discovered in 1959 by K. Grüter and S. Anderrüthi.

The assessment of VI, A2 should hold its own. Anyone who climbs this unusual route finds it a great experience. From the summit-plateau his delighted eyes can greet Palü, Bernina, the ice of the Silvretta and all the Parsenn; and when he scythes his way home through the valley of St Anthönien he can welcome that precious green mountain-home too. But would anyone celebrating such a hard-won victory have the kindly eyes to take in that remote, high valley, ravaged almost every year by avalanches; whose inhabitants have never given in and, in spite of all these tribulations, have always rebuilt their houses? There they stand, proud and clean as new pins, high up on the steep meadows; the true fortresses of an indomitable will to live.

Valley Reports Partnun, 1772 m (in the Prätigau). Tschagguns, 824 m (in the Montafon).
Bases Berghaus Sulzfluh (1769 m) on the Partnunstafel, private, serviced, some beds, 1¼ hours from St Antönien. Tilisuna Hut, ÖAV, 2208 m, serviced, 5 hours from Tschagguns or 2½ hours from Lift Grabs.
Starting Point At 2300 m at the left-hand junction of the pillar running up the first third of the Face; 1½ hours from Partnun. Time for the climb, for a two-man rope, 5–6 hours.
Descent Easily down northwards to the Tilisuna Hut. Easy but longer (Grade I and II) by way of the Scheienfluh South Ridge and Plasseggen to Partnun, 2 hours.
First Ascent M. Niedermann and P. Diener, 9/11.6.1957.
Guides/Maps RR *Rätikonführer* (AV series, German). LK 50M. Sh. 238 – Montafon (25M. scale map falls short).
Plate This picture taken by that splendid Swiss high-Alpine climber, Ruedi Homberger, shows the Scheienwand from the south-west. On the left, the rock-sliver, projecting from the Face and separated from the Face by a series of cracks. Slightly left of centre, the huge, often overhanging dièdre is seen slashing its way almost up to the summit-slab.

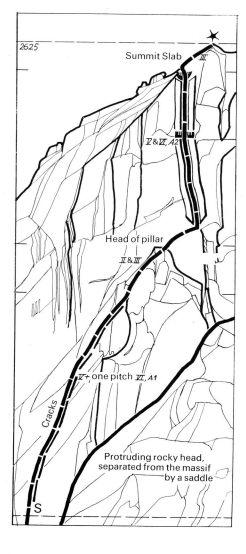

Rätikon
Sulzfluh 2817 m
South-West Face Direct
Grade VI−, A1/270 m from the start proper

Before the bright greyish-blue Sulzfluh limestone of the Eastern Rätikon range loses itself in the dark primitive rock of the close-grouped outliers of the Silvretta, there are three final giant walls standing grandly above the green rift of the St Antönien valley. They are the Sulzfluh, Scheienfluh and Rätschenfluh. All three weave a spell over the lover of extreme climbing. We are illustrating here the 'Direct' South-West Route up the face of the Sulzfluh, which arrives at the summit-ridge a little to the right of its highest point – in contrast to that opened up a year later, truly the 'Central' climb on the same face, which comes out to the left of the summit. This is seen better in a photograph in the Flaig guidebook than in our aerial photograph, taken from the west. There one can also see that the 'Direct' (Hiebeler-Bachmann, VI −, A1, 1949) deserves its name, while the 'Central' (Hiebeler-Brunold, VI −, 1950), attempting a parallel route to the 'Direct', in fact takes a more circuitous line. In any case, the name 'Central' is difficult to sustain in relation to the idea of a 'Direct'. There can be no doubt that both are splendid climbs, both enjoying the advantage of the famous, firm Sulzfluh limestone.

Our chosen 'Direct' can rarely be climbed with any pleasure in the early summer, because damp and icing pose difficulties in the big exit-chimney, to say nothing of soppy pigeon-droppings, alternating with the dampness and the ice. This is one of the reasons why the 'Central' is nowadays climbed more often. The pioneers used 20 pitons for our 'Direct' climb, whose route and its fearsome steepness are well shown in our aerial photograph. Today there are considerably more in position. The time taken by Toni Hiebeler and Franz Bachmann has since been reduced to 5–7 hours. 'Extremists' from Eastern Switzerland and also from places in the Vorarlberg prefer our climb in the late summer. Zürich climbers too, who today have swift access, by way of the Walensee into the St Antönien valley and up to the newly built Garschina Hut of the SAC, like to get to work on

the three main routes up the South-West Face, among which we include the Stanek-Neumann Route (IV and V), although it is not quite in the 'extreme' bracket, simply because it provides true 'pleasure-climbing'. On all the climbs on this Face we have the sun on our backs, which should not be forgotten any more than the proximity of the 3000-metre level, a feature one only notices when threatened by a break in the weather. There is no more chance of a quick turn-about and a swift abseil here than on the walls of the Civetta, though the descents from the summit to the Garschinafurka (II, 1 hour) or through the Rachen gorge to the Lindauer Hut (1¼ hours) or, in case of emergency, to the Tilisuna Hut near by (fully 1 hour) are comparatively easy. One might perhaps remember, having reached the summit, that the finest spring ski-run in the Rätikon plunges headlong down 2100 metres into the Montafon on the north side, and is possible till the end of May.

Valley Resorts Tschagguns/Montafon, 683 m. St Antönien, 1420 m, Partnun, 1772 m (motorable).
Bases Lindauer Hut, 1744 m, DAV, serviced, 2½ hours from Latschau, 4 hours from Tschagguns. Garschina Hut, 2201 m, SAC, no service, usually caretaker; 3 hours from St Antönien or 1½ hours from Partnun (accessible by motor).
Starting Point At 2550 m in the direct fall-line from the summit. First on to the cliffy projection (direct centre of the photograph) from the left (I and II), then slightly down to the right to the start of the entry gully. Not to be attempted when the rock is wet, because there is lichen in the chimney. The projection is half an hour from the Garschina Hut, or on the path to the Tilisuna Hut, 1 hours.
Descent Down the western gorge – Drusentor-Garschina Hut, 1¼ hours; Rachen-Lindauer Hut, 1½ hours; or by path to the Tilisuna Hut, 1¼ hours.
First Ascent T. Hiebeler and F. Bachmann, 28/29.7.1949.
Guides/Maps RR *Rätikonführer* (AV series, German). LK 50M. Sh. 238 – Montafon (25M. scale map falls short).
Plate The aerial photograph shows the western and south-western flanks of the Sulzfluh in the Rätikon. Right, below the West Summit (highest summit top left) you can see the chimneys and gullies of our 'Direct' South-West Face Route plunging almost vertically to the clearly recognisable cliffy projection with its rubble cap. The picture was taken from the west. A southern aspect (Plate 32 in the Flaig guidebook) shows that the wall fans out more broadly.

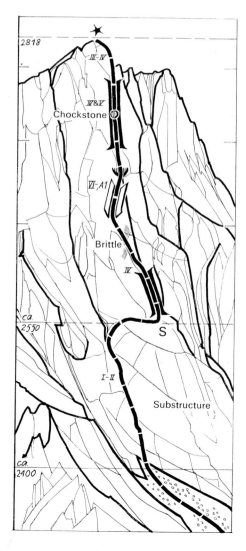

Tannheimer Group
Rote Fluh 2111 m
South Dièdre
Grade VI−, A1/250 m

The south walls of the Tannheimer Range between the Haldensee and the Lechdurchbruch are splendid climbing grounds. Here are routes to everyone's taste or mood, and the view from every face, ridge and summit is definitely more extensive than from the practice-climbs on the banks of Munich's Isar . . . Max Niedermann, that blasé Swiss specialist in first-ascents, visited the Tannheimer area once, climbed a few routes and commented: 'All very pleasant as a training-ground, but it all smacks of mere hill-country . . .' True, the height of the faces is minimal, but even climbs of 150 to 250 metres at the most amount to something, especially on limestone of almost unrivalled firmness and richness of holds, on south faces which dry out quickly after rain. It is possible to do many of the climbs from early spring well into the winter; many of them have been climbed by experts familiar with them in 15 to 20 minutes − against which, four climbers were fated to die of exposure or incompetence in stormy weather . . .

Our South Dièdre has become a fashionable target for the connoisseur, seeing that its VI − rating is no subject for contempt. Its start can be reached in half an hour from both huts on the southern flank. Its chief glory and delight is the big dihedral rift − a picture-book specimen − which, climbed as a VI before the 'Iron Age' practically without pitons, is today a profusely 'nailed' artificial A1. Even the roof was climbed then with only a single piton. Since then, there are plenty of pitons everywhere since ironmongery came into fashion and there is no longer any question of 'holds giving way', so often an excuse for failure . . . There are other interesting routes close by, on this sunny south face: the West Dièdre, pioneered by Kleemaier and Nieberle in 1955 (about VI, A1), and Loderer and Waitl's 1960 South-West Buttress, also a VI, A1. Who was that Waitl? The same tough Leonhard Waitl, from Füssen, the well-known German ice-hockey international, strong climber and brilliant exponent on ski . . . Coming back to the summit of the Rote Fluh, one's first look

over the other side takes in the favourite West Ridge of the Gimpel, with its surprise 'Come on, John − guts!' pitch (III+ or III−). Your second glance will seek out the Gimpel Hut, run by the once famous and even better-loved Franzl Fischer: but − horror of horrors! − it has been superseded by a 300-bed 'Alpine Hotel', which is of course very sad since an Alpine Hotel postulates faces 800 metres high, whereas our Rote Fluh only boasts a mere 250 . . . Two major cities are not so far away and their young generation of climbers swarms over the foothills in a flood . . . in spite of which, our South Dièdre has not yet been close-carpeted or provided with banisters.

Valley Resorts Nesselwangle, 1147 m, in the Tannheimer Tal. Possibly Musau, 818 m, in the Lechtal.
Bases Gimpel Hut, 1760 m, private, serviced, 1 hour from Nesselwängle. Tannheimer Hut, 1750 m, DAV, serviced, 1¼ hours from Nesselwängle. Otto-Mayr Hut, 1520 m, DAV, serviced, in the Reintal, 1 hour from the Musauer Alp.
Starting Point At 1850 m at the start of the slightly grassy terrace going slantwise up to the right. ½–¾ hour from Gimpel and Tannheimer Huts. Time for the climb, for a two-man rope 3–4 hours.
Descent On a marked path to the Judenscharte and down south-eastwards to the two huts (about half an hour).
First Ascent A. Kleemaier and L. Schuster, 16.5.1954.
Guides/Maps RR *Allgäuer Alpen* (AV series, German). AV 25M. Sh. 2/1, 2/2 – Allgäu – Lechtaler Alpen.

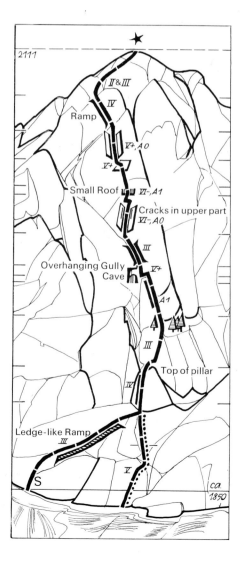

Wetterstein Range
Oberreintaldom 2371 m
North Dièdre (Gonda Groove)
Grade VI−, A1/300 m

For two generations climbers from Munich and Werdenfels have ruled over the Oberreintal and its famous little hut. The Oberreintaldom (formerly the Teufelsturm) was first climbed up its West Ridge in 1909 by that great pioneer explorer Anton Schmid and his friend Behrendt, but only attracted notice when artificial aids made 'extreme' climbing possible. It was its North Face, opposite the 'Squirrel Ridge' (Eichhorngrat) which signalled the arrival of the modern style. In 1936 Lesch and Prechtl found the first route up the left half of the face (V); in 1947 Martin Schliessler and Werner Fischer climbed it to the right of the buttress (VI) and created a considerable stir by their achievement. In 1952, however, Karlheinz Gonda came from Saxony and with Hans Hackel mastered the huge partly-overhanging rift, to the left of the buttress. This was an exploit of superlative technical skill never since surpassed. Sad to relate, only a year later this genius of climbing from the Elbsandstein range fell to his death with his Swiss rope-mate Uli Wyss, only 50 metres below the Eiger's summit. Heady with the sweet scent of success, they made one slight mistake and hurtled down the horrific Eiger North Face after climbing it successfully. Since that day the North Dièdre of the Oberreintaldom bears Gonda's name. Our sketch illustrates the route, while our photograph gives a true impression of the angle of the wall, which can justly be described as vertical. The larger of the two little pulpits shown in the sketch can be identified, lit by the sun, on the photograph, to the left of the buttress. The major difficulties continue up to that point, then the wet chimney which follows is easier. This Gonda Groove is today the favourite route on the Oberreintaldom, with its six in all, only one of which is below Grade VI.

You have to look out for rain; this shadowed north wall is slow to dry out. All the necessary pitons will be found in position on the face. In the approach-gorge beware of falling stones. The lower part of this gorge is climbed on its orographical right where footmarks are clearly visible . . . The descent route is a little difficult to see ahead and should be studied carefully in the guidebook. In early summer the gullies and scree-chutes leading down to the Oberreintal are often still covered by remnants of snow. When these are hard-frozen, the greatest care is essential . . . For a long time the little Oberreintal Hut was the residence of that prince among hut-keepers, Franzl Fischer; he ruled over his young courtiers with a sharp tongue, but a heart of gold – on the way to this purely climbers' hut, a notice-board warns weekend hikers against a visit. The hut is small, the breed of climbers likes to hide its true nature behind a noisy show of toughness. The warning should be heeded – after all, survival is what counts . . .

Valley Resort Garmisch-Partenkirchen, 715 m.
Base Oberreintal Hut, 1525 m, DAV, serviced; 4½ hours from Partenkirchen, 3¼ hours from the Partnachklamm.
Starting Point At about 1850 m in the deep gorge between the Eichhorngrat and the Oberreintaldom, just to the right (west) below the huge gully. A good hour from the hut. Normal time for the 300-metre gully some 3–5 hours for a rope of two.
Descent Down to the south (II) through rubble-chutes and gorges (somewhat confusing) south of the Oberreintaldom. Starts at the small saddle to the east of the summit (2371 m) but not south-eastwards till after the green saddle, then down the great couloir (1½ hours to the hut).
First Ascent K. Gonda and H. Hackel, 20.7.1952.
Guides/Maps RR *Wettersteingebirge und Mieminger Kette* (AV series, German). AV 25M. Sh. 4/3–Wetterstein und Mieminger Gebirge.
Plate The Oberreintaldom (formerly Teufelsturm), 2371 m (top right of centre) is nothing but a rounded step in the West Ridge of the Partenkirchener Dreitorspitze, which splits into two branches lower down. We are looking at the North Face, consisting of several vertical pillars. The Gonda Groove cuts up the shadowed part of the face behind the most central and strongest of the pillars. Below the North Face is the Western Gorge, on the left the Eichhorngrat.

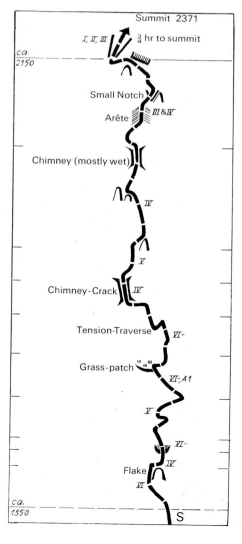

Wetterstein Range
Unterer Schüsselkarturm 2200 m
North Face (Schober Route)
Grade VI−, A1/250 m

As you go up in the shadow of those ancient maples surrounding the Oberreintal Hut on the way into the Schüsselkar, the mighty shape towering overhead is the Lower Schüsselkarturm: a vertical wall of Wetterstein limestone, whose solid structure reminds one of the monolithically smooth slab-armour of the Aiguille du Midi's South Face. Only late and far up do you notice that this apparently separate tower is closely joined at its base and back by an easy connecting ridge to the Oberer Schüsselkarturm and the Scharnitzspitze. Since 1938 there has been a 'Schober Route' up its 250-metre-high North Face. Michael Schober and Karl Münch took eleven hours and used only a few pitons on their first ascent. Every 'Sexogradist' nowadays hearing of a 'Schober' knows that the name speaks for its high quality. But, of course, this Michael Schober, who could never fall on a mountain, had to fall, a short time after his first ascent, in a war – and not even for a worthy ideal. His tower is not high and in no way comparable with equally well-known faces in the Eastern Alps; but a climber familiar with the route remarks: 'If you are used to climbing only 50 cm "free" to the next piton, that is no use at all here. Here the motto is: "fresh, fit, fearless and free!"'

Another regular frequenter of the Oberreintal, Manfred Sturm, comments: 'How even Michael Schober's innate talent for route-finding forced a way up this wall is astonishing. After the entry-crack there is no clearly defined series of cracks and no prominent corner to show the way ahead. And just at the point where the lower gully does become a feature, Schober traversed out to the right onto the face, at first sight crazily but, on reflection, with masterly sense, for it helped him to avoid the great overhangs barring the way. There are many such on this wall, to emphasise his route-finding sense. There is nothing prescribed here, on this small North Face, which demands complete involvement from its very first step, and never becomes easy. Every rope length on that climb has its special appeal.' These

remarks reveal a practical and knowledgeable judge, as the newcomer to the Oberreintal will appreciate the moment he starts the climb. The 30 metres to the first piton are climbed 'free', rightly marked VI− in our sketch. The rock is firm and good, as on all the climbs in the neighbourhood. Let us add one more well-informed opinion, that of Dietmar Ohngemach: 'The tower rises straight from the last green without any transition, like a wall. There is no rubble at its base. The Schober-route reminds one of the neighbouring climb inaugurated by two Munich men, Teufel and Herbst who, climbing free, also displayed a high degree of courage and an accentuated route-finding ability. One can only marvel!'

Valley Resort Garmisch-Partenkirchen 715 m.
Base Oberreintal Hut, 1525 m, in the Oberreintalboden, DAV, serviced; 4½ hours from Partenkirchen, 3¼ from the Partnachklamm.
Starting Point From the hut into the lower Schüsselkar and, right, to the foot of the North Face at about 1950 m, in the direct summit fall-line, where a grey crack 100 m high begins. Cairn. A good hour from the hut. Average time for the climb, for a rope of two, 4–5 hours.
Descent Down the South Ridge (normal route II) to the saddle before the Oberer Schüsselkarturm (15 minutes) then north-westwards into the upper Scharnitzkar, then down (cliffs) and on into the Oberreintalboden (1¼ hours from the saddle).
First Ascent M. Schober and K. Münch, 7.10.1938.
Guides/Maps RR *Wettersteingebirge und Mieminger Kette* (AV series, German). AV 25M. Sh. 4/3 – Wetterstein und Mieminger Gebirge.
Plate The Unterer Schüsselkarturm from the bottom of the cwm. In the fall-line from the summit it is possible to identify, in the left-hand part of the base of the wall, the slightly S-shaped crack-line couloir. It is steep and rather brittle, but it has to be climbed 'free' for the 30 m to the first piton.

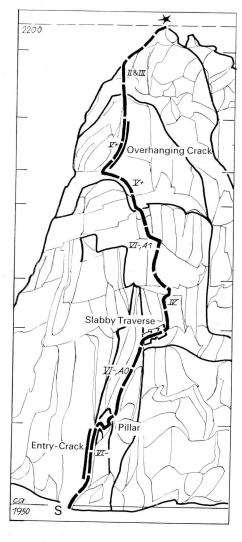

Wetterstein Range
AUSTRIA 38 Scharnitzspitze 2463 m
South Face Direct
Grade VI−, A0/260 m

Seen next to the compact, seemingly armour-plated limestone walls of the adjoining Schüsselkarspitze, the South Face of the Scharnitzspitze exhibits an almost friendly aspect. That is accounted for by the strong structure of its rock, with an inviting wealth of steps, ledges, cracks, chimneys and small gullies – almost as if the Scharnitzspitze were in the Kaisergebirge. Actually it stands between the noisy Werdenfelser Tal around Partenkirchen and the long-drawn-out quiet of the Leutasch. Sitting on its summit with, say, the 'Spitzenstaetter Route' (not to be despised) behind you, you can blink out happily into the distance and count the riches of the whole area: the many lonely and deserted farms under the Arnspitzen and Hohe Munde, the creased folds of the Karwendel valleys, then, over there, the snow-peaks of the Sellrain around the Lisenser Fernkogel. What frequenter of these south-faces in the Wetterstein ridges has not looked down and about, either contentedly, or longingly before a break in the weather? They have been chiefly Munich climbers, but also men of Innsbruck and Garmisch, who have early come to feel at home on the Scharnitzspitze. Here, Hannemann and Hoesch, Kadner, Pfann, Frey, Kuffner, Gretschmann and von Overkamp made their own climbing-garden, albeit it is only 260 metres high.

These devotees of pleasure-climbing were followed by the 'Men of the Extreme', looking (naturally, exactly like their predecessors) for the ultimate 'last problem on rock'. And they found what they were looking for. The 'Spitzenstaetter Route', known as the 'Spitz' for short, offers an avowedly 'modern' climb, though happily broken up by much free-climbing and following a logical line. It is not very long, but you are 'on it' for 3–4 hours. It is no mere stand-by when the weather is too unsettled for the Schüsselkar Faces. The route has character, which is to say that it is nowhere artificial and presents many unusual and fine pitches, as the sketch and the photograph will confirm. Compared with the straight upward line

of the 'Spitzenstaetter', the very sporting 'Eberharter-Streng Route' (classified in the guidebook at VI+ for all that) yields something out of the ordinary. It appeals to those with 'extreme' tendencies as the best way up, in spite of a loop to the right and a hanging-traverse. The climbing is still full of delights on its higher pitches and, at the gully which opens up there under the yellowish-red landslide-scar, there is another fascinating pitch, even if it is only a IV. Anyone who has nothing more 'serious' to do after the 'Spitzenstaetter' should have a quiet go at the Hannemann Route (V−) running up to its right, on which the young climbers of the period immediately after the First World War indulged their new passion for steep rock. It is another example of the pleasure of free-climbing.

Valley Resorts   Oberleutasch, 1180 m (Gaistal Inn). (bus from Garmisch-Mittenwald and Seefeld). Garmisch-Partenkirchen, 715 m.
Bases   Wangalm, 1753 m, to the south-west below the Scharnitzjoch, but private and not always accessible, 2 hours from the Gaistal Inn. 10 minutes below: Wetterstein hut c 1660 m, private, Austrian Mountain-Rescue Service, about 20 places, very obliging hut-keeper. Oberreintal Hut, 1525 m, DAV. thence over the Eastern Wangscharte to the foot of the wall (fully 2½ hours). Memorial hut of the AAVM (Munich), private, not accessible.
Starting Point   At 2200 m in the summit fall-line on the right-hand side of the substructure, 1½ hours from Wangalm.
Descent   Down the East Ridge (III−) to the Eastern Wangscharte, hour then either 3 abseils to the south (piton and block) or northwards into the Oberreintal.
Note   The climb is possible early in the year, this South Face drying out very early.
First Ascent   W. Spitzenstaetter and H. Baldauf, 1957.
Guides/Maps   RR *Wettersteingebirge und Mieminger Kette* (AV series, German). AV 25M. Sh. 4/3 – Wetterstein und Mieminger Gebirge.
Plate   The South Wall of the triple-headed Scharnitzspitze in the south comb of the Wetterstein Range. The route can easily be followed with the aid of the sketch.

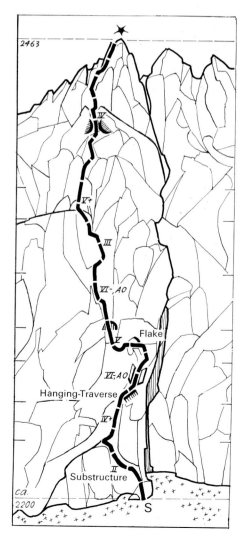

Wetterstein Range
Schüsselkarspitze 2537 m
South Face Direct
Grade VI, A1/350 m

It sounds like an exaggeration when a youngster says about this 'Direct': 'This is absolutely the *ne plus ultra* in free-climbing. A "direct" on a narrow line between beetling overhangs, but demanding the minimum of artificial aids. The rock is hard as nails, the climbing elegant and its 350 metres not too exacting for even the less-strongly muscled' . . . He was not speaking of the classic 'Herzog-Fiechtl' but of the South Face Direct. One might suspect a case of mistaken evaluation. The sense of shock simply underlines the progress in climbing-technique, the new aids, which make it possible to tackle the 'most extreme' with fewer misgivings . . . From the Scharnitzjoch this South Face looks utterly inhospitable, at once depressing and repellent, with its bulges and overhangs, now yellow, now black as ink, and all smooth as marble. The young climber will think so at first sight before he studies its structure with a critically calculating eye; later, this vertical wall will soon become nothing but a challenge. Here, once, stood all the important men of those earlier days. . . . When in 1912 Hans Dülfer hoisted the signal with his Fleischbank East Face triumph, the Munich pioneers came here to try their luck: Anton Schmid, Adolf Deye and Otto Herzog in the van. Schmid and Deye had to turn back at the 'Herzog Pillar'. Then, after the Fleischbank triumph, all the aces were suddenly here, Hans Dülfer himself, Tita Piaz and Paul Preuss. This élite had eyes for nothing but this Schüsselkarspitze South Face, thought of nothing but that name, which was pronounced with all the reverence of a bible-text.

Suddenly, on 26 September 1913, came the news that Dülfer and von Redwitz had climbed the West Face of the Totenkirchl. The repercussions were immediate: four days later, on 1 October, Otto Herzog and Franz Fiechtl accomplished their magnificent climb of the South Face, in spite of bivouacs, in spite of snow, but with a pendulum-traverse *à la* Dülfer and almost entirely by the most difficult of free-climbing. What was then 'the most

difficult on rock' has remained difficult and is still treated with respect. The 'Herzog-Fiechtl' is accepted and admired in spite of its roundabout route. It remains the classic test, the golden entry-gate to the young 'Extremist's' heaven. A look at the photograph and the sketch, as well as at others in the literature of climbing reveals that the old and the new, the 'Herzog-Fiechtl' and the 'Direct', share the same route up the 'Herzog Pillar' as far as the little '8-metre wall'. Says one of the enthusiasts: 'The "Direct" has been climbed without any of the latest technical aids. It demands less rope-technique and therefore more basic climbing-skill than the "Herzog".' Another writes: 'The "Direct" is definitely harder than the "Herzog", but "Rambo" would have had the guts for it, only not the right mentality . . . After all, the "Herzog" was the solution nearest to hand.'

Valley Resort Oberleutasch, 1180 m (Gaistal Inn), (bus from Garmisch–Mittenwald and Seefeld). Garmisch–Partenkirchen, 715 m.
Bases Wangalm, 1753, private, not always accessible, possibly milk. Better, Wetterstein Hut below, *c* 1660 m, private, Austrian Mountain-Rescue Service, 20 beds, obliging hut-keeper; 1½ hours up from the Oberleutasch. Oberreintal Hut, 1525, DAV, , in the Oberreintal, serviced; 4 hours from Garmisch.
Starting Point At 2200 m, close to the left of the prominent grey 'Herzog Pillar', 100 m high. In wet conditions start only to the right of the Pillar. Time for the climb, 4–6 hours.
Descent Down the West Ridge (III−) to the saddle before the West-Ridge Tower, then north-westwards to abseil-pitons, from which two 20-m abseils (care: overhanging), then onwards westwards to the Eastern Wangscharte Saddle. For the rest of the way, see route 38. Barely 1¾ hours from the summit. 50–70 minutes more on to the Wangalm or the Oberreintal Hut.
First Ascent K. Rainer and P. Aschenbrenner, 25.6.1939.
Guides/Maps RR *Wettersteingebirge und Mieminger Kette* (AV series, German). AV 25M. Sh. 4/3 – Wetterstein und Mieminger Gebirge.
Plate The South Face of the Schüsselkarspitze in the great southern range of the Wetterstein. Bottom right (to the left of the black slabs) the 100-m-high 'Herzog Pillar'. Left, at its base, our starting point. It is possible to trace both the 'Direct' and the 'Herzog-Fiechtl' on the picture.

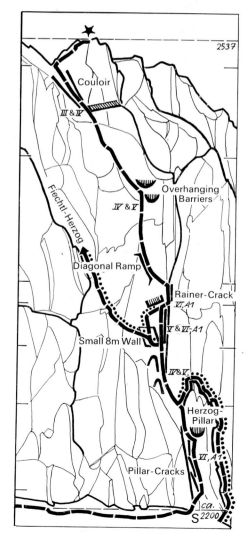

Wetterstein Range
Schüsselkarspitze 2537 m
South-East Face
Grade VI−, A1/400 m

Between Munich and Innsbruck, men have talked only of the 'South-East' since it capitulated, after a long siege, to two Rudolfs – Peters and Haringer. Dietmar Ohngemach, so greatly experienced on the Drus, the Engelhörner, in the Alpstein, Rätikon, Kaisergebirge and Dolomites (but now a family man, soon to graduate from 'extremes' to the role of a mere 'pleasure-climber') and a widely-informed, enthusiastic lover of mountains, accords it the highest praise: 'Why haven't I done the "South-East" every year? I had intended to ever since I first did the climb. This is the acme of rock-climbing, leaving no room for discussion why men go to the hills to climb!' . . . Long before Ohngemach and his peers tackled the great faces of the Civetta, the Kaisergebirge and the Wetterstein, a whole generation of their ancestors travelled regularly to the Wetterstein – on their bicycles or by train. There were no cars then: I myself pedalled with Leo Rittler, Hans Hintermaier and the others to the Partnach Ravine and went up from there into the Oberreintal. The great southern range of the Wetterstein, sweeping from the Plattspitzen, Teufelsgrat and Hochwanner over the Scharnitzspitze, Schüsselkarspitze and the Dreitorspitzen to the Musterstein, was in those days the highest aim of the Herzog brothers, Hannemann, Welzenbach, Fiechtl, Leberle, von Overkamp and Hösch: and, above all, of Anton Schmid, Adolf Deye and a few others who succeeded in climbing everything else – but not *all* the South Faces. The Schüsselkarspitze for one was left severely alone as 'impossible' . . . That has of course changed with the passage of time, as we can read in the climbers' guides and better still in the historic literature. But the 'South-East' has remained to this day a route greatly treasured by the 'Extremists'.

The easy approach, the absolutely reliable rock, reminiscent of that in the Kaisergebirge, its southern aspect, which allows the face to dry out quickly, and its great repute have assured the climb of a pre-eminent place, especially among Munich and Innsbruck climbers;

but the South-East Face has also become a 'run-of-the-mill thing', as you can confirm by reading the reports of recent climbers. Harry Rost, for instance, writes: 'Once an ideal route, it has unfortunately become poor and in part messed-up with pitons. The description in the guidebook is not always clear and some of the pitons simply lead one astray.' In Werner Goltsche's view, however: 'It had the same effect on me as the "Kirchl-West" – climbing of the most pleasurable kind.' Rudolf Peters and Rudolf Haringer were the first to capture the prize of that route, on which, in the previous year, Adolf Göttner, Martin Meier, Bertl Herbst and Hans Ellner were compelled only by rain and snow to beat yet another retreat, after two days. People today smile a superior smile about that; but even Napoleon had no rocket-launchers in his artillery . . . The East-South-East-Route of 1973 by Klaus Werner and Pit Schubert, which does not, it is true, affect our South Face, but commands an easy traverse into it, deserves mention as the latest achievement.

Valley Resorts Oberleutasch, 1180 m (Gaistal Inn). Garmisch–Partenkirchen, 715 m.
Bases Wetterstein Hut, 1660 m, private, Austrian Mountain-Rescue Service, 20 beds, obliging hut-keeper; 2 hours up from the Oberleutasch. Oberreintal Hut, 1525 m, DAV, in the Oberreintal.
Starting Point At about 2100 m near a rocky projection, at the lowest point in the base of the wall. 1½ hours from Wangalm, 2½ from the Oberreintal Hut over the Eastern Wangscharte. Time for the climb, for a two-man rope, 5–7 hours. Much elegant free-climbing.
Descent Exactly the same as for route 39, partly down the West Ridge (III−) to the Eastern Wangscharte.
First Ascent R. Peters and R. Haringer, 25/26.6.1934.
Guides/Maps RR *Wettersteingebirge und Mieminger Kette* (AV series, German). AV 25M. Sh. 4/3 – Wetterstein und Mieminger Gebirge.
Plate The South-East Face of the Schüsselkarspitze with the prominent 'Herzog Pillar' close to the vertical middle of the photographed. The start of the route is close to the little elongated island of rock (to its left) below the base of the wall (bottom right).

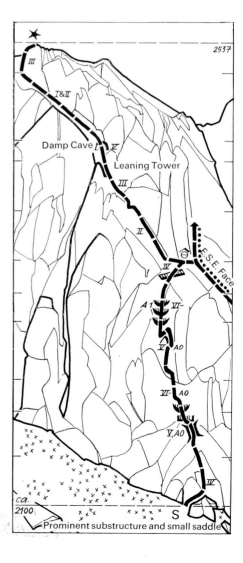

Stubai Alps (Kalkkögel)
Grosse Ochsenwand 2700 m
North-East Ridge Direct
Grade V+, A0/400 m

This huge North-East Face, rising sheer from the floor of the cwm offers three routes up its left-hand section alone (to the left of the rift defined by the shadow in our photograph). They are: the very fine 'North-East Ridge Direct', first climbed by Rebitsch and Novosansky in 1943 (Grade V+, A0), the start of which is close to the bottom left-hand corner of the picture; secondly, the new 'North-East Face Direct' (Zechel/Simon in 1964, Grade VI−) always keeping parallel with the outward-thrusting face buttress in the middle of the picture, starting close to the left of the projecting subsidiary base-formation; and third, the Laichner and Pertl 'North-East Pillar' (1944, still rated in the guidebook as VI), also starting on the substructure, then going up from the middle of the face diagonally to the right into the series of black rifts, with its exit behind the summit-buttress, visible up above . . . Our 'North-East Ridge Direct' (not to be confused with the 'North-East Pillar') is known to Innsbruck climbers as the 'Cold Ridge'. It offers the highly rewarding route, pioneered by the old master, Hias Rebitsch, on limestone relatively firm as the Kalkkögel go.

The start is at a little notch at the foot of the North-East precipice and goes up a slabby crack to the right to reach a debris terrace along which, to the left, you reach a narrow crack falling away in jutting overhangs. Circumventing these to the left, you go on up the crack till a ledge enables you to reach another curving yellow crack, bordered by a leaning slab. This crack is climbed till you reach the top of the slab, from which you keep on upwards for a few metres to the right, to reach the shoulder with a cairn on it, by way of yet another crack running up to the left. You then climb the deep groove starting a few metres to the right, then left again to a crack running up parallel with the ridge and up it to a second shoulder. From this, straight up to the crest of the ridge and over its flatter upper section to the northern summit and the summit itself. Our sketch, for which Pit Schubert and Manfred Sturm, two enthusiastic practitioners, are responsible, clearly gives

the essential details. Both are loud in their praises for this 'North-East Ridge Direct', shooting upwards close above the Adolf Pichler Hut in the upper Senderstal, from whose summit-rocks you look eastwards sheer on to the Schlick Alp and so into the lower reaches of the Stubai Valley.

Valley Resorts Telfes. 994 m, in the Stubai valley (train and bus from Innsbruck). Axams, 874 m (bus from Innsbruck).
Bases Schlicker Alm, 1643 m, inn, private, serviced; 2¼ hours to this point by motor from Telfes. Lift to Froneben or into the Schlick valley. Kemateralm, 1673 m, private, serviced; 2½ hours from Axams. Adolf Pichler Hut, 1977 m, AAĶI, serviced; 3½ hours from Axams, or 1 hour from the Kemateralm.
Starting Point At 2300 m, to the right of the lowest point of the arête, at a prominent gully. 1 hour from the Adolf Pichler Hut. Take care: the fine Kalkkögel rock can be brittle in places.
Descent Down the South Ridge, by way of the cwm and the Alpenklub Saddle to the Adolf Pichler Hut (1½ hours); or into the Schlick valley in 1½ hours.
First Ascent H. Robitsch and Novosanky, 1943.
Guides/Maps RR *Stubaier Alpen* (AV series, German) WCP *Stubai Alps*. AV 50M. Sh. 31/5 – Innsbruck.
Plate The North-West Face of the Grosse Ochsenwand with the North-East Ridge to its left. The starting point of our 'North-East Ridge Direct' can be clearly distinguished – the prominent gully to the right of the arête; as is also the gully in the middle part of the climb.

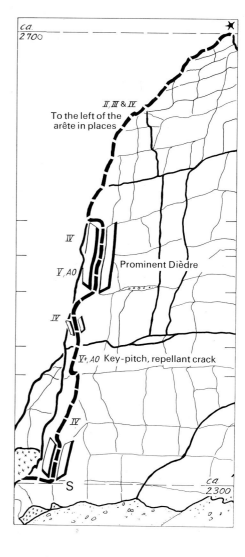

Karwendel Range
Kleiner Lafatscher 2635 m
North-East Dièdre Direct
Grade VI−, AO/400 m

The giant gully of the Kleiner Lafatscher runs up uncannily sheer to the south of the sloping roof of the Laliderer Walls, providing an eye-catching and nerve-shattering cynosure for guests frequenting the Hallerangerhaus which stands close below. This primitive phenomenon at first looks like a geometrical figure: to its left, the mirror-smooth, unbroken and absolutely vertical wall of stratified slabs and, to the right, as if welded on to it, the sharp upward-sweep of the slabby buttress. The bed of the dièdre cuts upwards so logically that it cannot help attracting the eye of every dedicated climber. Summoned by that magic spell, the Innsbruck chimney-sweep Matthias Auckenthaler (who loved to climb barefoot), and his friend E. Pirker started up the gully on 5 October 1930. They kept exactly to its hotbed, first on the splendid and easy rope lengths, later on the three extremely difficult ones up the gully-cracks of the upper, steeper part, whose overhangs eventually forced them out to the right. There are only 250 metres of the face's 400 left by the time you embark on the last rope lengths across the slabby traverse, first to the right then to the left, up to the exit along the North Ridge and the rubble-slog succeeding it. This limits the enthusiasm of our recommendation somewhat, as does the fact that the splendidly firm rock in the bed of the dièdre is followed by brittle stuff right at the top. These criticisms, however, do not downgrade the general impressiveness of the climb, which remains as tremendous as it looks in the photograph, especially when compared with the sketch.

There is another thing: the approach-march. There is either the very long way from Scharnitz to the Hallerangerhaus, which can only be reduced by a lift in the hut-keeper's jeep, or the 4-hour ascent from the Halltal to the hut, though you can of course approach it from the Hafelkar ropeway-station over the saddles of the Mannlscharte and Stempeljoch. To offset these drawbacks, all the approach-paths are exceptionally beautiful scenically, and the high-level route over from the Hafelkar makes

no demands on stamina. And if the Auckenthaler dièdre climb is not enough to satisfy the enthusiast, there are plenty of other 'extreme' face-climbs here to gratify his appetite. This great Karwendel Range, maligned for its brittle quality – falsely as is proved not only by the North Faces of the Laliderer Wall – offers other highly interesting routes on firm and reliable rock. Examples are the 1947 Hermann Buhl 'West Face Direct' (VI−, 300 m) on the north-west corner of the Spekkarspitze or Gomboz and Kienpointner's 1946 climb on the North Pillar of the Kleiner Lafatscher (VI−, at least 500 m), which is partly visible at the right-hand edge of our photograph. The way home into the Inn Valley through the magnificent Vomperloch is extremely beautiful. Moreover, the climb is relatively short; it can – and should – be done in the autumn, when the Hallerangerhaus is no longer full to overflowing, and the eye and spirit are enchanted by the lovely firework-display of the autumn colouring.

Valley Resorts Scharnitz, 964 m. Solbad Hall in Tirol. 560 m. Innsbruck, 574 m.
Bases Hallerangerhaus, 1768 m, DAV, at the north-west foot of the Specckarspitze, in the Hinterautal, serviced; 5 hours from Scharnitz, 4 hours from Hall, 4½ hours from Innsbruck–Hafelekar ropeway station, 2269 m, by the Goetheweg, Mannlscharte, Stempeljoch and Lafatscherjoch. Approach times can be cut by use of hut-keeper's jeep from Scharnitz or, possibly, drive up to Herrenhäuser, 1482 m, in the Halltal.
Starting Point At 2200 m near the big patch of rubble at the very foot of the gully, ½ hour from the Hut. Normal time for the climb to the summit for a rope of two, 3½–5 hours.
Descent South-eastwards down the slope which narrows gradually towards the ridge, over rubble and blocks to the Lafatscherjoch and the Hut, 1½ hours at the most.
First Ascent M. Auckentaler and E. Pirker, 1930.
Guides/Maps RR Karwendelgebirge (AV series, German). WCP *Karwendel*. AV 25M Sh. 5/2 – Karwendelgebirge.
Plate The Kleiner Lafatscher with its unique giant-gully, taken from the north-east from the vicinity of the Hallerangerhaus. Right, the North Face, top left the rubble and scree falling away to the Lafatscherjoch.

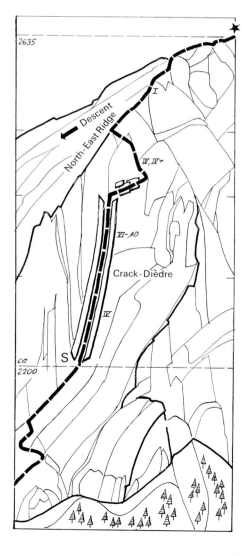

Karwendel Range
Lalidererwand 2615 m
North Face (Schmid-Krebs Route)
Grade VI−, A1/800 m

Between the maple-groves of the Kleiner and Grosser Ahornboden, those two dream-like 'fairy meadows' in the Karwendel, the barrier of the north-facing Lalidererwand plunges 800 metres down to the little Falkenhütte. The great North-Western Wall of the Civetta repels and frightens, but it is beautiful too; the north faces of the Tre Cime form such a glorious picture that they lose all their terror − not so this grim, dark wall between Hohljoch and Spielissjoch, rising from grey scree-chutes and grubby relics of snow-cones to the same sunny sky: it remains terribly depressing. It reduces one immediately to a small nobody at the foot of the huge, menacing mountain-mass overhead. What must have been the feelings of the first climbers who came to attempt this gigantic wall? . . . Three years before Toni Schmid fell to his death, climbing with Ernst Krebs on the Wiesbachhorn, he and the same companion climbed this Lalidererer North Face, directly up the summit fall-line, 800 metres of the steepest limestone, whose key-pitches are a very chancy roof-traverse and the 'Krebs Cracks,' which exact the toughest free-climbing skills. That was as long ago as 1929 and occupied only a single day, without a bivouac. Is there anyone who for a moment believes that those two, had they been young men today, would have given in to a Trieste, Su Alto, Cima Grande or West Face of the Dru?

Our 'Schmid-Krebs Route', like the neighbouring 'Rebitsch-Spiegl', is a long and difficult climb and still an outstanding Alpine achievement to this day. Route-finding flair, morale and physical condition, toughness in continuous difficult free-climbing, moreover on rock that is not always reliable, are indispensable considerations for both these climbs. You may be sure that the bivouac-box below the summit-ridge was not put there just because someone had money to spend. And a Ludwig Gramminger could have written massive tomes about his rescue-operations on this wall. The length of the climb alone − many climbers today, unlike its pio-neers, need a bivouac − and the danger from a break in the weather while on the face make this a very serious undertaking. Falling stones and wet rock can bring the climber into dire straits. That is why we have marked the two best bivouac-sites on our sketch. It will be easily understood that the greatest care for other parties on the face is essential, especially in the two chimney-gullies. Our photograph is plastic even in its shady parts; on it you can identify the first chimney, the roof-traverse and the 'Krebs Cracks,' while higher up, the strong sunlight throws up the gorge-overhang, first gorge, notch and yellow exit-couloir to perfection. Furthermore, it is not only the sombre, brooding appearance of the wall which reminds one of the Eiger's North Face. The footpath runs close beneath its base and on it the 'rubber-necks' marvel and at best shudder at the realisation of their own beautifully safe existence while, overhead, others are so courageously (but quite uselessly) exposing themselves to such terrible perils.

Valley Resort Hinterriss, 944 m (bus from Bad Tölz and Vorderriss).
Bases Falken Hut, 1848 m, DAV, on the Spielissjoch, serviced; 3½ hours from Hinterriss, 2½ hours from Eng (toll-road) Bivouac-box below the summit to the south.
Starting Point At about 1800 m, at the point where the base of the wall rises from the rubble brought down from the left-hand gullies, 35 minutes from the Hut. Time for the climb, for a two-man rope in top form and condition, 9–12 hours.
Descent Either down the craggy southern flank into the Rossloch and Hinterautal, thence to Scharnitz, 4–5 hours; or past the bivouac-box below the summit-ridge, westwards to the 'Spindlerschlucht' in the eastern North Face of the Ladizturm (III, beware of falling stones) and down 7 abseil pitches of 20 m each in a broad couloir and simple climbing down, 2–3 hours.
First Ascent E. Krebs and T. Schmid, 8.9.1929 (without a bivouac!).
Guides/Maps RR *Karwendelgebirge* (AV series, German). WCP *Karwendel*. AV 25M. Sh. 5/2 – Karwendelgebirge.
Plate The whole stature of the Lalidererer wall, taken from the north. By comparing the sketch and photograph exactly the key-pitches of the 'Schmid-Krebs Route' up this North Wall can be seen fully 800 m high.

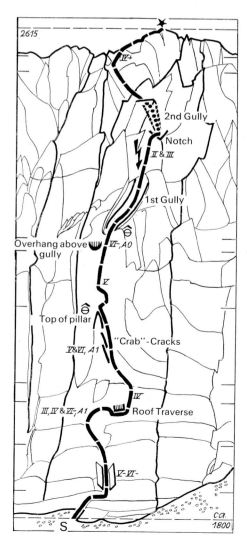

Karwendel Range
Lalidererspitze 2588 m
North Face Direct (Rebitsch-Spiegel Route)
Grade VI, A1/750 m

Right at the heart of the Karwendel the Lalidererwand and Lalidererspitze stand close together, features in a great sweep of mountain-wall – a cyclopean primaeval world above the green maple-groves in the valley. Their gigantic walls, scarred and riven in decay, rise vertically from stark, grey cwms. Even those who are not mountaineers can see beauty in this world of their own: Beethoven's fateful notes knock at the door of their world-consciousness. Joy, that 'divine spark', fills their hearts as they wander beneath these walls . . . For a long time Munich climbers have regarded the Karwendel as the most advanced school of climbing-skills. Anyone who has climbed a few severe routes on this uniquely stratified and not always firm Karwendel rock and has felt at home on it will very soon be an 'Ace' and rightly consider himself ready to trust himself in all other climbing areas. In spite of which, the Karwendel has not yet become fashionable. It is usually the 'loners' and the 'lovers', the 'great big idiots' who visit this recondite mountain-world to try their poetic luck. Listen to the names . . . Otto Herzog was devoted to this region of rocks for forty years and the barefoot climber from Innsbruck, Matthias Auckenthaler, remained head over heels in love with his Karwendel. Hias Rebitsch was for a long time the constant entrepreneur, the passionately dedicated 'arranger' of its modern exploration. With Meusburger he had dealt with the second ascent of the 'Schmid-Krebs Route'; fourteen years later, he climbed the lower half with Sepp Spiegl, then with Kuno Rainer the upper half, of our 'North Face Direct'. In 1947 Hermann Buhl and Luis Vigl, in a very protracted climbing-time, united the two halves, and the third successful party were Karl Lukan and Hausner from Vienna. In 1949 Rainer and Streng discovered the direct exit, an exploit denied Rebitsch. Study the photograph and the sketch: this North Face climb does not fall into a difficult lower- and an easier upper-half like the 'Schmid-Krebs Route' next door. Of its fully 750-metre height, 180 metres at least are V and VI, the rest all IV and V.

It has not yet become a fashionable climb and probably never will. You have always to reckon with faulty pitons. An assessment of the climbing-time as twelve hours is not excessive, and that stipulates fine, dry weather. The face, though not climbed till 1946, demands an unusual degree of very exposed free-climbing. There are no definite key-pitches, for everything is dicey, at the rope-traverse to the 'White Pillar', in the cracks on the 'Grey Tower' and at the gully-overhang. Beyond any doubt the climb belongs among the biggest and most serious free-climbs in the Alps; whoever has climbed it is a 'Tiger', an 'Ace' among mountaineers. He will have climbed a route on which that great climber, Angelo Dibona, has also done his stuff. Dibona solved every problem of his day as he met it, from the Spik North Face to the Ailefroide. Which gives our man something to think about.

Valley Resort Hinterriss, 944 m (bus from Bad Tölz, Lenggries and Vorderriss).
Bases Falken Hut, 1848 m, DAV, on the Spielissjoch, serviced; 3½ hours from Hinterriss, 2½ hours from the Eng (toll-road from Hinterriss). Bivouac-box below the summit to the south.
Starting Point A 1800 m, in the direct summit fall-line, at a recess in the wall below the prominent yellow cliffs, 20 minutes from the Hut. Take care when wet. Also take care not to send stones down on following parties.
Descent Either, uncomfortably, over craggy slopes southwards into the Rossloch, then through the Hinterautal to Scharnitz, 4–5 hours in all; or the normal route westwards and through the 'Spindlerschlucht' (III, with 7 abseils of 20 m each, then climbable slabs and steps) down to the foot of the wall and to the Hut, 2–3 hours from summit.
First Ascent Lower half: H. Rebitsch and S. Spiegl, 8.9.1946. Upper half: H. Rebitsch and K. Rainer, 20.7.1946.
Guides/Maps RR *Karwendelgebirge* (AV series, German). WCP *Karwendel*. AV 25M. Sh. 5/2 – Karwendelgebirge.
Plate The north Face of the Lalidererspitze, 2588 m. Right, the 'Herzog Ridge' (IV+).

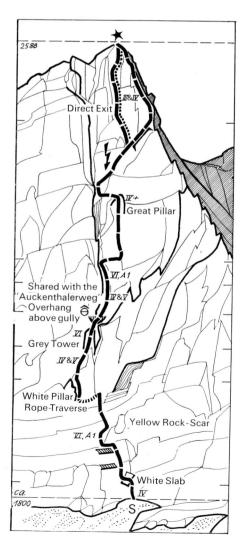

Rofan Range
Seekarlspitze 2240 m
North Face ('Y Crack')
Grade VI−, A0/400 m

The Rofan Range, between the Inn Valley, Achensee and the Schliersee foothills, pushes out green slopes on its south side to the very banks of the Inn; but to the north it breaks away into perpendicular limestone walls. Below them lie the quiet hollows around the old Alpmoos meadows in which nearly sixty years ago Munich climbing clubs built a kind of 'suburban' colony. Famous names: first Franz Nieberl, then Georg Leuchs, Josef Klammer, Hans Dülfer, Hans Fiechtl, Emil Gretschmann, Ernst Schmid, Herbert Eichhorn and others. They knew and loved their Kaisergebirge and their Wetterstein, but they always returned to the Rofan as to some favourite hiding-place. It was indeed a hiding-place full of dreams for that 'Poet of the Crags' from Innsbruck, Hias Rebitsch, the first man to climb the Direct Route on the North Face of the Lalidererspitze, one of the most stylish free-climbs of the modern era. In 1932 he and his brother Franz decided to have a go at the notably difficult and reputedly greasy 'Y Crack' on the Seekarlspitze, which Fiechtl and Schmid had already climbed in 1923. They mastered the 'Y' and reached the broad rubble-terrace, but at that point instead of making the great loop of the original route – 200 metres to the right along the terrace, then sharp to the left up the overhung ramp into the exit-chimneys – they took a direct line which soon leads leftwards from the terrace to another prominent ramp and later to narrow cracks (IV and V+), crossing the old route and leading straight up to the same exit-chimney.

The most interesting thing from a climber's point of view is the passage of the 'Y', which Rebitsch described in a somewhat lengthy but meticulously detailed article in vol. 4, 1967, of *Alpinismus*. It is essential to read it before attempting that North Face towering above those sleepy Alpmoos meadows, and also before one hears those voices prophesying woe: 'The "Y"? All slimy, horrid. Keep your hands off it!' Rebitsch must have heard them too, but he started up the climb (not without misgivings) and found the 'slimy' pitches

dry. The dark colour of the overhanging face had not led him to expect that. The lower slanting stem of the 'Y', two rope lengths of it with the abrasive effect of the smooth and holdless overhang at the breach in the crack, and the climb out into the bed of the funnel – all with the primitive climbing footgear worn at the time, and without a modern belaying-technique to safeguard them – was enough to give them all sorts of unpleasant moments. All the same, they did it. The rock is unbelievably compact and rough, even sharp-edged; it can often be black and wet. One has either to be very lucky, or not embark on the climb till autumn . . .

Valley Resorts Maurach on the Achensee, 958 m (train and bus). Steinberg by Guffert, 1015 m, to the north (bus from Jenbach and Tegernsee). Rattenberg on the Inn/Mariathal (Kramsach), 586 m.

Bases Erfurter Hut, 1834 m, DAV, serviced, ropeway station, otherwise 2½ hours from Maurach; or, Bayreuther Hut, 1600 m, DAV, serviced, 3 hours from Mariathal; or bivouac-possibilities in the Alpmoos cwm at the bottom of the wall (decayed alps) c 1780 m, reached in 1¼ hours from the Rosskogel lift coming from Mariathal and the Zireinersee.

Starting Point At about 1850 m at the foot of the wall to the right of the summit fall-line, 2½ hours from the Erfurter Hut, 1½ hours from the Rosskopf lift-station, 20 minutes from the Alpmoosalm (accessible in 2½ hours from Steinberg); or, in 2 hours from the Bayreuther Hut. Time for the climb, for a rope of two, 3½–5 hours, according to which route is taken on the upper part of the Face.

Descent On the south side by the easy normal way (i) to the Seekarlscharte or the Rosskarlscharte (20 minutes) or by the marked path back to the Erfurter or Bayreuth Huts in about 1½ hours.

First Ascent H. Fiechtl and E. Schmid, 22.10.1923 ('Y Crack'). 'Rebitsch Route' from the 'Y', 1.8.1932. Hias and Franz Rebitsch.

Guides/Maps RR *Rofanführer* (AV series, German). AV 25M. Sh. 6 – Rofangebirge.

Plate The North Face of the Seekarlspitze taken from the meadows. Left, Rosskarl Saddle and Gorge. A third of the way up the wall is the broad rubble-terrace. At its lowest point, just to the right of the summit fall-line, is the bottom end of the 'Y'.

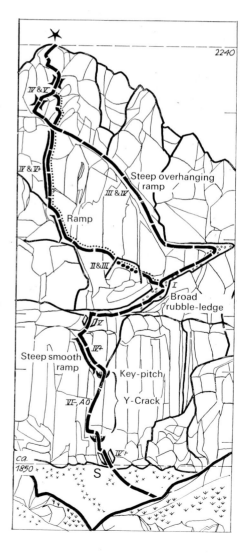

Zillertal Alps
Fussstein 3381 m
North Ridge
Grade V−/480 m

The Fussstein stands in the middle of the Tuxer Chain, equidistant from the Olperer and the Alpeiner Saddle. Close to it, on its south, the Schrammacher and Sagwandspitze link it with the main Zillertal (also the main Alpine) Range. Its summit-pyramid is supported by lengthy South-West, South and North-East Ridges, but the North Ridge rises abrupt and short from the ice of the Olperer Glacier to the summit. Our route is one of the easiest in this book, though the guidebook rates it at V, while our rating is of V −, and then only for one rope length. There is no controversy about its ranking as a perfect granite climb, for the most part on firm rock. It is a question of pleasurable free-climbing, though there are pitons, should they be needed. The granite is solid and sharp-edged, though there is a little too much rubble near the summit and on terraces and ledges. This calls for great care at these places, so as not to endanger parties coming up behind with falling stones. Certainly the first party up is the safest.

As the sketch shows, when read in conjunction with the photograph, the line of this route is almost plumb from the terrace where it starts, except where in mid-face a smooth wall of slabs enforces a 45-metre traverse to the right (with a resting-place on it), to join the route of the North-West Face Climb (Baumgartner, IV), which goes off up to the left again by means of cracks in the slabs. Our further progress is effected by staying on the ridge even at the key-pitch of a gully cutting through a roof-like overhang. Harry Rost says that most of the pitches in the granite look impossible to climb at first sight because the holds are well concealed, but that the solution is always found halfway up and from there on progress is surprisingly quick. Manfred Sturm, who did the climb with his wife, had a hair's-breadth escape at the bergschrund, which lies in deep shadow, because he had not taken crampons along a rock-climb. Both agree that it is a Grade IV, with only one pitch possibly V. It is a pleasant climb, interesting and also scenically exciting: a very different proposition from

the tough demands of the Sagwand Pillar standing opposite to the south — though good judges disagree about that one too . . .

Let us examine our photograph for the various routes: to the left of the North Ridge, outlined by sun and shadow, Paul Aschenbrenner and Wastl Mariner's 'North Face Direct' (partly VI −, but perhaps graded a little lower today) runs up in the shadow: to the right of the ridge, the upper part of Leo Brankowsky and A. Fluch's 1947 North-West Face Route (V and 600 m wall height) is visible. If you are in good condition you do not come down by the normal route, but add the glorious connecting ridge to the Olperer, the highest summit in the Tuxer Chain (II–III, one V pitch), to the left of the picture – but only when the weather is favourable.

Valley Resort St Jodok am Brenner. 1129 m (train and bus from Innsbruck).
Base Geraer Hut, DAV. 2324 m, close under the base of the Fussstein's South-West Ridge, 4½ hours from St Jodok, motorable to Innervals, thence only 2½ hours.
Starting Point At 2900 m to the east of the base of the ridge, where a prominent terrace-step goes up to the right, thence by the Olpererweg to the head of the moraine, then southwards. Care needed at the bergschrund. 2 hours from the Hut to the starting-terrace. Time for the climb, for a rope of two, 3–5 hours.
Descent By the normal way down the South-West Face (II) first down a big couloir to a cliff at a pulpit, then straight on over slabby steps, on the big ramp diagonally to the right into the cwm. 2¼ hours to the hut. Ideal descent route: the connecting ridge (II–III, 1 pitch V) to the Olperer, adding 1½ to 2 hours, only in settled weather, followed by a long descent.
Special Note Never start if the rock is iced. Care on the last rope lengths to the summit. Not to be undertaken in early summer.
First Ascent H. Frenademetz and K. Tschaler, 22.9.1935.
Guides/Maps RR *Zillertaler Alpen* (AV series, German). WCP *Zillertal Alps.* AV 25M. Sh. 35/1 – Zillertal Westliches.
Plate The North Ridge of the Fussstein, seen from below. Left bottom, the Olperer Ferner (glacier), top left the connecting ridge to the Olperer. To the left of the North Ridge, the North Face, to the right the North-West Face.

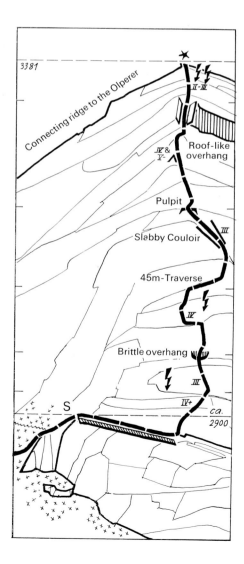

Zillertal Alps
Sagwandspitze 3224 m
North Pillar
Grade V+, A0/800 m

The dark north walls of the Sagwandspitze and Schrammacher, almost always in deep shadow, form a grim screen above the Alpeiner Glacier. It is hardly credible that the summits of these granite faces, slashed and streaked with ice, are relatively easy of access from the Pfitscher Joch on their further side, by way of the Stampflkees. The climber sitting comfortably outside the Geraer Hut in the sunshine looking doubtfully up at the Alpine horror-picture will only admit it is 'splendid' if he has not got to start up it next day. That is one of the reasons why the North Pillar Route to the Sagwandspitze arouses more controversy than any other climb in this book. Although it is the only 'extreme' high-Alpine climb in the main Zillertal chain, it seldom excites recognition. Some climbers talk and write of it as the 'Eigerwand of the Eastern Alps', as a 'rubbish-heap', calling it shattered and raising misgiving upon misgiving. All the same, this is what Harry Rost noted after climbing it: 'A first-class climb. Few pitons, 15 in all. Splendid free-climbing on sharp-edged rock. In part a mixed climb, according to the time of year. Not to be undertaken in bad weather.' Another good climber from Bad Tölz adds: 'A very difficult Eastern Alps mixed climb, but not one to delight the "Extremists".' The history of this North Face is rather a sad one. At one time the Sagwandspitze and Schrammacher were intended to provide the Geraer Hut with its classic climbs, but it never happened: the Fussstein and the Olperer have long won preference over them.

The North Face of our Sagwandspitze was first climbed in 1925. No great praise for that. Eight days before the start of the Second World War Aschenbrenner and Mariner collected the North Pillar. Very praiseworthy ... One thing is certain: this mixed climb is very long, very exacting and not for 'Extremists' only used to moving from one piton to another. So the artist in the 'artificial' may not be enthusiastic. But everyone who enjoys or even yearns for a great Alpine experience and is at home on extremely diffi-

cult high-level granite, should try this greatest of primitive-rock climbs in the Eastern Alps; even though every metre is not marked out by pitons, even though the rock is brittle in places and rubble interferes here and there. So, all in all, as witnessed by our photograph, this steep and lofty pillar genuinely qualifies for the 'superlative' cachet. Today Wastl Mariner, who first climbed it and at the time wrote a solemn but enthusiastic account, rates the greatest difficulties at only V+. Finally, no tough French climber who knows his Mt Blanc climbs would wish to add improvements to anything on the Sagwand Pillar. 'Mixed climbing on rock and ice' speaks for itself. The alleged brittleness is part of the risks of climbing, not only on the Sagwandspitze and Schrammacher. The genial hut-keeper will advise about the descent either to the Geraer Hut itself or straight down to Innervals.

Valley Resort St Jodok am Brenner, 1129 m (train and bus from Innsbruck).
Base Geraer Hut, DAV, 2324 m, 4½ hours from St Jodok; motorable to Innervals, these 2½ hours.
Starting Point At 2400 m in the Pillar's fall-line, which is bordered on either side by ice-couloirs. The first surge of the Pillar is 100 m above the southern Alpeiner Glacier. The start is up the right-hand couloir, 1 hour from the Hut. Time for the climb, for a two-man rope, 6–8 hours. (Only in settled weather.)
Descent On the southern side (normal route, I) by way of the Stampfkees and the Pfitscherjochhaus, 2½ hours from the summit. For especially good climbers: down the North-West Ridge and its northern flank (slabby) to the Alpeiner Glacier (III in places). 2½ hours.
Note Firm to the starting point, partly on rock, as also on the descent. The Pillar is brittle in some sectors. Do not start in icy conditions or doubtful weather.
First Ascent P. Aschenbrenner and W. Mariner, 20.8.1939, using the North-West Ridge as the descent-route for the first time.
Guides/Maps RR *Zillertaler Alpen* (AV series, German) WCP *Zillertal Alps*. AV 25M. Sh. 35/1 – Zillertal Westliches.
Plate The North Face of the Sagwandspitze, taken from the moraine above the Geraer Hut. Centre top, the main summit, extreme right a possible descent route.

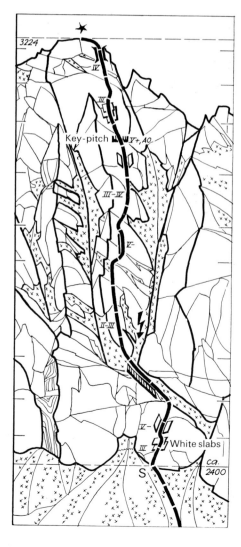

Zillertal Alps (Ahorn Range)
Grundschartner 3064 m
North Ridge (Mittergrat)
Grade V−, A0/750 m

One would like to suppress the adjective 'superlative'. 'But,' says Manfred Sturm, 'the North Ridge of the Grundschartner in the Zillertal must definitely rank with the Fussstein North Ridge as the two finest granite climbs in the Eastern Alps,' adding, sympathetically, '. . . a very lonely area, scenically tremendous – but a very hard mountain-day.' Our picture, taken by Jürgen Winkler, though suffering from the worst possible lighting conditions, reveals attractive aspects of this mighty, ice-plastered rock-pyramid, with the keen upward thrust of its sharp North Ridge . . . Here we are at the heart of the Zillertal Alps, between the Ziller and Stillup cwms, for the Grundschartner does not rise on the main Alpine backbone but from a northerly lateral chain, the Ahorn Range. Overnight accommodation at Häusling is at present very restricted, for a huge building-site has come to disturb its peace and quiet: but the cowherd folk up on the Bodenalm (1½ hours above Häusling) will take good care of you. Very early next morning there await you two hours of very trackless terrain to reach the start of the Ridge, involving a very, very long day ahead of you. You should be warned that it is not altogether easy to find the actual start of the Ridge, but if you keep your eyes open and use your tracking-sense, you cannot miss the point where its base rises between the two old snow-pans. After the first Grade IV pitch, you have to abseil down 3 metres into a notch. Till then there were just blocks, a riven step in the ridge and a sharp dark tooth – up to the abseil point. Then follow two easier rope lengths, before the ridge steepens into a precipitous slabby section (V−, Ao) with cracks in it – and immediately the 'extreme'-climber will call the sketch and guidebook to his aid.

Manfred Sturm says: 'More especially in the middle section of the Ridge there are possibilities – mostly to the west (right) – for turning difficult passages; but to use them is to deprive yourself of some marvellous climbing. Today it is usual to tackle these pitches direct. While the slabby crest of the Ridge provides firm rock all the way, the flanks on either side are comparatively brittle, eaten-into by two small hanging-glaciers, which give the Mittergrat (already architecturally prominent to the eye) its characteristically sharp structure – as can be well seen in the photograph.' Unfortunately the two pretty little glacier-hollows are gradually melting away . . . Up on our North Ridge there is a wealth of notches affording comfortable and safe stances, which is important to know. There is even leisure enough to enjoy the wide view out over the Bodental to the north, while your partner is doing the hard work . . . About 50 metres below the summit there are two possibilities. First, to the left on firm gneiss there are two elegant rope lengths (V−, Ao) – perhaps the finest on the whole climb; or, secondly, on the right, a 40-metre traverse leads to a chimney-crack (V−) followed by an easy exit.

The summit affords a vast panorama, but there remains before you a very long and not very easy descent. There is no marked track down into the valley, hardly any footmarks even. Here all depends on a good flair for the trail to help you find, directly after a left-hand traverse just below the summit on the south side, the Ebenkeesscharte, lying a long way over to the east. You keep on to the north-east down the upper slopes falling from Pts 2959, 2903, 2736 and 2721 – only occasionally tacking from south to north. You climb down on rock to the Ebenkees Glacier and then on down to the long valley-bed – to the Bodenalp and the care of the inkeeper at Häusling . . . This route on primitive rock is almost Western Alps in type, demanding, after 6 hours of extremely hard work, an unusually obscure descent, especially in overcast weather; nor is there any question of a hut, while provender for a modest appetite has to go along on the climb. And here the 'extreme' climber has to have a keen nose for the weather.

Valley Resorts Mayrhofen (Zillertal). 628 m (train and bus from Jenbach/Inntal). Häusling, 1053 m, in the Zillergrund, private inn. Overnight possibility: Bodenalm, 1672 m, in the middle Bodengrund, possibly hay, 2 hours from Häusling. No other available base.
Starting Point At the very lowest base of the North Ridge, at about 2150 m. You aim up out of the head of the valley to the left (not, as the *AV-Führer* says, to the right) and crossing the partly-vegetated base, reach the actual starting point on the ridge itself, 2 hours from the Bodenalm.
Descent Long and not easy: no path, no markings. You need a good nose for a trail to find the Ebenkeesscharte, 2721 m, which lies to the east (see the excellent AV map) directly after traversing to the left on the south side below the summit. Not till at the saddle must you strike northwards down into the Bodental. This descent route is longer, but less complicated, than that down the Kainzenkar to the east, leading to the inn 'in der Au'. Time for the descent c 3½ hours. Keep on studying the AV map and look out for snow patches.
Times 5–6½ hours for the climb from the Bodenalm. 3½ hours for the descent.
First Ascent P. Aschenbrenner and W. Mayr, 1928.
Guides/Maps RR *Zillertaler Alpen* (AV series, German) WCP *Zillertal Alps*. AV 25M. Sh. 35/2 – Zillertaler Mittleres.
Plate Looking up from the outer Bodengrund into the head of the valley and up to the North Ridge (Mittergrat) in the centre of the picture. To the left and right of the ridge, the Mitterkees (glacier). Our descent route (not visible in the picture) runs high up on the reverse (south) flank of the East Ridge, seen high on the left. The Ebenkeesscharte, which has to be crossed northwards, is just outside the top left-hand edge of the photograph.

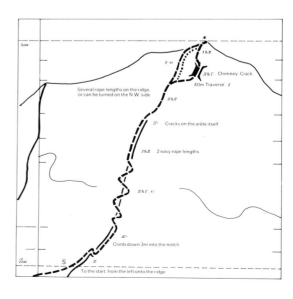

Kaisergebirge
Totenkirchl 2193 m
West Face (Dülfer Route)
Grade V+, A1/400 m

Hans Dülfer mastered the Fleischbank East Face in 1912, and the Totenkirchl West Face in the following year – the two classic routes in the Kaisergebirge. The way in which he captured the West Face of the Totenkirchl, the most famous rock peak in the Northern Limestone Ranges, at the height of his powers, is interesting. First of all, he knew that in 1907 Rudolf Schietzold had done a solo abseil down part of the face; secondly, after his success on the Fleischbank, Dülfer had unsuccessfully attempted the West with Werner Schaarschmidt in 1913. Thirdly, on 9 June 1913, he roped down the whole of the face alone, finding its central section impossible, seeing only smooth slabs. Fourthly, on 19 September, with Willi von Redwitz, Hanne Franz and Kunzen, he attempted the climb again, reaching the level of the pillar; Dülfer himself got across the smooth slab by a rope-traverse, today's 'Nose Traverse'; all in vain, they had to turn back. Fifthly, on 26 September he started up again with von Redwitz, two 40-metre ropes, 26 pitons and – his own fantastic ability. Seven and a half hours later the two of them were on the Totenkirchl Summit... It was not till 1919 that Georg Sixt, partnered by Karl Aichner, who had been wounded in the First World War, made the second ascent. Next came Paul Diem and Karl Schüle. Soon more and more climbers congregated at the foot of this wall, mastering the '17-metre Crack', 'Nose-Traverse', 'Zig-zag Wall', 'Gorge Traverse' and the exhausting exit-cracks; and the fame of the face rang far out beyond the Lesser Alps.

It is essential to study the guidebook before starting up it. There are also some interesting commentaries from today's young climbers. Harry Rost, for instance wrote: 'A fine long route, every inch of which has to be climbed. Some of the pitons sticking there could be dispensed with.' Immo Engelhardt writes: 'The stratification of the rock doesn't help much and there are fewer jug-handle holds than on the other big climbs in the Wilder Kaiser. The route is not easy to find. Very many climbers

go astray directly after the Winkler Gully.' 'This,' says Manfred Sturm, 'was the first triumph of the piton at the decisive Alpine divide between Paul Preuss and Hans Dülfer, and yet a shining example of great free-climbing technique. Unlike so many modern "Direttissimas", Dülfer's ideal "Direct" was wrested from the face, not engineered up it. An ideal example of a great classic limestone climb, in spite of the great "Nose-traverse".' And this is Dietmar Ohngemach's opinion: 'The route lies so well hidden that it calls for great experience in taking the right line and in the use of equipment to find it. Dülfer's "17-metre Crack", his "Nose-" and "Gully-Traverses" make the climbing population very inquisitive; but not many of them are aware that after the "Gully-Traverse" there is still an interminable summit-gully demanding great guts.' And this is important: even in the Winkler Gully at the bottom, there is a key-pitch (V–), which cannot be avoided; only after it can one climb out to the left on to the West Face.

Valley Resorts Kufstein, 503 m, in the Inn valley. St Johann in Tirol, 690 m (from where bus and motors to the Griesenau, 727 m; thence toll-road to the Grieseneralm, 1006 m).
Bases The Stripsenjochhaus, 1580 m, ÖAV, at the Stripsenjoch, serviced; 4½ hours from Kufstein or 1½ hours from the Grieseneralm parking-place. Hinterbärenbad (Anton Karg Haus), 831 m, in the Kaisertalboden, ÖAV, serviced; 3 hours from Kufstein.
Starting Point At about 1750 m at the bottom of the Winkler Gully, 1 hour from the Stripsenjochhaus, 2 from Hinterbärenbad. Tracks in the upper recess. Time for the climb, for a rope of two, 5–7 hours. Note: the 'Summit Gorge' is not a gorge but rather a gully.
Descent By the 'Führerweg' (II), following the cairns and plentiful foot-tracks. Summit to Stripsenjoch 1½–2½ hours, according to how much 'traffic' there is on the normal route.
First Ascent H. Dülfer and W. von Redwitz, 26.9.1913.
Guides/Maps RR *Kaisergebirge* (AV series, German). WCP *Kaisergebirge*. AV 25M. Sh. 8 – Kaisergebirge.
Plate The Totenkirchl in the Kaisergebirge, with its West Face. To the right, running up diagonally from the bottom centre to the right, the Winkler Gully deep in shadow and Kaiser history. Top right, the South-East Ridge; left, the terraces of the North Flank (normal route).

Kaisergebirge
Vordere Karlspitze 2261 m
East Face (Göttner)
Grade V+, AO/250 m

The East Face of the Vordere Karlspitze and the West of the Bauernpredigtstuhl confront each other across the Kübelkar to the south of the Ellmauer Tor – two nearly classic Kaiser faces, the only qualification being in respect of their relatively low heights. They are two climbs first made during the great era of late exploration in the Kaisergebirge, while free-climbing was held in great esteem and was none the less beginning to compromise with the new techniques based on artificial aids. Had it not, there could have been no new routes. This favourite one on the East Face of the Vordere Karlspitze which, halfway up, meets the 'new-style' 1953 route of M. Kramheller and H. Schmidt, is a purely 'sporting' climb. The wall looks exactly as shown in the picture: now smooth as marble, now plentifully riven and scored, bordered on the right by the rift of the Matejak Chimney (our abseil descent-route) and provided up in the middle with a prominent triangular slab – highly inviting for the 'extreme' climber, but a brutal shock for the uninitiated hiker who has to pass its foot. The great right-to-left traverse – at whose start one is forced to climb down – is a delicate passage. It uses the grassy terrace which, broad in places, slashes across the whole East Face, cutting it in two. If there is a question of a key-pitch, it must surely be the one on the right-hand lower half of the face where, after the second overhang, you have to get up into an overhanging chimney-crack by means of a hanging-traverse to the right, soon followed by a similar but easier traverse to the left around the arête.

The climbing is continually exposed and exhausting – in spite of the pitons. The new East Face Route, a direct, purely technical variant, is also shown in the sketch by an additional dotted line. It follows an ideally plumb line, classified at VI –, AI. All the same, we recommend our somewhat more circuitous route, which has earned its own reputation among the multitude opened up in the Kaisergebirge, and has become a great favourite – perhaps on account of those lovely traverses. The good climber who is also conceited

comes into his own here, for this climb is in full sight, close above the hikers' path leading to the Ellmauer Tor. Here he will find a plentiful audience and many 'ooh's and 'ah's; and while climbing he can send down many a charming insult into the gaping void. Nobody will be able to 'get at him'. After dealing with the final chimney-crack, the usual practice is to traverse a short way eastwards to the Matejak Chimney, and abseil down it. If you do that, the climb is really only a half-day tour. The East Face catches the sun early and dries out quickly after days of rain. If you start early enough, you can tack on another climb after your half-day, depending on your fitness and the weather. The Bauernpredigtstuhl – the old 'West Face' – might be a good idea . . .

Valley Resorts St Johann in Tirol, 690 m (bus to Griesenau, toll-road to the Griesneralm). Dorf Going, 773 m, Dorf Ellmau, 812 m (bus from St Johann and Kufstein).
Bases Gaudeamus Hut, 1267 m, DAV, serviced, below the Kübelkar, 1½ hours from Going or Ellmau. Grutten Hut, 1620 m, DAV, serviced, 2½ hours from Ellmau or Going (if car is taken to the Wochenbrunner Alm, the ascent on foot is only 1½ hours). Wochenbrunner Alm, private beds.
Starting Point At 1900 m to the left of the prominent Matejak Chimney 150 m high in the East Face, 15 m left of its mouth, 1 hour from the Gaudeamus and Grutten Huts. Time for the climb, for a two-man rope, 2½–3 hours.
Descent If the climb is continued up the South-East Ridge (III) to the summit, the descent is down the normal way (I), following the footmarks, to the Ellmauer Tor in 1 hour. Better and shorter: swift abseil down the abseil-piste of the Matejak Chimney.
First Ascent M. Meier, A. Göttner and H. Biegler, 21.5.1935.
Guides/Maps RR *Kaisergebirge* (AV series, German). WCP *Kaisergebirge* AV 25M. Sh. 8 – Kaisergebirge.
Plate The whole of the East Face of the Vordere Karlspitze seen above the Kübelkar in the Kaisergebirge. At the right-hand edge of the picture, the Matejak Chimney, for the most part used as an abseil-route.

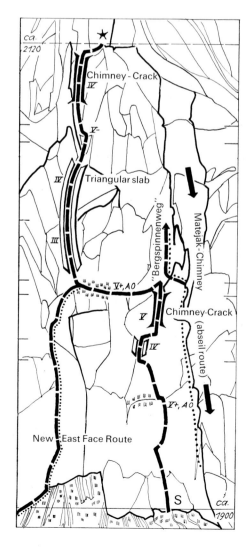

Kaisergebirge
Fleischbank 2187 m
East Face (Dülfer Route)
Grade V, A0/350 m

The summit crest of the Kaisergebirge, fashioned out of light-coloured, firm Wetterstein limestone, runs from west to east and is split at its centre as by a sword-slash. At that exact spot, above the Steinerne Rinne, two huge, precipitous walls face each other in such close proximity that the climbers on them can – from the Fleischbank or the Predigtstuhl – carry on conversations with each other across the horrid abyss between them. It is impossible for the ordinary visitor coming from the south and seeing those smooth, towering, slabby walls, with their bulges and overhangs, for the first time from the Ellmauer Tor, to take it all in. The climber, looking at those walls closely can at least discover cracks, grooves, ramps, and as he looks further and further up, all sorts of chimneys, pillars, and gullies – but for someone else, unable to take in the primaeval immensity of the scene, it remains shapeless. Perhaps one in a thousand who look up from the Steinerne Rinne knows about the history of climbing on those walls from having read Alpine literature – according to which this rift is pregnant with both tragedy and the highest human joy. High fortune has ruled here in two senses of the word . . .

The East Face of the Fleischbank, today long assured as the classic testing-ground and still the delight of keen 'V-graders' remained virgin till 1910. Then Otto Herzog and Adolf Deye made the first attempt on it. They only got as far as the cave above the entry-terrace and there they left hanging a little red rag. It was intended to scare people away, but it had quite the opposite effect. On 25 October 1911, Georg Sixt (the younger) and Hans Fiechtl got across the first big slab-traverse, but had to turn back and endure a bivouac in a storm standing, unsecured by pitons, on minute footholds – unaware in the pitch-darkness that they were only a few metres above the bed of the cwm. Only a few days later, Hans Dülfer and Werner Schaarschmidt climbed the face and labelled it 'by far the hardest climb in the Kaiser'. Dülfer, that master-cragsman, did not rate the two rope-

traverses, but the exit-cracks which follow, as the key-pitches (see sketch). The face had capitulated. It was climbed in 1912 by seven parties; today it ranks as the forerunner of 'modern' climbing. It is climbed frequently, but is less decorated with pitons than other faces. Many claim that the decisive holds have become more difficult owing to the panic-sweat of far too many an assailant. Be that so, this classic route, entailing for the most part free-climbing, with its almost perfect vertical line (normally needing 30 pitons, which have been in position for a long time), remains a great favourite even among those who know nothing of its early history. For Munich climbers it is of course their own 'rock-patch', but many a famous mountaineer has come to climb it in our own day and, deeply impressed, to confirm its ancient reputation. Here they can learn the 'rope-traverse' technique with which Dülfer not only opened up the East Face of the Fleischbank but also a new epoch in climbing. For many years a fine possibility lay hidden between the Dülfer Route and the Noichl-Wörndl 'East Face Direct': Pit Schubert and Udo Pohlke discovered it in 1975 so, to the other two routes, was added the 'New East' – climbed more than thirty times during its first year.

Valley Resorts Kufstein im Tirol, 503 m. St Johann in Tirol, 690 m. Ellmau, 812 m.
Bases Gaudeamus Hut, 1267 m, DAV, serviced; 1½ hours from Ellmau. Stripsenjochhaus, 1580 m, OAV, serviced; 4½ hours from Kufstein, 1¼ from the Griesneralm, 1006 m.
Starting Point At about 1850 m in the Steinerne Rinne (1½ hours from the Stripsenjochhaus) at a point where a prominent terrace cuts horizontally across the smooth wall from left to right.
Descent The normal route by the Schöllhorn couloir to the Fleischbank Saddle, 2134 m (II), traverse to the Christa Saddle, then by the 'Herweg' (III, with one abseil pitch) into the Steinerne Rinne (1½ hours).
First Ascent H. Dülfer and W. Schaarschmidt, 15.6.1912.
Guides/Maps RR *Kaisergebirge* (AV series, German). WCP *Kaisergebirge*. AV 25M. Sh. 8 – Kaisergebirge.
Plate The East Face of the Fleischbank, taken from the West Face of the Predigtstuhl, opposite.

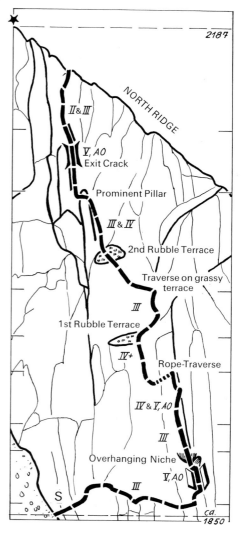

AUSTRIA 52

Kaisergebirge
Fleischbank 2187 m
South-East Dièdre
Grade VI, A1/300 m

What an odd name this is for one of the most famous rock-peaks in the Eastern Alps! The Predigtstuhl on one side and the Totenkirchl on the other and in between a compact bundle of vertical limestone slabs winging up into the Tirolese air. It is no fat giant like the Totenkirchl, with broad ledges all over it and only really precipitous at the back but, like the Predigtstuhl, a slender tower-structure. Its East Face presents a 400-metre limestone wall, almost vertical, terrifyingly smooth and often jutting out into overhangs above the shadowed gorge of the Steinerne Rinne. The name is a beacon-light. Four times first-ascents of routes on the Fleischbank's East Walls were hailed as the 'Ultimate on Rock'. In 1912 Dülfer and Schaarschmidt broke the barrier; they were the first to practise the 'rope-traverse' technique which brought them success. In 1913 Dülfer mastered the vertical Dülfer-Crack up to the Fleischbankscharte in an incredibly daring solo effort; in 1925 Wiessner and Rossi, lavishly supplied with pitons, climbed the long-besieged South-East Face (Emil Solleder and Kolb followed them up in $4\frac{1}{2}$ hours), and in 1944 Moser and Weiss demonstrated the new style of perfection-climbing with artificial aids in the South-East Dièdre: they were the first to use bolts, thus introducing those controversial shafts, as they were later to become, into the Kaisergebirge long before the climbers from Saxony. Hardly anyone remembers that now! . . .

Common sense asks the question 'Why didn't they stop at the end of free-climbing?' The human animal just can't do things like that. So nowadays many an 'Extremist', as gifted and as enthusiastic, cheerfully climbs from piton to piton, but for many of them the final pitch isn't important any more: they opt out at the grassy slab before the overhanging crack and climb out leftwards to the saddle. 'Well, hadn't they done the famous dièdre? There was only one difficult rope length left to do.' The proliferation of pitons has made many a talented free-climber a little careless . . . And yet look at that monstrous knife-edged recess from the Steinerne

Rinne, from the Ellmauer Tor — what an experience in itself! . . . One of its admirers recalls: 'I once climbed the North Ridge and paused on the Hintere Goinger Halt for a short rest, and looked across. There was a man on almost every stance in the dièdre, everywhere on the East and West Faces was packed with climbers. Suddenly, there was a roar in the Steinerne Rinne — deeply moving. Someone had started the climbers' song. Everyone joined in, from every wall they joined in and sang, roaring it out . . . it was quite something.' The direct start, by the way, demands the very hardest free-climbing and, after the 'Needle's-Eye' of the extremely difficult traverse out of the dièdre, there is still a Grade VI—, A1 waiting for you in the overhanging crack on the 'Great Slab' (seen shining-white and smooth in the photograph), to say nothing of the summit overhead, which presumably forms part of the climb . . .

Valley Resorts Kufstein in Tirol, 503 m. Ellmau. 812 m, St Johann in Tirol, 690 m.
Bases Stripsenjochhaus. 1580 m ÖAV, serviced. Gaudeamus Hut, 1267 m. DAV serived; 1½ hours from Ellmau. Grutten Hut, 1620 m. DAV serviced; 2½ hours from Ellmau or 1½ hours from the Wochenbrunner Alm (motorable).
Starting Point At 1880 m in the fall-line of the dièdre (1½ hours from the Stripsenjochhaus or 1¾ hours from the Gaudeamus Hut) — or by avoiding the difficult entry-cracks from out on the left. Time for the climb, for a two-man rope, 5–7 hours.
Descent As for route 51. by the normal way: Schöllhornrinne to the Fleischbankscharte, traverse to the Christascharte, then by the 'Herrweg' (III, one abseil pitch) into the Steinerne Rinne.
First Ascent P. Moser and W. Weiss. 2.7.1944.
Guides/Maps RR *Kaisergebirge* (AV series, German). WCP *Kaisergebirge*. AV 25M. Sh. 8 – Kaisergebirge.
Plate The Fleischbank (centre top of the picture) seen from the Ellmauer Tor. To the right centre, our dièdre, which can profitably also be studied on the East Face picture accompanying route 51. To the left, close to the dièdre, the South-East Face climb and the 'Dülfer Crack' leading up to the Fleischbankscharte.

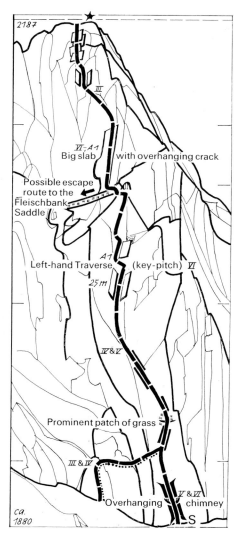

103

Kaisergebirge
Predigtstuhl 2115 m
West Face (Schüle-Diem + Haslacher-Behringer)
Grade V+, A1/300 m

The vertical limestone walls above the narrow trench of the Steinerne Rinne have made it the potter's wheel for the development of the modern climbing technique. It would be possible to write books and books about the magnificent, typical, incredibly daring routes on these faces of the Kaisergebirge, smooth as walls, soaring vertically and – the outstanding feature which accentuates this geological freak – rising so closely opposite each other. In this unique gymnasium of the Northern Limestone Ranges, we have chosen an unusual combination of two famous routes on the Predigtstuhl. We start up the 'Schüle-Diem Route' on the West Face of the North Summit till its interesting continuation up the West Gully and then, after the exposed 'Downward Traverse', change over into the bed of the West Gully on to the upper and finest part of the 'Haslacher-Behringer Route' on the West Face of the Central Summit. This is the acme of refinement, giving us the supreme treasures of the Predigtstuhl's delights at one bite. Our sketch gives bare but, in the circumstances, exact information, when compared with the photograph.

Of the 1921 'Schüle-Diem Route' (immediately repeated by Fritz Bechtold and Willi Merkl) we pick out the luscious dièdre with the daring traverse leading out of it; from the 'Haslacher-Behringer Route' the cracks, the slab and the couloir overhanging it, which make the West Face of the Central Summit into a *crème de la crème* of 'extremes'. The total height of the face is about 300 metres; a twosome in good condition should take about 4 or 5 hours. It is V+ and Ao almost all the way, there is hardly any relief of III and IV. The limestone is a true sample of the Kaisergebirge's rock, firm and reliable. All the pitons are there – far too many of them. The most exhausting feature of the climb is undoubtedly the 'Schüle-Diem Dièdre', the largest array of pitons is that on the 'Haslacher-Behringer'. Until recently this was known as the 'Lackner-Langer Dièdre'. Fritz Schmidt discovered the error. Lackner and Langer climbed the easier dièdre in the

West Wall Gorge, but the error managed to survive fifty years in the literature of Alpine guidebooks. Dietmar Ohngemach is probably speaking for the mass of Kaiser climbers when he says: 'Whoever climbs this combination of two routes can be sure he has enjoyed the finest pitches in the whole Kaiser Range. I have done it in the spring, when our noisy enthusiasm lorded it over the silence down in the Steinerne Rinne and also in high summer, in front of an audience jamming the track down below. It was always something of a knee-twister, but always enormous fun. We laughed and fooled about, and at the famous 'Misery-holds' on the Central Summit brought to an end all north-face solemnity . . .' Which proves that extreme rock relaxes the soul.

Valley Resorts Kufstein, 503 m. St Johann in Tirol, 690 m (bus/motor to the Griesenau, 727 m). Going, 773 m, and Ellmau, 812 m (bus from Kufstein and St Johann).
Bases Stripsenjochhaus, 1580 m, ÖAV, serviced Gaudeamus Hut, 1267 m, or Grutten Hut, 1620 m, both DAV, serviced.
Starting Point At about 1800 m in the Steinerne Rinne (1 hour from the Stripsenjochhaus, 2 hours from Gaudeamus and Grutten Huts) to the left of the fall-line of the North Summit, below the West Gully of the Predigtstuhl, which comes down in a narrow crack.
Descent Abseil down the Botzong chimney (III) to the hollow in the West Wall and on into the Steinerne Rinne, or over the summits of the Predigtstuhl and the Angermannweg (normal way, III−) to the Ellmauer Tor (all about 1 hour from the summit). Fixed abseil pitons in the Botzong chimney.
First Ascents P. Diem and K. Schüle, 1921. Haslacher and Behringer, 1926.
Guides/Maps RR *Kaisergebirge* (AV series, German). WCP *Kaisergebirge* AV 25M. Sh. 8 – Kaisergebirge.
Plate The Predigtstuhl in the Kaisergebirge, above the Steinerne Rinne. We are looking at the entire West Faces, from the North Summit, 2092 m (top centre) and Central Summit (to the right of the North Summit). The Central Summit overlaps the Main Summit.

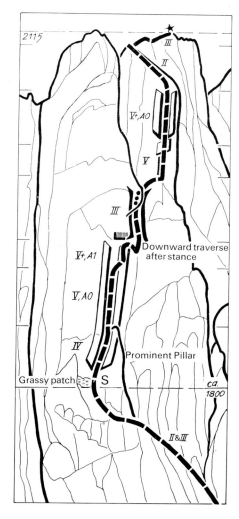

Kaisergebirge
Bauernpredigtstuhl 2119 m
West Face (Lucke-Strobl Crack)
Grade VI−, A0/220 m

The Lucke-Strobl Crack up the smooth face of the Bauernpredigtstuhl is a show-piece among modern 'extremes', highly rated, highly respected. Anyone who possesses the skill and the condition takes this crazy route undocumented. Admittedly, it is short, but it is one of the most attractive of the modern Kaiser routes. Looking back to the first ascent, remember that the first critical crack at the start, which was the decisive factor in making possible the mastery of this gigantic, polished slab leading up to a bulging roof, was climbed 'free' by our two pioneers of that time. Later, an enormous block of wood facilitated the first difficulty, and its 'loss' had to be paid for dearly at the Gaudeamus Hut . . . Later still the crack was further relieved of its terrors by a ladder of pitons. One can only say: thank God! None of the stock excuses such as 'the critical hold had disappeared, etc' will pass muster here. The Lucke-Strobl Crack remains a rousing rock-climb and every 'Sexogradist' in his prime should do it.

This is its brief history: the first climb of the Bauernpredigtstuhl was on 30 September 1900, by the Munich bookseller, Emil Mönnich, and Michael Kainel. It must have been a dramatic performance, since it was recorded by Nieberl. The famous climbers Hans Pfann, Adolf Schulze and Georg Leuchs traversed the mountain in 1901 (up by the South-West Gully, down by the North-East). The North Ridge (III) was climbed in 1904, after which there was a long gap. It was in 1930 that the thunder-clap detonated: Leo Rittler and Alfred Drexel, using a number of pitons, climbed the South-West Arête (VI−), the Rittlerkante. Poor Leo, ever unemployed, ever lucky on mountains! Then, in 1934, came today's 'Old West Face' (VI−), immediately reported as one of the great climbs, crack-climbing *par excellence*. Fritz Stadler, the third man to climb it, has left a brilliant account of it (*ÖAZ*, 1950, 41) . . . Thirteen years were to pass before the 'Lucke-Strobl', in 1947. A 'non-Extremist' who stands at the foot of the wall today and can bear to look vertically upwards without suffering an attack of vertigo, will understand all – or nothing. The unbroken exposure of this perpendicular wall – given a piton here, a wooden wedge there – must be conceded. All in all, it can be truly said, taking a comprehensive view of all the 'modern' developments, that here, in their own climbing-ground of the Kaisergebirge, shared by Munich and Innsbruck, decisive deeds of daring were waged and won, to enable today's standard of the Alpine 'Sixth Grade' to be achieved. The old descent down the North-East Gully was always a risky affair; brittle, muddy and filled with ice well into high summer – a perilous ice-couloir, which spelled death for many a climber who had succeeded in making the ascent. The Rescue-Service, called into being by the DAV (at Pit Schubert's instigation) has therefore constructed a new way down the little wall to the south of the Bauernpredigtstuhl.

Valley Resorts Going, 773 m, or Ellmau, 812 m (bus from St Johann and Kufstein).
Bases Gaudeamus Hut, 1267 m, DAV, serviced; 1½ hours from Ellmau or Going. Grutten Hut, 1620 m, DAV, serviced; 2½ hours from Ellmau or 1½ hours from the Wochenbrunner Alm (motorable to here).
Starting Point At about 1900 m in the left part of the base of the wall, not far from the path up from the nearby Ellmauer Tor. Time for the climb, for a rope of two, 3–4 hours.
Descent Abseil 20 m north-east of the summit, then southwards (marked) to abseil pitons, 4 abseils of 20 m and then follow clear track-marks down into the cwm.
First Ascent K. Lucke and H. Strobl, 29.6.1947. The right-hand 'Old West Face Route': G. Gotthardt and H. Told, 1934.
Guides/Maps RR *Kaisergebirge* (AV series, German). WCP *Kaisergebirge*. AV 25M. Sh. 8 – Kaisergebirge.
Plate The Bauernpredigtstuhl, here showing us its smooth West Face, stands in front of the Northern Törlspitze, like a tower. On the left we look into the North-East Gully and on the right we have the sharp profile of the Rittlerkante (South-West Arête) before us. In the solid limestone face we can discover the narrow cracks, bulges and overhangs of the 'Old West Face' (to the right) and of our 'Lucke-Strobl' (to the left). To the right of the Rittlerkante, the South-West Gully and still further to the right the 'Little Wall', down which runs the new descent-route.

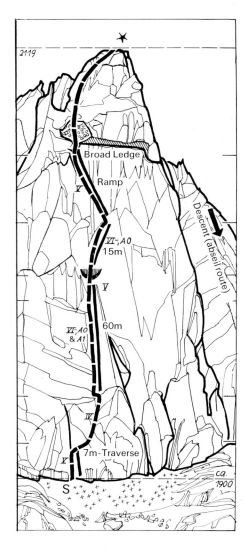

Kaisergebirge
Maukspitze 2227 m
West Face (Buhl)

Grade VI, A1/350 m (Easier if the 'Woll/Woll' pitch is avoided)

Hermann Buhl called his first ascent of the Maukspitze's West Face one of the most precarious and exciting of his early years. That was in 1943 with Wastl Weiss from Kitzbühel, who had already come to grips with the wall. Several attempts on the part of others to repeat their success came to grief at the vital key-pitch because one of the new pitons had broken off and, to make matters worse, it was an essential, irreplaceable little piece of rock-ironmongery. Only Karl Gomboz and Buhl's Innsbruck friend, Hugo Vigl, succeeded in making the second ascent, an operation which took them eleven hours of climbing time: that was on 2 October 1948, with the help of additional artificial aids. They turned the critical pitch with the greatest difficulty by traversing above it, close under the bulge, hammering piton after piton. Kuno Rainer and Erich Streng did exactly the same when they completed the third climb, taking seven hours for the whole face. After the first two relatively easy rope lengths at the start, you find yourself straight away in a partly overhanging chimney, which looks like a crack from below. That brings you at once to the critical pitch, the 'Woll/Woll' ('Yeah, Yeah') (VI), an overhang in the chimney-crack, which opens outwards. It is essential to study the route in the guidebook, photograph and sketch. I will quote one of two interesting remarks made by younger 'Extremists' of today. Werner Schertle says: 'The climb has been robbed of its extremely difficult key-pitch by excessive use of pitons. No very great difficulties now. Good firm rock, good pitons.' This is what Erich Griessl writes: 'The "Woll/Woll" is VI, but the gallery of pitons bypassing it isn't really the "Mauk" any more. And the "Woll/Woll gets harder all the time by being polished more and more.' Here is Manfred Sturm's view: 'This is an extremely difficult Kaiser climb, but it has been too highly rated for the last ten years. The "Woll/Woll", if climbed free, is the most difficult pitch and, when wet, of extreme difficulty. Buhl's traverse, climbed free, has been considerably eased by today's piton-

traverse ... compared with the walls above the Steinerne Rinne, the Mauk climb is now an oasis of peace.' Dietmar Ohngemach, however, comments: 'Whoever has down-graded the Mauk-West should climb it again in five years' time. You simply can't downgrade it.' Harry Rost's dry observation is: 'Nothing startling. There is a fine, difficult 90-metre crack soon after the start. The route is heavily pitoned.'

When talking of Buhl's favourite West Face, one should not overlook the tough, delicate climb of the Spengler Chimney, on its firm, dry, yet difficult rock (at its solidest in early autumn), which connoisseurs regard as neither easier nor less beautiful. And no less beautiful is the arresting picture – looking out to the south – of the snow and ice of the Glockner Group, rising above the as yet dark-green ski-slopes around Kitzbühel.

Valley Resorts St Johann in Tirol, 690 m (station) or Going, 773 m (bus), or Ellmau, 812 m (bus), or Kufstein.
Bases Gaudeamus Hut, 1267 m, DAV, below the Kübelkar, serviced, 1½ hours from Going or Ellmau. Ackerl Hut, 1695 m, ÖAV, below the Ackerlsporn, unserviced, AV-locked; new Ackerl Hut, 1446 m, at base of spur 3 hours from Going or Ellmau. Across from the Gaudeamus Hut, 1¾ hours, marked path.
Starting Point At about 1900 m to the right of the start of the Spengler Chimney (prominent dark rift in the West Face). 1½ hours from the Gaudeamus Hut, ½ hour from the Ackerl Hut. Normal time for the climb, for a two-man rope, 4–5 hours.
Descent By the normal way (I) to the Niedersessel (partly marked-and protected path). Summit to Ackerl Hut about 1½ hours. Summit to Gaudeamus Hut, 2½ hours.
First Ascent H. Buhl, H. Reischl and W. Weiss, 22.8.1943.
Guides/Maps RR *Kaisergebirge* (AV series, German). WCP *Kaisergebirge*. AV 25M. Sh. 8 – Kaisergebirge.
Plate The West Face of the Maukspitze in the Kaisergebirge. Cutting vertically through the left of the face, the deep rift of the Spengler Chimney. Studying the sketch and photograph together will make the route of our climb clear throughout from the direct and only starting point.

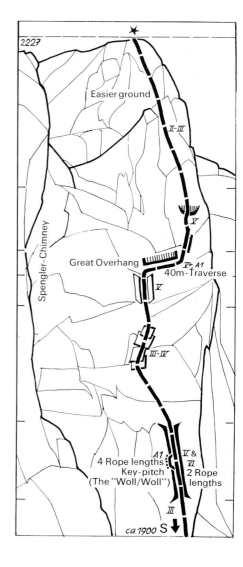

Berchtesgaden Alps (Reiteralm)

Grosses Grundübelhorn 2096 m
South Dièdre
Grade VI−, A0/500 m

The limestone plateau of the peaceful Reiteralm, between Junger Saalach and Hintersee resembles a rhomb placed on its apex. At its southern point, high above the lonely Hirschbichl Pass, closed to traffic, stand the Mühlsturzhörner and the Grundübelhörner side by side. Their southern slopes are interesting; the way up is lonely, its scenery enchanting, but long and tedious. There are steep runnels and hollows, and clumps of woodland-scrub, sufficiently impenetrable to please our friends the foresters and hunters, but about which some climbers are inclined to grumble. The uphill approach to the South Dièdre of the Grosses Grundübelhorn, which has so quickly become well-known, is at times difficult to find and indisputably long. A very exact study of the guidebook is advisable. If you are traversing from the old approach-route over the Halsgrube and Teufelskopf to the start of the climb, you have, just short of the South Arête, to cross a horrid trench, where you will find some assistance from a wire-rope, running down to the bed of the runnel, left by an earlier climber – or you can rope down some 40 metres into the bottom of the trench and climb up again directly opposite. The whole approach takes 3–3½ hours from Hintersee. The route of the actual climb follows the natural line up the South Dièdre, on rock which remains ideally firm all the way up to the exit; but caution is necessary in wet conditions, when the lower part of the climb, whose cracks have to be climbed 'free', become much more difficult.

Route-finding presents no difficulty. It is the prototype of the kind of route which, thanks to the use of two bolts, but otherwise not over-pitoned, yields a splendid climb. This is a case where a bolt need not be considered an object of execration. The difficult tension-traverse out to the left occurs in the third rope length, and for it the second on the rope should have a 6-metre long spare line available. The stances are excellent, the free-climbing first rate and enjoyable. Nearly all the necessary pitons are there, on the face and in the Dièdre. The upper gully-crack affords delightful high-grade climbing (IV). The descent into the Halsgrube to the north is I and II, first down the Wagendrischlkar and then to the right over steep, trackless and overgrown steps to the Böselsteig and so into the Halsgrube. Werner Schertle's opinion: 'Unlovely, difficult and lengthy approach. Even today the free-climbing is of extreme difficulty, on magnificent rock, but the route is, unfortunately, short, only about 250 m to where it emerges into the South Ridge Climb.' Manfred Sturm writes: 'A modern rock climb, even including a few bolts, but otherwise purely classical in type. Difficult free-climbing pitches, but on very good rock. It confirms that there are still rewarding routes to be discovered today.' One of the interesting things is the utter silence of the surroundings. Close opposite, a half-dozen very steep couloirs fall from the Hochkalter and Hocheisspitze. At the beginning of May they yield the most recondite snow-gullies and ski-runs: among them, as if in a dead world, the splendid chaos of the Hirschbichltal.

Valley Resort Hintersee near Berchtesgaden, 790 m (bus Berchtesgaden–Ramsau–Hintersee).
Base None. Inns and hotels at Hintersee. Bivouac-site on the way up, 30 minutes below the start.
Starting Point At about 1600 m, reached by traversing from left to right up a gently inclined ramp to the start of the Dièdre above the triangular slab. Time for the climb, for a two-man rope, 3–4 hours.
Descent The route up ends exactly where the South Ridge ends, a long way from the summit. Anyone with a sense for terrain avoids going up to the relatively obscured summit, but ropes himself down through the chimneys of the South Face.
First Ascent Rudi Bülter and Michael Gröll, 24.6.1967.
Guides/Maps RR *Berchtesgadener Alpen* (AV series, German). KK 50M. Sh. 14 – Berchtesgadener Alpen.
Plate Looking into the South Dièdre of the Grosses Grundübelhorn in the Reiteralm Massif. The start is well marked by the triangular ramp. The start of the neighbouring 'South Ridge Climb' (IV+) in the exact centre of the picture, to the right below the tree-top. Top left: the long, easy ridge up to the summit.

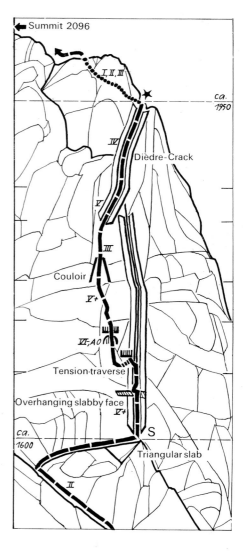

Berchtesgaden Alps (Reiteralm)
Grosses Mühlsturzhorn 2235 m
South Arête Direct

Grade VI, A1/350 m

The South Ridge of the Grosses Mühlsturzhorn is at the same time the southern edge of the great limestone massif of the Reiteralm between Junger Salaach and Hintersee–Ramsau. As shown in our picture the fine, unusually steep limestone of this arête is very much like a piece of the Kaisergebirge. There cannot be anything more dramatic than its big corners, huge slabs, dark caves, prominent cracks and other delectable obstacles for the 'extreme' climber. Our direct South Arête Climb calls for both respect and reverence — respect because this fearsomely difficult climb was first made as long ago as 1936, reverence because the two very young men who did it, Toni Kurz and Anderl Hinterstoisser were to meet their brave but horrifying deaths on the North Face of the Eiger soon afterwards . . . The climbing is as lovely as it looks and less exhausting than one might at first think. That sage of the mountains, Bernulf von Crailsheim, who wrote the text in the guidebook, considers the 75-metre dièdre 'gigantic' and classifies the climb as the most rewarding in the Berchtesgaden Alps. He goes on: 'Many exhausting cracks and overhangs, much free- as well as piton-climbing — and it was done over forty years ago! Our "artists" of today would be lucky to open up such a climb.' Werner Schertle writes: 'The approach is good. There is airy climbing, in part of great difficulty, on the slightly-sloping giant slab — really an extreme climb to enjoy. The rock could not be better, the line is perfect, though there is a little too much artificial climbing.'

One joint study of the sketch and the photograph, and you will be ready to start; you can't go wrong. The approach to the start from the peaceful Grundübelau is fabulously beautiful, without any kind of exaggeration. And when you take a rest below the sheer black precipice or at one of the three caves (there is water at the first), or on the top of the pillar above the long gully, on a warm, soft autumn day, before or after the first snowfall, you can listen to the roaring of the stags down in the woodland-thickets below — an

uncanny, primaeval sound. A sound like everything here in this mercifully hidden Nature reserve – 'the forest primaeval'. Finally, a good tip: there is a convenient bivouac-site close to the way up, near a prominent small tree, about half an hour below the start of the climb. A rope of two needs 4–6 hours for the climb, but one should take the relatively long approach into account. The old way down, to the north, through the Wagendrischlkar is scenically beautiful, but a long 'slog'. It is much quicker by way of the piton-route down the South Chimney, installed by the DAV Rescue-Service (well marked, demanding use of doubled rope); a good hour if you have foregone the last 100 metres of the climb.

Valley Resort Hintersee, 790 m, near Berchtesgaden–Ramsau (bus).
Base None. Inns and hotels at Hintersee. Bivouac-site below the start.
Starting Point At about 1850 m close to the left of the South Ridge's base (to the right in the picture), where you have to tackle a huge black re-entrant in the wall. The approach takes about 2½ hours from the ruined Engertalm, 959 m, at the head of the valley (1½ hours from Hintersee); then following route 167 in the guidebook (not very well marked), up the unusually lovely Schaflsteig, till you can look across to the foot of the wall; then through trenches to the ramp out of the cwm (see picture).
Descent ·Northwards into the Wagendrischlkar as in route 206 (II) in the guidebook, then eastwards to the Böselsteig and over the Halsgrube to the Hintersee (at least 2½ hours). Or better, after 300 m of the climb, abseil down the southern chimneys to the left (pitons in place, marked) thus saving oneself the last final 100 m (I and II) to the summit.
First Ascent Toni Kurz and Anderl Hinterstoisser. July 1936.
Guides/Maps RR *Berchtesgadener Alpen* (AV series, German). KK 50M. Sh. 14 – Berchtesgadener Alpen.
Plate Looking at the South-West and South Faces of the Grosses Mühlsturzhorn above the Hirschbichltal near Ramsau. Top left, seemingly lower, the Main Summit, top right the South Arête Summit. Bottom right, our starting point. Our 'Direct' keeps to the left of the Arête.

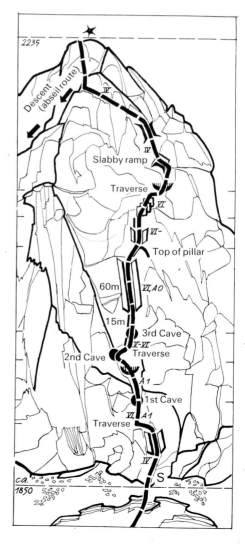

Hoher Göll 2522 m
West Face (Kleiner Trichter – 'Small Funnel')
Grade VI−, A0/450 m

The slab armoury of the Hoher Göll's West Face lies hidden between the Mannigrat and the West Ridge itself; a huge vertical half-circle of surging lime-stone walls above the green floor of the Scharitzkehlalm, lying flat as a board at its base. Inset in this wall, so rich in structure yet so solid in slabs, are two noticeable funnels – the 'Grosser Trichter' and 'Kleiner Trichter'. Both give their names to famous Göll climbs; the former to the oft-repeated route first climbed by J. Aschauer and J. Kurz in 1922, the latter to the more recent climb opened up by Gauder and Helminger in 1943. The key-pitch on both climbs is the rope length leading up to the lower end of the respective funnels. A compari-son of the sketch and the photograph will immediately help the reader to recognise this; the guidebook too requires careful study, as some of the pitches depend on minutiae. The 'Kleiner Trichter Route', as a whole, can be described as a fine, delicate piece of free-climbing, whose classic style is beyond reproach. The hardest part is the key-pitch at the complicated entry to the bed of the funnel. When you have eventually done with the 'ups and downs' on the steep, solid slab below the Funnel's lower outlet and reached the starting point for the 'Pendulum Traverse'; and when the leader has ef-fected that movement, then the second man can follow on the taut traversing rope used for the 'Pendulum'.

It should be noted that there is no chance for retreating after the with-drawal of the pendulum-rope. You have to move up at once by free-climbing (V−) to the next stance, a distance of quite 20 metres. The part-chimney, part dièdre on the left flank of the Funnel then provides another 4–5 rope lengths of not too easy free-climbing before you reach a small notch, where the actual climbing finishes. From there on, you proceed up the broken rocks to a patch of rubble, then up to the left to the so-called Gölleiten, where you find a path to the summit. The climb, from start to finish, offers no chance of going astray, since the route appears absolutely logical and appropriate to the firm, safe rock up which it runs. The stances are good. If you do not wish to follow the rock-and-rubble route to the summit, you can keep to the left (eastwards) at the Gölleiten and steer along a marked path towards the Kehlsteinhaus, from where buses go to Berchtesgaden during daylight hours. On the other hand, if you go up to the summit of the Hoher Göll (an extra 400 metres from the top of the climb), in order to survey the Salzachtal, the Dachstein Range, the Steinernes Meer, Watzmann and Hochkalterstock, instead of taking the Pflugtal Descent, you can go down the Alpeltal to the Alpeltal Hut, where there is a bus. That takes two hours more, but has the advantage of offering great personal satisfaction.

Valley Resorts Berchtesgaden, 573 m, or Vorderbrand, 1100 m (bus and ropeway).
Bases Scharitzkehlalm, 1046 m, in the upper Endstal, private, serviced, limited overnight accommodation. Alpeltal Hut near Vorderbrand, 1100 m, TVN, unserviced, caretaker, 29 beds and 60 sleeping-places.
Starting Point At about 1650 m, at the left-hand edge of the rubble-cone, about half-way between the starting points of the Grosser Trichter and West Face Direct Routes. 1½ hours from Scharitzkehl, 2¼ from the Alpetal Hut (the way down does not pass the starting point). Time for the climb, for a rope of two, about 5 hours. Excellent stances.
Descent South-east from the summit to the Göllscharte, then down north-westwards circuitously, passing close to the Pflughörndl and steeply down into the Pflugtal, then along the old hunters' path into the Endstal (fully 2½ hours). Many clim-bers of the 'extreme' routes on the West Face of the Göll traverse above the Funnels, i.e. at the end of their actual climbs, northwards through the broken rock, so as to climb or rope-down the old West Face way or through the Zellerschlucht (to the left of the 'Grosser Trichter'). Only pos-sible if closely familiar with the terrain.
First Ascent Gauder and Helminger, 1943.
Guides/Maps RR *Berchtesgadener Alpen* (AV series, German). KK 50M. Sh. 14 – Berchtesgadener Alpen.
Plate The West Face of the Hoher Göll above the Endstal, with 'Grosser Trichter' and 'Kleiner Trichter' in the left half of the picture.

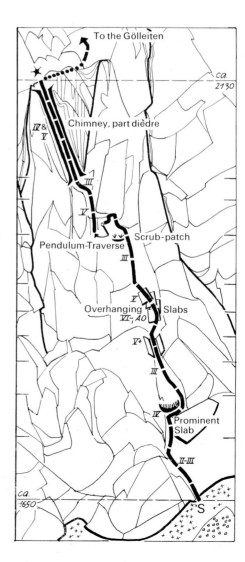

Dolomites (Brenta Group)
Cima d'Ambiez 3102 m
East Face (Via della Concordia)
Grade VI, A1/350 m

The stark lump of the Cima d'Ambiez – between the Bocca d'Ambiez and the Bocca d'Agola – unfolds its broad, vertical East Face, fearsomely striped by black water-streaks, opposite the Punta l'Ideale – a graceful tower in the outliers of the Tosa Massif. Between them lies the slowly shrinking d'Ambiez Glacier. From the base of the East Face, and from the summit too, there is a wide view southwards down to Lake Garda and Monte Baldo. Our picture was taken from a couloir just by the north foot of the Punta l'Ideale, showing at the bottom one or two crevasses in our miserable little glacier and, close to them, the two water-marks in the base of the East Face, the left hand of which marks the start of our Via della Concordia. The name was given to it because on 30 June and 1 July 1955 two parties, both attempting the first ascent, joined together and succeeded, after great difficulties, in achieving it as a combined rope. The time of seventeen hours of actual climbing, the bivouac which became unavoidable, the hammering of 18 pitons and four wooden-wedges give some idea of the character of this explicitly modern climb. If the term is appropriate, its delectable key-pitches are a delicate 25-metre traverse to the left quite low down and the dièdre with its overhangs waiting for you high up on the face. Horst Wels has given a detailed description in the Brenta guidebook. We are adding a short commentary by the Munich climber, Willi Schröttle of the HTG-élite of the Oberland Section, who made the third ascent with Wels. He says: 'The holds on the 25-metre traverse are small but plentiful and it affords most enjoyable climbing. The wooden-wedge dièdre is an almost perfect example of splendid bridging-technique and involves fully 40 metres of unprotected ascent, though you could of course provide intermediate belays by using more wedges. My general impression is of a very delicate and varied "extreme" rock-climb.'

The photograph and sketch reveal further resting-places on this Brenta route, which has so quickly attracted a high reputation, decorated in the mean-time with 30 pitons (so far as is known, the first party only left nine). The line taken by this climb, which demands so much fine free-climbing, is ideal: it follows the vertical thrust of the dièdre. Halfway up the face, above the 'Wet Chimney', a fairly broad terrace offers quite a good bivouac-site. Once above the dièdre you are on the upper bastion, riven into terraces by lateral bands, of this Fortress of the Brenta, safe in the knowledge that an easy, quick descent awaits you.

Valley Resort San Lorenzo di Banale, 785 m. South of Lake Molveno (bus from Trient or Madonna di Campiglio).
Base Agostini Hut, 2410 m, private, in the upper Ambiez Valley, serviced; 4½ hours from San Lorenzo (jeep, motorable to the Upper Prato pasture, 1819 m).
Starting Point At about 2670 m, roughly in the fall-line of the prominent dièdre which cuts through almost the whole East Face and ends in broad, black water-streaks above the base of the wall. Time for the climb, for a rope of two, 5–7 hours.
Descent By the normal South Ridge Route (II), a descent of about 400 m. First, climbing down to the saddle between the Cima d'Ambiez and the Denti d'Ambiez, then a ledge-traverse below the South-East Face back to the Agostini Hut. Plenty of cairns. About 1½ hours to the Hut.
First Ascent A. Oggioni, J. Aiazzi, A. Aste and A. Miorandi, 1955.
Guides/Maps CAI *Dolomiti di Brenta* (Italian). AC *Dolomites West*. TCI 50M. Sh. D64 – Gruppo di Brenta. KK 50M. Sh. 73 – Brentagruppe.
Plate The massive East Face of the Cima d'Ambiez in the Central Brenta Group. To the left centre of our picture you can follow our 'Via della Concordia'. Close to its left – in the space before the next prominent water-streak – is the East-South-East Route of M. Stenico and M. Girardi, first climbed in 1941.

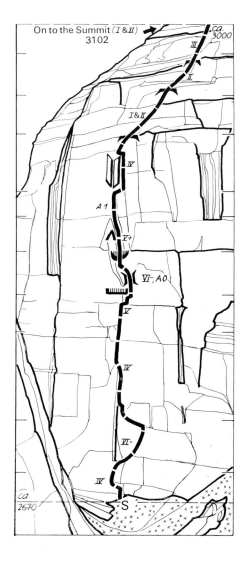

Dolomites (Brenta Group)
Crozzon di Brenta 3135 m
North-East Pillar ('Frenchmen's Pillar')
Grade VI, A1/800 m

As you come out of the Brenta valley, the scene is immediately dominated by the Crozzon di Brenta, first in the guise of a huge, steep, staircase-like arête, then as a massive, broad projection from the Cima Tosa behind it. When at last you are sitting at ease outside the hut kept by that famous Brenta-host, Bruno Detassis, himself one of the great pioneer climbers here, with the melodies of the local climbers' choir from Trient ringing in your ears, you can see nothing but this single fearsome Colossus of a mountain. Its solid limestone walls, 800 metres high, are seamed with fine but distinct horizontal bands; so rich is its architecture that it has attracted every 'extreme' climber since Paul Preuss's day. Then, suddenly one is bewildered to discover the delicate, slender little 'Aiguille' of the Guglia di Brenta directly opposite it. What a contrast! The guidebooks and the literature of mountaineering will tell you how many attempts, successful and otherwise, those two faces have witnessed. Here we will only quote the sovereign expert's view of Pit Schubert (3rd ascent with Klaus Werner) of the 'Frenchmen's Pillar': 'This is the biggest free-climbing route in the Brenta.'

In opening up this elegant climb the two Frenchmen, J. Fréhel and D. Leprince-Ringuet, demonstrated that the Alps are by no means 'worked out', nay more, that there is a hint of new territory to be conquered on the face of the Crozzon, so marvellously pioneered by them. The rock in the difficult passages is absolutely firm and the hand-holds are often the jug-handles of a fairy-tale, but the exposure is terrific and there is any number of impressive glimpses into the abyss. There is the advantage of much unexpected free-climbing, many of the pitches being Grade V without pitons. The climb has become at least as great a favourite as the Via delle Guide ('Detassis Giordani'). Nor are there any route-finding difficulties, unless they are met with on the way down; but that fairly long descent, once dreaded, as is evidenced by numerous little bivouac-walls along the many notches in the connecting-ridge to the Cima Tosa, is plentifully marked by cairns, and footmarks

are an additional aid. However, it is only sensible to start down it if there are at least 2 hours of daylight left. Otherwise the night should be spent in the bivouac-box at the summit. The descent does not pass the starting-point. It is more than ten years since the first ascent, so all the necessary pitons have been supplied in the meantime. though happily not too many. So much for the 'Frenchmen's Route' – once your appetite is whetted, you should study the ample choice of other fine 'extreme' routes in the guidebook and the BK-chart of neighbouring climbs. The glorious Via delle Guide is there for the taking and the amusing Aste Dièdre. Most visitors to the Crozzon's Summit come up by the splendidly firm North Ridge (IV). Every one of them immediately looks across in one direction, down onto the Guglia: his eyes riveted on the incredible – that classic 'column of rock', one of Nature's pranks. Those who have come back to climb it again will confirm its grading – VI, A1!

Valley Resort Madonna di Campiglio, 1515 m (bus from Bolzano or Trient).
Base Brentei Hut, 2182 m, CAI, above the Val Brenta Alta, on the Sentiero Bogani, serviced; fully 3 hours from Madonna di Campiglio; but motorable as far as the Vallesinella Inn (also jeep), whence only 2¼ hours.
Starting Point At 2300 m, to the right of the cowl-like substructure, just an hour from the hut. Time for the climb, for a rope of two, 7–9 hours.
Descent Back along the connecting-ridge to the Cima Tosa (III–) in 1½ hours by way of saddles and the west side of several towers. Plenty of cairns and foot-tracks. From the Cima Tosa, according to the guidebook, by the normal way down to the Tosa Hut, +3 hours. Bivouac-box on the summit.
First Ascent J. Fréhel and D. Leprince-Ringuet, 4.8.1965.
Guides/Maps CAI *Dolomiti di Brenta* (Italian). AC *Dolomites West.* TCI 50M. Sh. D64 – Gruppo di Brenta. KK, 50M. Sh. 73 – Brentagruppe.
Plate The 800-m-high North-East Face of the Crozzon di Brenta, showing the ice-couloir, 50° inclination in its upper sector, to the Cima Tosa. To the right, the North-East Pillar with the 'Frenchmen's Route' easy to follow in the centre of the picture. Easily identifiable too are the cowl-like substructure and the exit on to the North Ridge Route (close to the left of the uppermost shoulder on the right).

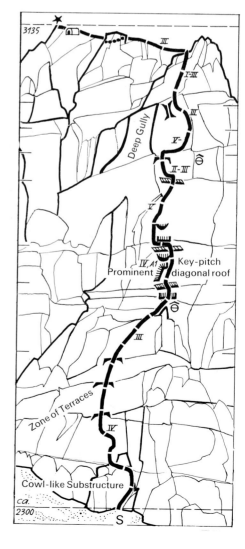

Dolomites (Brenta Group)

Guglia di Brenta (Campanile Basso) 2877 m
South-West Dièdre and South-West Face
Grade V−, A0/300 m

Here is a mountain which dares to lay claim to being impressively slender, smooth and again truly vertical, as if erosion and the shattering and destructive forces of ice did not exist. This Guglia will not collapse. Our route combines two climbs, the South-West Dièdre and the fine variant above it on the excessively sheer summit-block, first climbed by Charles Meade and his French guide, Pierre Blanc. They are joined by the 'Shoulder'. Here, too, we meet the normal route, which spirals its way up the whole of this rock-Colossus and runs from the North Face (Strada Provinciale) – in shadow on the photograph – to the Shoulder. The South-West Gully must be definitely graded at V−, Ao, as also the Meade-Blanc continuation up the South-West Face. Knowledge of our 'extreme' leadership leads us to believe that they smile a superior smile at these routes, which they assess at only IV and IV, Ao, because the impetus of their ambitious spirit only cares to look at the very highest limits. They cast enthusiastic glances on our Civetta walls, consider the Marmolada's South Face and the Northern Faces of the Tre Cime, but flip through the pages illustrating our routes in the Kaisergebirge and the Wetterstein only a hair's-breadth less difficult . . . and they will never forgive our Fusstein North Ridge, this very Guglia di Brenta, the Punta Fiames and the Arête of the Rosskuppe. We accept their superior view because we see everything and understand everything and take thought for those second- and third-class 'Extremists' who, dazzled and exalted by the beauty and impact of Alpine experiences, are not anxious to look so exactly at the little differences . . . Once and for all, here we have the Alpinist's 'Wonder of the World' since the turn of the century, which offers the real joy of a free-climb late in the autumn (when the Tosa Hut is no longer full to overflowing).

The route is clean-cut and therefore easy to find . . . but the dièdre looks difficult, oppressive to the spirit, and so many have allowed themselves to be led astray into traversing out to the right, where it looks easier at first but turns out not to be by any means to be so. So, straight on up the dièdre! Anyone standing on the Sentiero Otto Gottstein (part of the Bocchette path) in the middle of the North-West Face of the Brenta Alta (the face in the shadow at the right of the picture) and suddenly catching sight of the whole narrow South Face of the Guglia, can see, close below him, the start up the 'Fehrmann Dièdre'. From these he can follow and study the route up the entry-ramp, through the gully, up into the chimney groove and from the shoulder above it, past the resting-place, the 'Albergo al Sole', almost to the very top. A mountain-lover could want no finer object for his studies. The gully is arranged for the express purpose of straddling; the rock in the cracks, on the ramp, in the gully and the chimney is everywhere firm, but so vastly exposed that there can be no cause for complaint on that score.

Valley Resort Madonna di Campiglio, 1515 m. Thence motor to the Vallesinella Inn.
Bases Tosa Hut. CAI, 2491 m, 2 houses, serviced, heavily visited, 120 sleeping-places/beds; 3½ hours from Vallesinella. Brentei Hut, 2182 m, CAI, 2½ hours from Vallesinella.
Starting Point At 2550 m in the cwm below the Bocchetta del Campanile Basso, between the Guglia and the base of the Brenta Alta, to the left of the pillar which leads like a ramp to the 'Fehrmann Dièdre'. Approach from the Bocca di Brenta (downhill) ½ hour. Time for the climb for a rope of two (to the summit), 4–5 hours. You will need all of it.
Descent By the normal route (Ampferer–Berger) III and IV. Several abseil-rings in position to the Bocchetta del Campanile Basso (longest abseil 20 m).
First Ascent South-West-Dièdre: R. Fehrmann and O. P. Smith, 27.8.1908. South-West Face: C. F. Meade and Pierre Blanc, 19.8.1909.
Guides/Maps CAI *Dolomiti di Brenta* (Italian). AC *Dolomites West.* TCI 50M. Sh. D64 – Gruppo di Brenta. KK 50M. Sh. 73 – Brentagruppe.
Plate The narrow slender rock-column of the Guglia di Brenta, taken from the north-west. To the right in shadow the North-West Face of the Cima Brenta Alta. Next, to the left, the South-West Face of the Guglia with (high up) its characteristic shoulder, where we change from the Fehrmann to the Meade Route, crossing the 'Ordinary' climb.

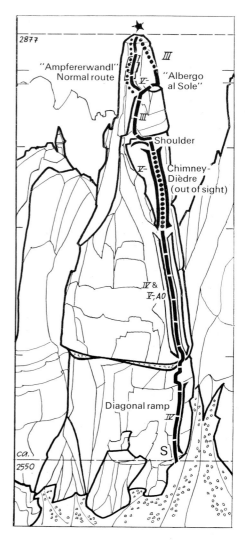

Dolomites (Brenta Group)
Brenta Alta 2960 m
North-East Dièdre
Grade VI−, A1/450 m

No human being can respond to Nature's greatest phenomena with small reactions. Great matters excite great responses . . . Anyone moving northwards along the Orsi Path between the Bocca di Brenta and Bocca di Tuckett – be he hiker, 'extreme' climber or footsore enemy of Nature – will experience a heavenly shock on reaching the Sfulminikar; for there he will see those comically contrasting, adjoining limestone mountains – the huge Cima Brenta with its broad walls and deep gullies, as if carved by the hand of some giant and next to it, the delicate, slender stone column of the Guglia di Brenta. One man will simply catch his breath, another, feeling the full effect of this unique contrast, will savour a starry moment of Alpine glory with every nerve in his body . . . The Guglia is out of sight, just outside the right-hand edge of our photograph. All we see is the terrific rift sundering two compact walls, the simplicity of whose architectural structure is almost beyond comprehension. Every 'extreme' climber has been caught in its spell. They come again and again to attempt that gigantic dièdre, which actually splits the face from its very foot to its summit roof, as the 'last problem in the Brenta Group'. The North-East Face Route (VI− today), made as long ago as 1934 by B. Detassis, U. Battistata and E. Giordani, failed to satisfy any more; and there was the dièdre, beckoning with its incomparably perfect line. It capitulated in 1953, when two Italians from Monza, A. Oggioni and I. Aiazzi, mastered its difficulties, always approaching those of the Cassin Route on the Cima Ovest, in eighteen hours. On the two difficult thirds of the wall they needed 120 pitons, but hardly any on the easier third up above. It was not till the fifth ascent that it was done without a bivouac, and the route was regarded as an unusually tough example of free-climbing . . .

This 'picture-book' dièdre, as an enthusiastic 'Extremist' has called it, certainly offers the climber in prime condition a truly 'picture-book' climb. As soon as you are past the first rope length,

– in an uncomfortable bouldery chimney – you find yourself in the Brenta-climber's heaven, slabby cracks, overhanging chimneys, groove after groove. It is all climbable by marvellous bridging and friction techniques. True, there are a few piton-pitches but they are comparatively easy, so that you never feel you are doing them by 'machinery'. It is exciting: when you have safely reached some piton you tatt around everywhere in perplexity for the continuation of the route, reflecting, trying everything, till, suddenly, there it is, and most surprisingly attractive – at least for the élite with the necessary muscle. A note for the worthy craftsman: Bypass the very first dièdre rising from the floor of the cwm. The sketch shows that you then keep to the bed of the great dièdre all the time. It is not till all the main difficulties are behind you that you veer to the left out of it, to finish the climb over the rounded rib bordering it on the left, up into the summit-gorge, and so to the top.

Valley Resorts Madonna di Campiglio, 1515 m. Molveno, 864 m.
Bases Tosa Hut, CAI, 2491 m, serviced; 3½ hours from Madonna di Campiglio, by way (motorable) of Vallesinella, Brentei Hut and Bocca di Brenta; or from Molveno (chair-lift to 1525 m) 4½ hours on foot, 3 by chair-lift, through the Val delle Seghe and past the Selvata Hut.
Starting Point At about 2500 m in the fall-line of the gully, ¾ hour from the Tosa Hut first eastwards along the Orsi Path, then northwards into the enormous cwm (Busa degli Sfulmini) until the whole of the gigantic dièdre is seen overhead, then over rubble and snow. Time for the climb, for a rope of two, 7–10 hours.
Descent Down the South Flank, heavily rubble-covered, on the tracks of the normal route (I), to the Bocca di Brenta. Well-cairned. A full hour from the summit to the Tosa Hut.
First Ascent A. Oggioni and J. Aiazzi, 25/26.7.1953.
Guides/Maps CAI *Dolomiti di Brenta* (Italian). AC *Dolomites West*. TCI 50M. Sh. D64 – Gruppo di Brenta. KK 50M. Sh. 73 – Brentagruppe.
Plate The Cima Brenta Alta, seen from the north-east, with the Sfulmini Cwm below. To the left of the vertical centre of the picture we see the North-East Dièdre, huge and slashing up the 450-metre face in unbelievable strength. Our route remains in the very bed of the dièdre all the way to the 'Yellow Roof'.

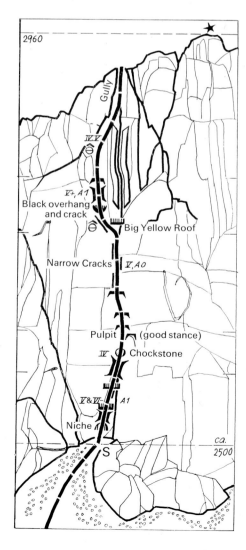

Dolomites (Catináccio or Rosengarten Group)
Roda di Vael (Rotwand) 2806 m
South-West Face (Buhlweg)
Grade A2, VI/400 m

Every summer the motorists turn aside from the Costalunga Pass road, close-by, to get as near as possible to the walls of the Catináccio, impelled by the guilty conscience and manifold troubles of the 'only-by-car' brigade. But genuine climbers come too, making for the Aleardo Fronza Hut and then through the 'Gartl' to the Vaiolet Hut, on their way to the Seiser Alp . . . A glance at our photograph will prompt the guess that their journey has something to do with this daunting 400-metre face and its smooth masonry. This has little connection with earlier attempts to climb it for the first time, all bound to fail in the 'pre-ironmongery' days. Even if Angelo Dibona himself, who was interested in the whole of the Alps from the Špik to the Ailefroide, not just selected specialities, took part in them. No, in 1958 this excitingly smooth and vertical wall had suddenly become a burning problem. At the start of July 1958, Dieter Hasse and Lothar Brandler, teaming-up with Lehne and Löw, had mastered the revolutionary 'Direttissima' on the Cima Grande. Very naturally they now turned to this Red Wall, which had, from the technical angle, only just become a possibility – if they took bolts along. It needed three whole days and three bivouacs in hammocks; it needed preparation with spare line, brought up from below by the ground-party, and an immense assortment of pitons to effect that first-ascent early in September 1958.

Their success led to the route being christened the 'Buhlweg', the 'Hermann Buhl Memorial Route'. Then followed the commentaries: 'harder than the Livanos on the Cima Su Alto'; 'harder than the Torre Trieste South – the Andrich route on the Civetta, the Marmolada South-West and Cassin's climb on the Cima Ovest'. The 180 pitons and screws, the wooden-wedges and toe-loop paraphernalia of those first climbers speak for themselves; but the less than dyed-in-the-wool enthusiast will still be speechless to discover so much purely pleasurable free-climbing there. A good Lowlander, Immo Engelhardt from Nuremberg declares:

'Very delicate to the bivouac. Later on, a tiring hassle with pitons, but quite good fun if "griffifi" are used, for the pitons are all firm.' Charmingly, he adds: 'The only available bases are tents or some very comfortable hay-ricks beside the Costalunga Pass.' It is only fair to the nice couple who look after the Paolina Hut to point out that one doesn't do so badly there either. Taking all in all, let us rejoice over Dieter Hasse who, during that great 1958 season of his, was still reaping so rich a harvest. His climbing career in Saxony, which grew into that of a great Alpine mountaineer, was thick with successes on the little stuff as well as the great. Someday we shall all be reading with suspense and enjoyment a book about the life of this man, now well into his forties . . . The 'Hasse-Brandler' was not the end of the chapter; the Italian Clubs took plenty of pickings: Maestri-Baldessari, 1960; De Francesh-Franceschetti, Romanin-Vurich, 1962, and Schott-Abram in 1967 – all hit the headlines. Can the Roda di Vael now sleep in peace?

NOTE: This route had changed recently owing to a large rockfall. It is still climbed but it includes more difficult climbing than when this was written.

Valley Resort Nova Levante, 1182 m (bus from Bolzano) on the Costalunga Pass road.
Bases Carezza Hotel (Carezza al Lago), 1670 m, private. Catináccio Hut, 1950 m, CAI, chair-lift from the Carezza Hotel's car-park, thence ¾ hour; 2½ hours on foot all the way. Paolina Hut, 2150 m, private, very pleasant; by chair-lift or 1 hour from the Pass road.
Starting Point At 2400 m, to the right of the blackish, 60-m-high substructure, a little to the right of the fall-line, ½ hour from the Paolina Hut. Time for the climb, for a rope of two, about 10 hours.
Descent Down the North Ridge (I) to the Vaiolon Pass and back to the huts, 1 hour from the summit.
First Ascent L. Brandler and D. Hasse, 8/11.9.1958.
Guides/Maps CAI *Sassolungo – Catináccio – Latemar* (Italian). RR *Dolomitenführer*, vol. I (AV series, German). AC *Dolomites West*. TCI 50M. Sh. D56 – Val Gardena, etc. KK 50M. Sh. 59 – Sellagruppe – Marmolata. IGM 50M. Sh. 027 – Bolzano (divisible into six 25M. sh.).
Plate The architecturally-smooth south-west face of the Rhoda di Vael in the Southern Catináccio Chain.

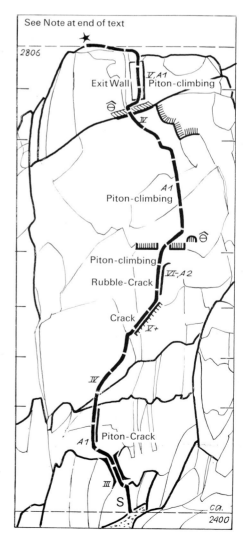

Dolomites (Catináccio or Rosengarten Group)
Catináccio 2981 m
East Face Direct (Steger)
Grade VI−, A0/600 m

Two very contradictory pictures establish the character of the complete Alpine masterpiece called the Catináccio Group – first the aspect of the three Vaiolet Towers streaming skywards like filigree-work as seen from the 'Gartl'; secondly, that of the broad, massive, fortress-like East Face of the Catináccio with its black square below the right-hand of the two immense rock-funnels. These two unforgettable pictures are responsible for that fame of the group . . . even an 'Extremist' cannot shut his eyes to that. It seems only natural today that so magnificent a 600-metre wall should have invited the opening up of numerous routes. Not so, however, when in 1896 two British climbers, the Revd A. G. S. Rayner and J. S. Phillimore, with their guides Antonio Dimai and Luigi Rizzi reached the summit by way of the 'Wiener Schnitzel Buttress' in the left section of the East Face. That caused a sensation, just as when in 1899 G. B. Piaz climbed its upper part by a tremendous diagonal route – solo! The Kiene Route followed in 1909, and the next great sensation came in 1929 with the mastering of the first 'extreme' climb straight up to the summit by the plumb-line falling from it. This is the route we have chosen: it was climbed by Hans Steger, with Paula Wiesinger and other friends on 26 and 27 August 1929, and still ranks as a particularly fine 'free' climb of great stylishness.

Our photograph and sketch clearly reveal the unique character of this route, made possible by the presence of three parallel but almost vertical cracks. Its description can be broken up into three parts: in the first and hardest (VI−) height is gained by 150 metres of almost pure crack-technique, of which, strictly speaking, only the two rope lengths leading to and over the two overhangs qualify for a grading of VI−, A0. In the second part, after the traverse into the central chimney-crack, which is often missed because of a misleading piton (it is essential to study the route-description meticulously here), there follow nearly 250 metres of III and IV, with a few pitches of V. On the third and last, the

triangle between the rock-gullies has to be climbed, followed by the hidden chimney leading out onto the summit (V+). The line is not only perfect; its character is unique – definite reasons for the affection in which this exacting climb is held . . . One can hardly mention the classic routes on the Vaiolet Towers by comparison: for all the refinement of those tower-climbs, their brevity downgrades them too much. The 600 metres of the climb to the Catináccio are a unique phenomenon in this area. At every resting-place there is only one view and no climber ever fails to take it in – it is the prospect eastwards to where the Marmolada presents a picture-book profile – her flat roof of ice to the north, her gigantic, vertical rock-precipice to the south. It is impossible to take one's eyes off her.

Valley Resorts Pera, 1326 m, and Vigo, 1391 m, in the Fassa Valley.
Bases Vaiolet Hut, 2243 m, CAI, serviced; 3 hours from Pera or 1 hour from the Gardeccia Hut, 1949 m, private. Motorable from Mazzin by toll-road since 1975; or else, chair-lift Vigo–Ciampedie, 1998 m, then by path via Gardeccia to the Vaiolet Hut in just 2 hours.
Starting Point At just 2400 m, at the base of the wall, slightly left of the fall-line, from where you can see the start of the crack above a projecting grey pillar. 1 hour from the hut. Time for the climb, for a two-man rope, 5–6 hours.
Descent By the North Ridge and West Face (normal route from the west III−) to the Santner Pass, 2741 m, and back through the 'Gartl' to the Vaiolet Hut, 2 hours.
First Ascent H. Steger, P. Wiesinger, F. Masè-Dari and S. Lechner, 26/27.8.1929.
Guides/Maps CAI *Sassolungo – Catináccio – Latemar* (Italian). RR *Dolomitenführer*, vol. I (AV series, German). AC *Dolomites West.* TCI, 50M. Sh. D56 – Val Gardena, etc. KK 50M. Sh. 59 – Sellagruppe – Marmolata. IGM 50M. Sh. 027 – Bolzano (divisible into six 25M. sh.)
Plate The Catináccio (top left) revealing its great East Face. Our route follows the series of cracks straight up to the summit between the two prominent rock-hollows, in a vertical line. The North Summit is seen to the right.

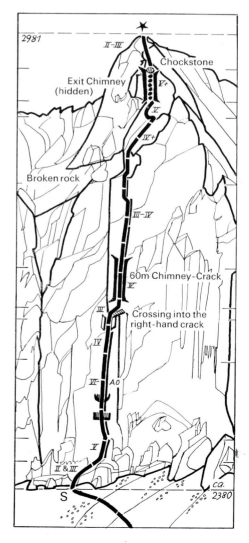

Dolomites (Sella Group)
Piz di Ciavázes 2828 m
South Face Direct (Micheluzzi-Castiglione)
Grade VI−, A0/500 m

At the point where the Val di Mesdi and Val Lasties slash the great keep of the Sella fortress into two halves as by a sword-thrust, the enormous walls of the Ciavázes and the Sass Pordoi present one of the most characteristic but unique spectacles in the Dolomites. Our picture shows one half, the southern front of the Piz di Ciavázes, split horizontally by the Gamsband, vertically by two deep perpendicular rifts, as by the hand of some master-builder. An additional touch of style lies in the fact that there is no sharp summit sitting on top of this monstrous wall as opposite on the Punta delle Cinque Dita, but a flat, rubble-covered pyramid. The Micheluzzi Route snakes its way up between the two rifts, marked by a famous, sensationally-exposed 90-metre traverse – to the Gamsband (which, when the upper half of the face is icy, always offers a comfortable escape-route) – and then rather more simply but taking the local line, up the upper bastion. Pit Schubert, who assembled the details for many of the route-sketches in this book, opened up a modern and highly-praised route through this huge South Face, climbing with his rope-mates of many years' standing, Klaus Werner and Karlheinz Matthies; yet he recommends this Micheluzzi-Castiglioni route as the finest and most interesting on the wall. Of course there are more difficult routes (some of them had to resort to 200 pitons) and there is a choice of a dozen or more on the South Face – but our 'Micheluzzi' is the most suited to the concept of a modern classic climb. The glorious traverse already mentioned has hardly a parallel in the Alps.

Buhl's direct variant, which breaks up the rhythm of the climb and misses out the traverse, has not met with any acclaim. The general situation is best absorbed from the splendid article by Hans Stutzig in *Bergkamerad*, vol. 1, 1966, but it does not include the Schubert route; it gives the history of the face up to that year. The fact that the 'Micheluzzi' dates back to 1935 reminds us of the 'upsurge' of the 'Sexogradists' in the Civetta at the same time. It was in 1956

that Cesare Maestri dared to climb the face solo, and 1964 brought the first climb by a woman, Vitty Steinkötter. All of which speaks volumes for its highly important example of a free climb. Our experts Dietmar Ohngemach and Manfred Sturm testify: 'Today the Gamsband is practically regarded as the "summit", since the "nice" climbing is on the lower half and the wall can be reached easily because of its favourable position. It has consequently gone down the scale to something of "practice-climb" status. The upper half is still icy during the early part of the year, or at the very least wet and, all in all, harder for step-cutting than the lower part. One should add that the South Face, though it dries out quickly, has a snow-roof at its top, whose melting waters activate stone-falls just at the peak of the climbing season.'

Valley Resorts Canazei in the Val di Fassa, 1465 m. Selva in the Val Gardena, 1567 m.
Bases Sella Hut, 2179 m, CAI, serviced, car park and camping-site in the rock city. Maria Flora Hut, 2240 m, private, serviced, on the Sella pass road.
Starting Point At 2250 m in the left half of the base of the central face, in the fall-line of the dièdre which is closed by a kind of roof. Approach 20 min. Time for the combined climb of the lower and upper halves, 7-9 hours in favourable conditions.
Descent Along the protected very exposed Pössnecker Path, whose finely engineered course ends at the foot of the face to the north of the Sella Towers.
First Ascent L. Micheluzzi and E. Castiglioni, 29.9.1935.
Guides/Maps CAI *Sassolungo – Catináccio – Latemar* (Italian). RR *Dolomitenführer*, vol. I (AV series, German). AC *Dolomites West*. TCI 50M. Sh. D56 – Val Gardena, etc. KK 50M. Sh. 59 – Sellagruppe – Marmolada. IGM 50M. Sh. 028 – La Marmolada (divisible into six 25M. sh.). AV 25M. Sh. 52/1b – Langkofel – Sella – Gruppe.
Plate The complete South Face of the Piz di Ciavázes above the Sella pass road. The 'Gamsband' cuts across the centre of the face horizontally. At the left-hand edge of the picture the saddle leading to the Second Sella Tower.

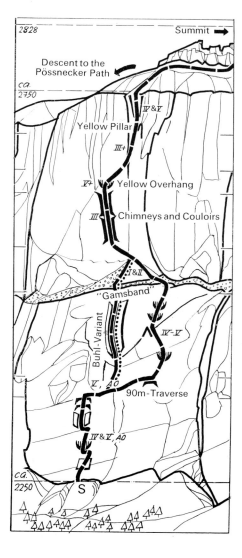

Dolomites
Marmolada di Penia 3343 m
South-West Face (Soldà)
Grade VI, A2/550 m

Curiosities arising from the terrific movements of the Earth's crust are more especially noticeable in the high Alps than down below among the meadows, woods, thickets and streams . . . Besides housing the Tre Cime, Vaiolet Towers, Guglia di Brenta, the Alpstein's limestone waves and the Via Mala, the Alpine curio-cabinet contains the freak of the Marmolada. From the nearby Civetta or from the Catináccio she looks impressive: to the south an almost perpendicular, smooth rock-wall more than 500 metres high, to the north a gently flowing glacier . . . but when you stand on the Ombretta Pass, close to the base of those South and South-West Faces and crick your neck trying to look upwards, you may well stop breathing for sheer astonishment. The very name Marmolada arouses respect and stimulates the imagination. Looking at the thing in detail, one cannot grasp that this gigantic wall, twice split transversely and decorated by mighty columns and rifts, above which lowers the rim of a glacier, can possibly invite climbing. But it does, more than ever today. The many excellent Civetta-climbers always regard the Marmolada's slabby walls with greedy eyes, and it is mostly not too long before they turn up at the starting-points on the Ombretta Pass. Both faces, the Penia and the Rocca, retained their reputation as 'by far the hardest of all' for a surprisingly long time. Clearly the very readable horror-stories published about the ascent of the huge South Pillar, with full details of its gorge, roof, bottle-neck pitches and hazards from ice and water, have sustained that reputation. Or have they?

A recent climber says: 'It was great. We froze, we bivouacked, we starved; it was icy and it was dangerous.' He also says: 'Hats off to Soldà in 1936.' On the other hand, all the great Dolomite climbs which remain interesting in today's ambience were made at that very time, except the late vintage of the magnificent routes on the Tre Cime . . . The writer and his rope-mate came down to the valley, half-dead from exhaustion, after two days' battle with that Soldà Route. Staggering up to the hut, we met two Italians, who had done the Buhlweg and wanted to do the Soldà. We, who had done the Soldà, had planned to do the Buhlweg. We exchanged advice and reminded the Italians of the very icy state of the exit in cold weather. Then we parted. After climbing the Buhlweg, we Germans learned that one of the Italians had died on the Soldà Route, the other had escaped with his life. That South Face remains the ultimate test. Even moderate icing-conditions in the great exit-rift can impose unimaginable difficulties: to say nothing of the fact that for fully 40 metres before you get to it you are climbing up a waterfall . . .

Valley Resorts Canazei, 1465 m, in the Val di Fassa. Malga Ciapela, 1428 m, below the Val Ombretta.
Bases The Contrin Hut, 2016 m, CAI, serviced, 2 hours from Penia Ombretta (Falier) Hut, 2080 m, CAI, serviced; 1¾ hours from Malga Ciapela. Bivouac-box 'Marco dal Bianco' near the Ombretta Pass, 2750 m, CAI, 6 sleeping-places; 2 hours from Contrin Hut, 2 hours from Ombretta Hut.
Starting Point At about 2760 m at the Ombretta Pass, 2704 m, 1¾ hours from Contrin Hut. Climbers' tracks to the starting point to the left above the pass. Time for the climb, for a rope of two, 8–10 hours, in favourable conditions.
Descent Down the West Ridge, partly protected by iron ladders (II) to the Marmolada Saddle, 2910 m, then down to the Contrin Hut; 2½ hours from the summit. Or, down the glacier.
Note The South-West Face, like all the climbs on the Marmolada's South Wall, cannot be undertaken before the late summer, and is at its best in autumn, with a bivouac. In a normal summer the difficulties are greatly increased by the wet coming down from the glaciated summit-ridge or because of the icing of the exit-cracks and the runnels above the great terrace. There is a good bivouac-site on the big (second) terrace.
First Ascent G. Soldà, U. Conforto, 29/31.8.1936.
Guides/Maps CAI *Sassolungo – Catináccio – Latemar* (Italian). RR *Dolomitenführer*, vol. I (AV series, German). AC *Dolomites East*. TCI 50M. Sh. D56 – Val Gardena, etc. KK 50M. Sh. 59 – Sellagruppe – Marmolata. IGM 50M. Sh. 028 – La Marmolada (divisible into six 25M. sh.).
Plate The south aspect of the Marmolada di Penia above the Ombretta Pass (centre below). Close to the right of the middle of the picture, the pillar and the gorge separate the South Face from the South-West Face.

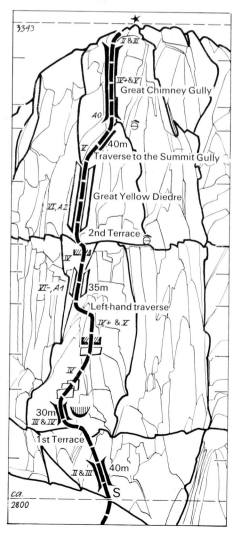

Dolomites

Marmolada di Rocca 3309 m

South Face Direct (Gogna)

Grade VI, A1/800 m

In the first edition of this book (1970) we dealt with the Marmolada by the Soldà Route on the South-West Face of the Penia summit (VI, A2) and the 'Vinatzer-Castiglioni' on the South Face of the Rocca summit (VI, A2), both of which date from 1936. Since then all the top climbers of our day are agreed that in a 'beauty-competition' the new 'Gogna Route', made in 1970, would win the crown. Our sketch shows what Gogna and his three rope-mates, Alemand, Dorigatti and Giambisi, achieved on 26 and 27 August 1970. Pit Schubert's opinion is: 'by far the finest route on the Marmolada'. After many days of preparation, the 'Gogna Route', lying a little to the left (west) of the admittedly difficult 'Vinatzer', was discovered in 26 hours of climbing-time: it leads straight to the summit and for this extension of the vertical they used more than 100 pitons, 7 wooden-wedges – 53 belaying-pitons being used for 33 rope lengths – but not a single bolt of any kind . . . Almost all the material for the repetition of the climb was left on the face by the first party: the climb is VI, A1. Schubert, who with that splendid climber Klaus Werner made the fourth successful attempt, speaks in all seriousness of a 'fabulously interesting climb' and expresses surprise that this classic possibility remained undiscovered for such a long time. His fine commentary continues: 'As far as the great band halfway up the face there is nothing but perfectly firm Kaiser-type rock with several delicately devised rope-traverses (the longest about 6 metres).

A great advantage of the new route is that on its upper part there is no water, no ice and no falling stones (unlike the other routes on these faces). It goes straight up the prominent pillar falling from the Punta di Rocca. To the very last metre it offers splendid, at times difficult, climbing. On the great band there are bivouac-sites sheltered by over-hangs. Not to be underrated, since there are certainly many more difficult pitches than on the 'Vinatzer', even if the most difficult ones are definitely easier than those on the latter. Nearly all the pitons are good and firm. Between ourselves,

the 'neighbouring' problem was not known only to the Italians. Dieter Hasse, at that time barred from serious climbing by a cartilage operation, had also had his plans for tackling it – vol. 12, 1970 of *Alpinismus* carried Pit Schubert's complete report at the time, from which I have quoted. So, as our final word: cheers for Alpinism itself and cheers for that meticulously clear journalist of the 'Extreme' – Pit (because he is so utterly reliable), my ideal collaborator in this hazardous climbing-tome.

Valley Resorts Canazei, 1465 m, in the Val di Fassa, with the villages of Penia and Alba. Malga Ciapela, 1428 m (new ropeway station), below the Val Ombretta.
Bases Contrin Hut, 2016 m, CAI serviced; fully 2 hours from the head of the Val di Fassa. Ombretta (Falier) Hut, 2080 m. CAI, serviced, on the east side of the Ombretta Pass; 1¾ hours from Malga Ciapela. Bivouac-box 'Marco dal Bianco' near the Ombretta Pass, 2750 m, CAI, 6 sleeping-places; 2 hours from the Contrin Hut, 2 hours from Ombretta Hut. Summit Hut in the saddle.
Starting Point At about 2500 m a little to the east and below the pass, directly to the right of the bottom centre of our picture. You start up a red, very difficult chimney (hidden in the photograph) and climb to the left up to the block. Time for the climb, for a two-man rope, provided conditions are good, vary at about 10–12 hours.
Descent Over the Punta di Penia (the crossing is protected by a wire rope) down the West Ridge to the Marmolada Saddle and so to the Contrin Hut (3 hours), or down the glacier (track mostly visible) to the Ferdaia Pass (and Inn). In case of emergency, to the ropeway-station and down by cable-car to Malga Ciapela.
First Ascent A. Gogna, B. Alemand, A. Dorigatti and A. Giambisi, 27/28.8.1970.
Guides/Maps CAI *Sassolungo – Catináccio – Latemar* (Italian). RR *Dolomitenführer*, vol. I (AV series, German). AC *Dolomites East*. TCI 50M. Sh. D56 – Val Gardena, etc. KK 50M. Sh. 59 – Sellagruppe – Marmolata IGM 50M. Sh. 028 – La Marmolada (divislbe into six 25M. sh.).
Plate The South Face of the Marmolada di Rocca, showing the menacing cornices on the summit-ridge. Starting point, bottom left. Exit, direct up the arête of the second tower, sharply defined by light and shade, to the summit, clearly visible in the background.

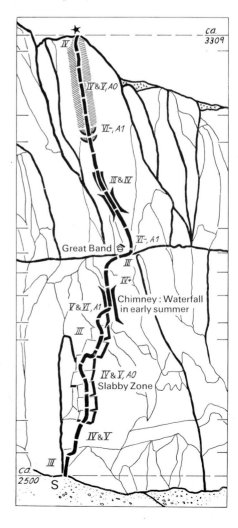

Dolomites (Pala Group)
Sass Maor 2816 m
East Face
Grade VI, A1/1000 m (with 400 m of substructure)

This famous East Face in the Southern Pala Group – close behind the equally celebrated 'Schleierkante' (Scarf Arête) of the Cima della Madonna – is, as it were, a 'Senior' among the 'extreme' routes in the Eastern Alps. It is remarkable for its solid wall 1000 metres high and its VI rating, which holds till this day. Still more remarkable is the history of its first ascent, achieved by Emil Solleder (whose nickname among the ski distance-runners was 'Spike') and his buddy from Rosenheim, Franz Kummer. No sooner had Solleder and his friend Gustl Lettenbauer climbed the North-West Face of the Civetta in 1925 than he heard from Gunther Langes that there was an equally difficult problem on the Sass Maor. So, on 2 September 1926 they came to the foot of that mountain to look for a solution of its huge chimney-corner, visible from a great distance. By noon they had dealt with the 400 metres of slabby substructure to where the actual face starts with an enormous, vertical, yellow shield. On its lower part they found pitons and fragments of rope, left by earlier attempts; then came a questionable-looking corner. Solleder, in the lead, got 8 metres further than his predecessors, but was then forced to abseil. Then, although it was already 5 pm, he tried a different pitch. At this point the mists enveloped them. In the half-darkness Solleder mastered the decisive problem by getting out of the corner to its right, then turning the lower cliff by two stiff traverses, and back into the corner below the overhang. That circumvention in the half-darkness constituted an Odyssey of climbing-technique, marking the most hazardous key-pitch of those days – in terms of free-climbing. Then they lit a lantern and with it in their teeth, defeated the long series of cracks in the chimney, fought their way in total darkness up the lengthy ramp above it and reached the top. There they bivouacked in dire misery and spent a freezing night. The various objects which make today's bivouacs reasonably comfortable did not exist at that time: even if they had, Solleder and Kummer would not have been able to afford

them . . . but one of the great Dolomite faces had capitulated, and, one might add, well before its time.

For a long time it was feared, and even avoided, because of its occasional passages of brittle rock; today it is a great favourite and highly regarded. The best time for this climb is from the end of June, not earlier, to the end of September. The whole substructure is free-climbing, clear of any trouble, but none the less worth some previous study. An exact study of the descent is advisable beforehand, the route to the saddle between the Sass Maor and the Cima della Madonna, as well as its confusing continuation down the southern gorge. You will find a few abseil-pitons, but no one should merely trust to luck after a very difficult and exhausting climb of a wall 1000 metres high.

Valley Resorts Fiera di Primiero, 713 m, in the Cismon Valley, of San Martino di Castrozza, 1467 m (bus from Predazzo over the Rolle Pass).
Base None. Possibly Pradidali Hut, 2278 CAI, at the top of the Val Pradidali, 3½ hours from San Martino over the Passo di Ball. From Fiera di Primiero through the Canali and Pradidali Valleys 5 hours (bus to Rifugio Cant. d. Gal. private, 1167 m, then only 2¾ hours).
Starting Point At 1800 m. Climbers' path from Pedemonte, 20 minutes to Val Cimerlo; then over slabby rock to the shoulder of the substructure. The actual start is on the grassy saddle joining the substructure to the East Face. The substructure is 400 m high. Time for the climb, for a two-man rope, 8–10 hours.
Descent By the normal route (III) to the saddle between the Sass Maor and the Cima della Madonna; down the southern gorge (abseil pitons) and then by path to the Pradidali Hut.
First Ascent E. Solleder and F. Kummer, 2.9.1926.
Guides/Maps CAI *Sassolungo – Catináccio – Latemar* (Italian). RR *Dolomitenführer*, vol. I (AV series, German). AC *Dolomites East*. TCI 50M. Sh. D60 – S. Martino di Castrozza. KK 50M. Sh. 76 – Pale di S. Martino. IGM 50M. Sh. 045 – S. Martino di Castrozza (divisible into six 25M. sh.).
Plate The East Face of the Sass Maor in the Pala Group with its 2816 m summit top left. To the right the summit of the Cima della Madonna, 2733 m, with the 'Schleierkante' (the 'Scarf Arête') leading up to it, easily identifiable, its profile deeply shadowed.

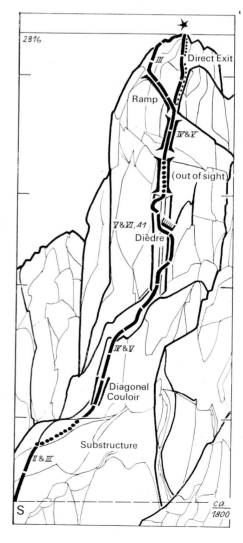

135

Dolomites (Pala Group)
Cima Canali 2897 m
West Face (Buhl-Herweg)
Grade V+, A0/500 m

At first sight, the Cima Canali above the Pradidali Hut baffles spirit, comprehension, intellect and even simple courage. For there, from a forsaken cwm of rubble, its huge, solid cathedral-columns shoot 500 metres up into the blue sky, perpendicular, bare of all horizontals – yet decorated by all the rock-climber's superlatives, as yet invisible to the eye ... Our route runs for more than 400 metres, perpendicular as a plumb-line, up to the central of the face's many pillars and marks the finest of Hermann Buhl's first-ascents; a pure free-climbing route of the highest grade, almost old-fashioned, since only four pitons (all, with the usual consideration, still in position) were used. Maybe by now there are six or eight, but even that is no great number on so high a pillar. One climbs overhang after overhang and it is only occasionally that the second climber sees his leader, the leader never his second. Nothing but the rope, dangling over the roofs and projections, unites them. The rock of the Canali's West Face is iron-hard, rough and entirely reliable. Anyone who knew Hermann Buhl can imagine how on 9 September 1950 – just three years before his seldom-equalled solo-ascent to Nanga Parbat's summit – he bridged and clawed his way, cat-like, up this crack, to shout down his 'Up you come!' at the end of each rope length. The circumvention to the left marked on our sketch as an alternative possibility belongs to the original Simon-Wiessner climb; Buhl and Herweg followed their route and only diverged from it above our shaded and dotted variant, climbing down a little way to the right to get into the bottom of the 'Buhl Riss' or 'Crack'. Simon and Wiessner on the other hand moved out from here into the gully bordering the pillar to its north.

To reach the 'Buhl Riss' by that route is an extremely difficult and dubious matter. The Italians who made the second ascent in 1957 tackled the 40 metres of sheer vertical below the start of the actual crack and got up it after a tremendous struggle. According to Erich Griessl, Heinz Steinkötter and Horst Grabner, this new direct rope length is possible thanks to a very narrow crack in the yellow wall. Somewhat brittle in places, it needs four pitons (only one on the first ascent) and demands the best possible condition. Presumably controversy will long continue as to whether this difficult 40-metre short-cut or the continuously-overhanging 38-metre pitch above the third and fourth overhanging roofs inside the 'Buhl Riss' constitute the key-pitch. In any case it is a dream climb for great experts in free-climbing, on which the doubled rope is only necessary for safeguarding purposes, with a few pitons and karabiners thrown in. In misty conditions the way down can be very worrying if you miss the cairns leading to the Forcella Canali. So, back to the guidebook once again!

Valley Resort San Martino di Castrozza, 1467 m (bus from Predazzo and Fiera di Primiero).
Base Pradidali Hut, 2278 m, CAI, serviced, at the top of the Val Pradidali. Over the Passo di Ball from the Rosetta ropeway – station in 1¾ hours or on foot from San Martino through the Val di Roda in 3½ hours.
Starting Point At about 2400 m at the foot of the face in the fall-line from the 'Buhl Riss' or 'Crack', to the right of the cliffs at the bottom of the gorge falling from the Forcella Wilma, ½ hour from hut. Time for climb, for a rope of two, 5–7 hours.
Descent Down the South Ridge (II) to the Forcella Canali. From there down the diagonal couloir seen on the right of our picture to the foot of the face. Plenty of cairns. 3 hours from the summit.
First Ascent West Face: F. Simon and F. Wiessner, 28.7.1927. The 'Buhl Crack': H. Buhl and H. Herweg, 9.9.1950.
Guides/Maps CAI *Sassolungo – Catináccio – Latemar* (Italian). RR *Dolomitenführer*, vol. I (AV series, German). RR *Pala-Gruppe* (Klein series, German). AC *Dolomites East*. TCI 50M. Sh. D60 – S. Martino di Castrozza. KK 50M. Sh. 76 – Pale di S. Martino. IGM 50M. Sh. 045 – S. Martino di Castrozza (divisible into six 25M. sh.).
Plate A show-picture of the Pala Group in the Dolomites: the pillars of the Cima Canali rising like organ-pipes above the Pradidali Hut. To the left of the vertical middle of the picture is the notably thick pillar with the steeply falling-away arête, which shows the 'Buhl Crack' from its start down below on the yellow face. On the extreme right the descent couloir.

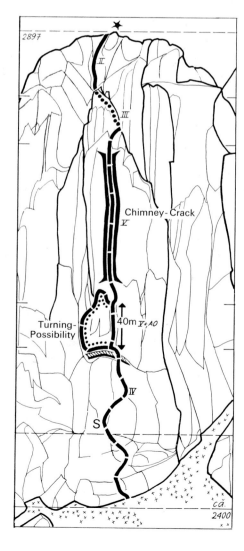

Dolomites (Pala Group)
Campanile Alto di Lastei 2830 m
West Face
Grade VI−, A1/330 m

When in 1894 that great work in Alpine literature, *Die Erschliessung der Ostalpen*, appeared, there was not a word mentioning the Northern Pala Group, which stretches eastwards in a long thigh-like crest from the Cima della Vezzana to the Passo Lucan. Nobody had heard of the three Lastei Towers, rising above the Mulaz Hut, hidden in the bouldery, isolated cwm at their feet. When in 1899 the first tower was climbed, it was still called the 'Great Cencenighe Tower'. As our photograph shows, the towering walls of the North and West Faces soar in exciting steepness above the Focobon Glacier of which, admittedly, only some traces of snow remain. It was, for the most part, Munich climbers, tried and proved in the Wetterstein and Kaisergebirge climbs, Adolf Deye, Otto Herzog, Spindler, Fiechtl, Bechtold, Merkl and Müllritter who opened up new climbs in this area before and after the First World War; the Italians, Castiglioni, Battisti and before them Andrealotti, followed and today the modern Italian climbers are hard at work to upgrade this out-of-the-way field of climbing. Paradise in the terms of the modern 'extreme' technique.

On 29 June 1929 Martin Pfeffer (a friend and rope-mate of Leo Maduschka's) and Erwin Kaup made the first ascent of the rugged West Face of the highest Lastei Tower, straight up to its summit, since the gigantic dièdre invited and constrained them to that line. If you compare the photograph and the sketch you can easily detect the comfortably sunny West Face and the way up it. The start is from the snow-gully up a pitch of IV in a 15-metre crack, then over rubble up a steep ramp and steep slabs to the inhospitable grass-terrace. From it, cracks go straight up with a V pitch and an energetic traverse to the right – leading to the 'downward ledges' – which is always difficult to find. After a loop out to the right you reach the foot of the great dièdre, which requires three rope lengths of exposed but splendid climbing and leads to a big cave. This is passed on the left and one immediately comes to a polished slab, which you traverse some 4 or 5 metres to

the left and then straight up for about 10 metres (the key-pitch) to a stance. This passage should still be assessed at VI−, A1. The narrow course of an easier chimney follows, then, on the summit, you can enjoy complete solitude. The rock is sound and the holds are fairly plentiful. The pioneers had few pitons with them, free-climbing was the watch-word and remains so on this fine route. The descent to the Passo Lucan is (especially in a mist) rather complicated for, after descending the chimney on the north flank to the saddle between Cima Mezzo and Cima Alto and going down the couloir, to the east, you have still to cross to the Passo Lucan along the eastern foot of the towers and only then down from it by a steep grass-couloir below the western precipices. Only then do you go uphill again to the comfortable Mulaz Hut opposite.

Valley Resort Falcade Alto, 1298 m, at the head of the Val Biois, below the Valles Pass and San Pellegrino Pass (11 km from Cencenighe and Agordo, bus).
Base Mulaz Hut, 2571 m, CAI, serviced, north-east of the Mulaz Pass; 4½ hours from Falcade, 2¼ hours from the Baita Segantini over the Rolle Pass.
Starting Point At 2500 m, 40 minutes from the Mulaz Hut across the little Focobon Glacier (bottom centre of our picture) below the West Face. Start up the rocks on the east side of the gully directly in the fall-line of the huge vertical rift. Time for a rope of two, 4½–6 hours.
Descent On the northern side (II) down the Oberwalder Chimney to the Lucan Pass and so back to the Hut, first crossing the little saddle between the Campanile Mezzo and the Alto, 1–2 hours.
First Ascent M. Pfeffer and E. Kaup, 27.6.1929.
Guides/Maps CAI *Sassolungo – Catináccio – Latemar* (Italian). RR *Dolomitenführer*, vol. I (AV series, German). RR *Pala-Gruppe* (Klein series, German). AC *Dolomites East*. TCI 50M. Sh. D60 – S. Martino di Castrozza. KK 50M. Sh. 76 – Pale di S. Martino IGM 50M. Sh. 045 – S. Martino di Castrozza (divisible into six 25M. sh.).
Plate The Campanile Alto di Lastei, just north-east of the Mulaz Pass and Hut, at 2830 m the highest of the three Lastei Towers, which terminates the Eastern Pala Chain. High up, the enormous rift falling vertically down this fine West Face from the saddle close to the summit.

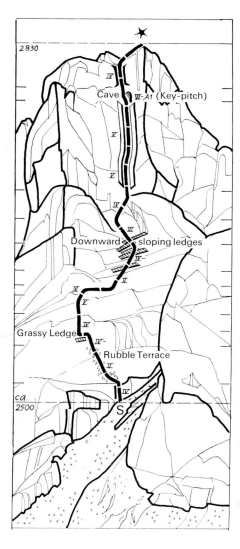

Dolomites (Eastern Pala Group)
Monte Agner 2872 m
North Ridge
Grade V+, A0/1600 m

From the primaeval Alpine parks any-where round the Vazzoler Hut in the Civetta you will see it over and again, over there to the south, the incomparably slender sweep of Monte Agner's North Ridge, 1600 metres in height, difficult from its very base, and offering countless opportunities of losing your way . . . Celso Gilberti was the first to climb that enormous ridge in August 1932. Six months later, only twenty-three years old, he took his doctor's degree, but in June the following year he fell to his death on the Paganella . . . Every visitor to the Civetta comes under the spell of that North Ridge; he hears this and that about it and one day he wants to climb it. What he hears is that it is the route of the extreme contradictions – one of the longest in the Alps but leading to a summit less than 3000 metres high. The rock is sound and firm but difficult, sometimes exceedingly so. Down below, where you are already climbing, you have to contend with the scrub-thickets and are furious you have left your secateurs behind – how useful they would have been! The dimensions are enormous and again and again the description proves that you have gone astray – but it hasn't been right for a long time and after long periods of internal worry you find you are back on the right route after all. It is best to trust your own instinct here. The climbing is marvellous, but not everywhere – there is dangerous ground in between. As a whole it is wonderfully romantic for 'Extremists' in skill and stamina, a great alluring Alpine adventure.

If you arrive late on the flat summit-pyramid, you can see, as night falls, the exhaust flames from the oil-refineries near Venice. Then you feel your way down the descent-path, partly protected by wire-ropes, for half an hour to the little bivouac-box, tired, exhausted, as if you had just climbed something like the East Face of the Watzmann. But the 'Watzmann-East' is a parquet floor compared with the savagery on this Agner Ridge, on which one needs to possess a truly animal path-finding sense, must be as muscularly agile as a

cat and, above all, must have unparalleled endurance. And that counts thrice-over if you cannot rely on settled weather. The time needed by a good pair is from 10 to 12 hours. It is impossible to take the ridge in less, for your rucksacks have to go all the way up with you. A question often raised is the length of the approach to the foot of the ridge. If you have been lucky enough to find the way, the shortest possible time is an hour. In the approach-card issued by *Alpinismus* it says something about 4 to 6 hours from the Col di Pra to the start of the climb, which is quite excessive or meant for invalids. The best thing is to follow the scree-bed (the bed of the torrent) which falls from the right (west) of the Monte Agner and is crossed by the road for private cars. Then up the scree-bed to the substructure with its scrub, and if you follow the foot-trails to the left you will get to the notch where the climb starts.

Valley Resorts Taibòn, 640 m, north of Agordo. On the descent: Frassenè, 1082 m, west of Agordo.
Bases None. Two small inns at San Luciano, 756 m, or hayricks, or else possibly lodgings in peasants' houses at the head of the valley, motorable; or the bivouac-box at the foot of the North Face, near to the starting point. CAI, 4 sleeping-places. Bivouac-box Giancarlo Biasin, 2700 m, CAI, open, ½ hour below the summit on the normal descent.
Starting Point At 1200 m in the wide re-entrant at the foot of the ridge, formed by separate teeth. Down the valley from the Col di Pra, cross the stream, up through the woods in the old wood-rides to the right, but soon trackless southwards straight to the base of the ridge in the Vanet del Piz. Also straight up in the fall-line of the starting point from the hayricks in the valley of San Luciano. Trail-finding sense essential; there is no track. 2 hours at the most from the valley.
Descent By the West Ridge to the Forcella del Pizon, protected as far as the bivouac-box (½ hour). Then southwards to the left down the gorge to the grass-ridge 300 m lower down, steeply down a parallel gorge to the left, then across the Agneralp, 1612 m, or Malga Losch, to the Scarpa Hut, 1742 m, CAI, serviced, and into the valley.
First Ascent C. Gilberti and O. Soravito, 29.8.1932.
Guides/Maps CAI *Sassolungo – Catináccio – Latemar* (Italian). RR *Dolomitenführer*, vol. I (AV series, German). RR *Pala-Gruppe* (Klein series, German). AC *Dolomites East*. TCI 50M. Sh. D60 – S. Martino di Castrozza. KK 50M. Sh. 76 – Pale di S. Martino. IGM. Sh. 045 – S. Martino di Castrozza (divisible into six 25M. sh.).
Plate In the centre the North Ridge of Monte Agner. Bottom, left centre, the steep green substructure, directly over the vertical 25-metre gully with its difficult pitches.

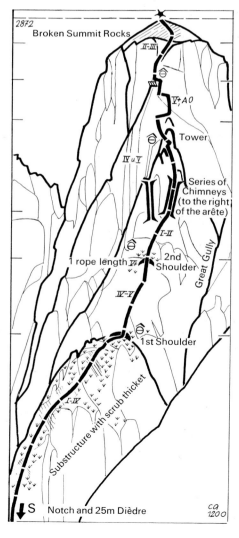

Dolomites (Civetta Group)
Torre Venezia 2337 m
South Face (Tissi)
Grade V+, A0/500 m

There can be nothing finer for a man wearied by the grime of a great city's 'civilisation' than to arrive in the fairy-garden around the Vazzoler Hut and to find himself in that healing chaos which time immemorial and the absence of human beings have preserved there. The mighty towers of rock pierce the sky with terrifying upthrust; the larch-gardens with their close-grown fragrance, the thickets of the mountain-forests, the murmur of waters and the lush greenery are all there for one's comfort and delight. One devoted visitor to the hut wrote in the visitor's book: 'The loveliest spot on earth – I would like to be buried here . . .' Others have achieved the very wish he expressed, and the memorial chapel for those who have died on the Civetta houses many an unforgettable name. Truly climbing is a great sport and a noble passion! . . . The question arises – Torre Trieste or Torre Venezia – which is the finer tower? Without doubt the Trieste from the Valle dei Cantoni is the harder. But which wall has the greatest charm – maybe that of the Cima della Busazza? All the same the South Face of the Torre Venezia is one of the few true walls: a single complete entity, solid, difficult; its daunting stature sweeps up fully 500 metres to its broad, flat summit. The climber who feels the urge to stand on that monolithic face, ready to trust the splendidly firm rock, with its many holds, sure that he will in good time discover the critical one to further the next move, will find the 'Tissi' a deeply fascinating Dolomite feast of clinging, climbing and bridging . . . Struggles are always rewarding: be it on the Andrich–Faè South-West Ridge or the Ratti–Panzeri South-West Face, which leads so daringly over the fearsome landslide-zone, or the savage South Dièdre, attempted as long ago as 1960 by Biasin and Melucci, but whose problem was not solved till, in 1974, Pit Schubert, Klaus Werner and Aloisius Wojas, following the continuation of the Dièdre, mastered the 25-metre widely-bulging overhang and then the summit-face direct . . .

Each of those routes can be followed on our photograph. There are climbers who jib at the long substructure leading up to the first big traverse, or the deep exit-chimney up which one can crawl the wrong way, but which can also be climbed by straddling outside. On the whole, the character of this classic example of a Civetta climb approaches perfection; it is 500 metres of free-climbing for the expert connoisseur and it follows an ideal line. Even the traverse, – if one climbs down to it at the right elevation – can be done 'free', always supposing its pitiless exposure leaves you the eyes to look for the holds. No, whatever is said, this route is a 'Superlative' which, in Civetta terms, is saying quite something, even if a few new practitioners of the piton-gallery brigade just give it a cursory glance and pass it by. The Dolomite rock of this South Face is so prolific in firm holds that, as an observant climber has very properly remarked, you can go anywhere on it – a thing you can't do with piton-galleries . . . We could also discourse at length on the giant hearth-chimney of the Vazzoler Hut, where wine, women and song spur one on to new adventures . . . but our higher nature scorns lesser experiences.

Valley Resort Listolade, 682 m, (bus from Agordo, Alleghe and Cortina d'Ampezzo).
Base Vazzoler Hut, 1714 m, CAI, serviced; 3 hours from Listolade up the Corpassa Valley, by private car to the Cabana Trieste then 1½ hours to the Hut.
Starting Point At 1850 m, ½ hour above the Vazzoler Hut at the foot of the wall (bottom right in our picture) only a little way to the right of the edge of a huge landslide whose immense scar is the hall-mark of the Torre Venezia. Time for the climb, for a rope of two, 5–7 hours.
Descent Down the normal East Route (II, one pitch of IV, abseil, pitons available), from the great circular band to the bottom of the face, a descent of 300 m; summit to hut 2½ hours.
First Climb A. Tissi, G. Andrich and A. Bortoli, 20.8.1933.
Guides/Maps CAI *Dolomiti Orientale*, vol. I, parts 1/2 (Italian). RR *Dolomiten-Kletterführer – Civetta* (GF series, German). AC *Dolomites East*. IGM 50M. Sh. 046 – Longarone (divisible into six 25M. sh.).
Plate The South Face of the Torre Venezia, the southern corner-stone of the Pelsa Chain of the Civetta Group. It is possible to distinguish the South-West Ridge, South-West Face and the 'Tissi Route'.

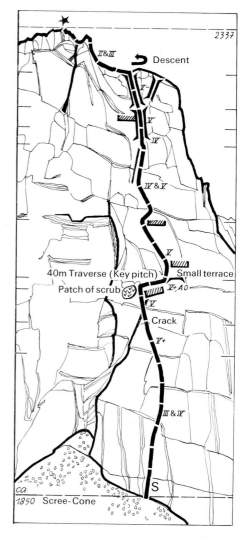

Dolomites (Civetta Group)
Torre Trieste 2436 m
South Face (Carlesso-Sandri)
Grade VI, A2/650 m (A3 when the pitons are missing)

As one goes up to the Vazzoler Hut from Listolade it is not easy to realise, at the first overpowering sight of the Torre Trieste – which is only a 700-metre appendage to the huge bulk of the Busazza – that the 'Very Ultimate' in rock-climbing awaits one here. In the competition of the last thirty-five years for that 'Ultimate', the Civetta routes have come off even better than the 'Tre Cime'. On the Torre Trieste three routes were thrown into the passionate argument: the West Ridge (V+, Tissi, Andrich, Rudatis, 1931), the magnificent South-East Ridge (VI, A2, Cassin-Ratti, 1935: see sketch) and the South Face (still VI, A2 today, Carlesso-Sandri, 1934). The 'Carlesso' won the day and nowadays every 'Extremist' dreams of it. The grading it has of VI, A2 appears in this book only six times. Our South Face is the longest of the six – enough said! Seen from the Vazzoler Hut the Torre stands quite clear and you can see every detail on its roofs, in the yellow cliffs of the wall and on both of the prominent lateral ramps, whose horizontal terraces provide escape-routes to the right. But from the hut door you can also assess the difficulties and tribulations which' await you on that South Face, mostly well warmed by the sun's rays. During 1973 and 1974, the whole route was entirely stripped of its pitons. By whom? One can only repeat the rumours. Be that as it may, Peter Bednar climbed it in 1975 and provided the excellent description in *Bergsteiger*, vol. 9, 1975, with which we checked the grading given in our sketch as in force summer 1975. In 1975 there were many genuine VI pitches to be climbed free, certainly more than on any other route in this book. If by any chance the pitons go missing again, their restoration over the whole route could mean an A3!

The once greatly feared descent by way of the abseil-route from the Cozzi Saddle has now been provided with normal pitons and no longer poses any problems. Against that there is the tip given by Signor Da Roit, the amiable keeper of the Vazzoler Hut, that it is simpler to go down below the saddle

into the hanging Valle delle Sasse. By all means take the hut-keeper's advice. In our sketch we have marked the bivouac-sites – they are, incidentally, important aids to survival. Embark on this hardest of all the climbs described in this book convinced that you are in for a very long example of its kind. You can hardly hope to avoid a bivouac, and the 'South Face thirst' is a renowned feature of the 'Carlesso'. You can gain a first impression of the difficulties of the climb from the photograph and the sketch; a second from reading the knowledgeable literature of the guidebooks; a third at the tables of the Vazzoler Hut, by way of the usual 'grapevine'. It may shock one man, enlighten another. Let it be freely admitted that there has been a long conflict of opinion whether the difficulties of this climb exceed those of the Cassin Route on the Cima Ovest and Soldà's on the Marmolada South-West Face. The difference may have been settled among the few 'extreme' climbers really qualified to judge.

Valley Resort Listolade, 682 m (bus from Agordo, Alleghe and Cortina d'Ampezzo).
Base Vazzoler Hut, 1714 m, CAI, serviced, in the lower Valle dei Cantoni; 3 hours from Listolade up the Corpassa Valley, motorable to Cabana Trieste, thence 1½ hours to the Hut.
Starting Point At 1800 m, on the upper end of the steep, partly scrub-covered substructure, best approached from the right; 1½ hours from the Hut. Time for the climb, for a two-man rope, at present 10–12 hours, in the absence of pitons considerably longer.
Descent Eastwards (IV+) to the Forcella Cozzi, then abseil route into the cwm (pitons provided). Study the abseil route carefully in the guidebooks. Length of abseil 450 m. Time from summit to hut, depending on conditions, 3½–5 hours – see important advice about a second abseil route in the main text.
First Ascent R. Carlesso and B. Sandri, 7/8.8.1934.
Guides/Maps CAI *Dolomiti Orientale*, vol. I, parts 1/2 (Italian). RR *Dolomiten-Kletterführer – Civetta* (GF series, German). AC *Dolomites East*. IGM 50M. Sh. 046 – Longarone (divisible into six 25M. sh.).
Plate The Torre Trieste, the dominating corner-pillar of the Cantoni Chain, showing its South Face. To the left, the West Ridge and the South-West Face.

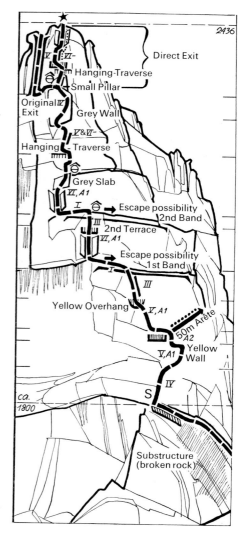

Dolomites (Civetta Group)
Cima Su Alto 2900 m
North-West Face (Gabriel-Livanos)
Grade VI−, A2/800 m

'Hoch Empor' ('Excelsior!') is the name of an 'Extremist' Munich Club. Su Alto is that of the mountain climbed for the first time by two of its members, Merk and Schneider – the corner-stone rising just where the magnificent Pelsa branch thrusts away from the main ridge of the Civetta. Let us glance back a moment . . . the Civetta had to be discovered three times before it became well known. The Munich climbers Späth, Hübel and Oberhäuser crept into it as long ago as 1903 and came there repeatedly till 1907. Then came the Great War and it was forgotten. In 1925 a new generation of 'Hoch Empor' men arrived: Solleder and Lettenbauer, to unravel the mysteries of the North-West Face, while their club-mates Rittler, Schneider, Leiner and Merk climbed and reconnoitred. In 1933 no German climbers; but King Leopold of the Belgians joined Tissi, Andrich and Rudatis on their rope. At the same time an extraordinary thing happened hardly noticed by the world. Between 1931 and 1936, an élite of brilliant Italian climbers, Rudatis, Castiglioni, Cassin, Ratti, Andrich, Faè, Panzeri, Bortoli, Carlesso, Menti, Tissi, Comici, Soldà, Sandri and Benedetti had climbed those extreme, classy routes, which were not discovered by their northern neighbours, the Germans, till after the Second World War. What a turn-about! It was only then that Europe's many 'Extremists' came to consecrate this new citadel of 'extreme' climbing in the Eastern Alps. Only then was a new conception of modern climbing introduced . . . and it was left to two Frenchmen, Gabriel and Livanos (the latter climbing with his wife) to climb, in 1951, this North-West Face of the Cima Su Alto, which today holds such a prominent position. At the time their climb set a new standard, not to be eclipsed till, seven years later, Dieter Hasse and his friends set a still higher one with the 'Direttissima' on the Cima Grande.

The Su Alto climb starts with difficult and dangerous climbing (if the rope be dispensed with!) up the big substructure, followed by some 400 metres which cannot be climbed in a hurry: 8 to 10 hours is the average time required and a bivouac is often obligatory. Below the 150-metre reddish-yellow dièdre, which is the hall-mark of the route, there is a cave and above its roof a convenient bivouac place in case of emergency. Progress on this verticality is mostly slow. Waiting on its stances while the leader slowly masters the difficulties, you have plenty of time to look around. You can send your kind regards across to the Marmolada's armoury of ice-crowned rock, dreaming . . . then suddenly there are gasps, agitated scratting, the clink of ironmongery, and you wake up. That man up there has reached a stance, and you hear the familiar 'Up you come!' . . . Right at the top, cause for real fury: the exit-chimneys are brittle in places and you utter your bitter complaints – only no one is listening. Our splendid picture allows us to follow every detail of the route exactly, as well as the four others on the Cima de Gasperi and the Su Alto (among them the old Ratti-Vitale).

Valley Resorts Alleghe, 980 m (bus from Cortina d'Ampezzo and Agordo). Listolade, 682 m (bus to Alleghe or Agordo) on the descent.
Bases Tissi Hut, 2281 m, CAI, serviced, on the Col Rean, below the foot of the face of the long-drawn-out precipices of the Civetta's North-West Walls; 3¼ hours from Alleghe (see route 76), the Vazzoler Hut, 1714 m, CAI, serviced, at the exit from the Valle dei Cantoni into the Val Corpassa.
Starting Point At about 2100 m at the foot of the substructure which is broken into by numerous diagonal cracks, ¾ hour from the Tissi Hut, 1¾ from the Vazzoler Hut. In the picture the substructure is distorted, being magnified beyond its real size in comparison to the whole face.
Descent Down the East Flank (II−) first northwards towards the Cima de Gasperi, then to the south, crossing a deep couloir, then across ledges and steps down to the 'Giazzer' and on this tiny glacier down into the Valle dei Cantoni and to the Vazzoler Hut (2 hours). In no circumstances take the old abseil-route described in the older guidebooks.
First Ascent G. Livanos and R. Gabriel, 9/11.9.1951.
Guides/Maps CAI *Dolomiti Orientale*, vol. I, parts 1/2 (Italian). RR *Dolomiten-Kletterführer – Civetta* (GF series, German). AC *Dolomites East.* IGM 50M. Sh. 046 – Longarone (divisible into six 25M. sh.).
Plate Cima de Gasperi (top left) and Cima Su Alto (close to the top centre) with their North-West Precipices, and the Cima della Terranova to the right.

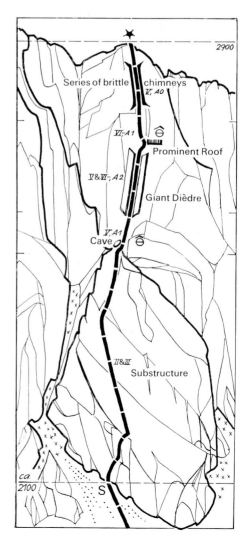

ITALY **75** **Civetta 3218 m**

North-West Face (Solleder-Lettenbauer)

Grade VI−, A1/1100 m

The drum-roll which greeted Emil Solleder and Gustl Lettenbauer in 1925, when they astonished mountaineers all over the world by climbing the Civetta, is still reverberating. Whatever else has been discovered, sought after and climbed for the first time on fine straightforward routes and so-called sporting climbs on those four magnificent ridges which meet in all their majesty at the Civetta's main summit – nothing can compare with that climb of the North-West Face, not even the Comici 'Diagonal', which should really be called the 'Direttissima' starting at the base of the Punta and eventually joining the Solleder Route. The latter route, on which there is not much pleasurable climbing, which is often brittle, difficult to find and, finally, keeps a drenching in store for you in its main gully, is really one of the great undertakings in the Alps. Fifty-four years old in 1979, it still ranks as the classic test, for it demands the toughest determination all the way up the 1100 metres of the face. True, there are much more difficult routes close by – between the Torre Valgrande and Punta Tissi, or between the Cima de Gasperi and the Torre Venezia for instance – than this 'Solleder', which was mastered on 7 August 1925 in fifteen hours at a stretch without a bivouac, employing 12 pitons for belaying purposes, two of which Solleder used for the wet overhang.

It is a boon and a blessing that this great and truly major climb has been so well described in the Hiebeler guide. Incidentally, the proof of Toni Hiebeler's expertise lies in his first winter-ascent of the face with his friends, whom he led with spectacular discipline from start to finish, establishing a new standard. Total application is the watchword on any climb on this huge Civetta Face, where perpendicular column is followed by perpendicular column. All its routes demand the utmost. Here the beautiful, fairy-tale mountain scenery is fused with the toughest and most exalting sport known to modern man. Leo Maduschka gave his life for this most gripping experience on Solleder's Wall. It is a dangerous

face, on which stone-falls and cataracts menace the climber; everyone who gets back safe and sound to the tiny Torrani Hut must feel happy. The chimneys in the 'Exit-Gully', presenting one difficulty after another, seem never-ending. Everyone with any experience knows what that must mean when mist, rainstorms or fresh snow materialise. The greatest respect for and familiarity with the structure of the wall, the finest equipment and superlative technical skill – none of these is sufficient – as many a sad event can witness. Here, all a man can give is the requisite, and on top of that he needs a good slice of climber's luck.

Valley Resort Alleghe, 980 m (bus from Agordo and Cortina d'Ampezzo).
Bases Coldai (Sonino) Hut, 2135 m, CAI, serviced; 3 hours from Alleghe. Tissi Hut, 2281 m, CAI, serviced, goods-ropeway from Masarè; 1½ hours from the Coldai Hut. Torrani Hut, 3130 m, CAI, open, emergency accommodation; 15 minutes eastwards below the Civetta Summit.
Starting Point At 2200 m on the gable of the triangular pillar in the substructure. 1½ hours from the Coldai Hut, ¾ hour from the Tissi. Time for the climb, for a two-man rope, 9–12 hours.
Descent Down the Eastern Flank (I) marked and protected, passing the base of the Torrani Hut to the Tivan Path and by it to the Coldai Hut, 2 hours.
Note This gigantic face demands the highest degree of condition, endurance and route-finding flair. A bivouac is often essential. Especially good equipment is called for because of the damp. Exhausting free-climbing with relatively little technical assistance.
First Ascent E. Solleder and G. Lettenbauer, 7.8.1925.
Guides/Maps CAI *Dolomiti Orientale*, vol. I, parts 1/2 (Italian). RR *Dolomiten-Kletterführer – Civetta* (GF series, German). AC *Dolomites East*. IGM 50M. Sh. 046 – Longarone (divisible into six 25M. sh.).
Plate The North-West Face of the Civetta, top right centre. Next to the right, the Piccola Civetta. With the assistance of the sketch our Solleder Route can easily be followed, as can the so-called Comici-Benedetti 'Direttissima' of 1931 and the Philipp-Flamm 1957 Route on the Punta Tissi (Quota IGM).

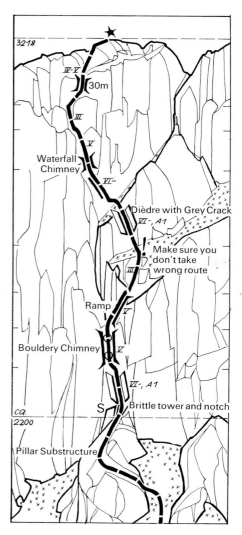

Dolomites (Civetta Group)

Punta Civetta 2920 m

North-West Face (Andrich-Faè)

Grade VI−, A2/750 m (The key-pitch can be turned: in which case VI−, A1)

There are two famous routes running up the North-West Face of the Punta Civetta from its wedge-like base to the summit, in amazingly direct line. The left-hand one, to the west, the Andrich-Faè, reaches the ridge to the west of the summit and can be recognised in the photograph as a skein of narrow cracks and chimneys, the Eastern one to the right, the Aste-Susatti, comes out to the right of the summit and is remarkably clear in the picture as a black crack-groove. Both are today rated as VI−, A1, share an approach route and are both very stylish free-climbs, differing in the number of pitons used ... Our chosen route was first climbed as long ago as 1934 by Alvise Andrich and Ernani Faè, and was immediately acclaimed as one of the purest and finest free-climbs in the Dolomites; its magnificent line, straight as a die, is dictated by a system of cracks. The key-pitch, a holdless slab, can be turned a little way to the left (VI−, A1). The rock is firm. Experts can climb the substructure unroped. An interesting note in the guidebook states that this 'Andrich–Faè Route', taking all its difficulties into account, is rated higher than Soldà's route on the South-West Face of the Marmolada or Cassin's on the North Face of the Cima Ovest! An additional comment by Dietmar Ohngemach: 'Ten years ago it carried an aura of one of the hardest routes ever. That doesn't make sense. Its cracks, slabs and gigantic chimneys offer pure climbing delights, while demanding 100 per cent morale and a very good physical condition.'

If you start very early, a competent party in favourable conditions should be able to do the climb without a bivouac, right through in a single day. An aid to that is the Via Ferrata, leading eastwards from the summit to the Tivan Path and so back to the Coldai Hut. Further important advice: the final chimneys with their overhangs before you finally climb out onto the circular terrace 50 metres below the summit, are almost always wet, often icy, even in July. You have to reckon on that. Finally, the parallel route mentioned above, the 'Aste–Susatti' (also VI−,

A1) was, unbelievably, not climbed for the first time till twenty years after the 'Andrich–Faè'. It, too, is a perfect exercise in the perpendicular. That says a great deal for those two brilliant climbers, who finally made the first ascent and whose names are linked with so many climbs once 'modern', now considered 'classic'. And just one more weighty piece of advice from Joachim Schneider, who has climbed the route: 'There is danger from falling stones when other parties are at work overhead. The sketch shows clearly that the only easy terrain is on the substructure. Once the difficulties begin there is not one pitch below V (a fact which will be gladly overlooked).'

Valley Resort Alleghe, 980 m (bus from Cortina d'Ampezzo or Agordo).
Bases Coldai (Sonino) Hut, 2135 m, CAI, serviced, 3 hours from Alleghe. Tissi Hut, 2281 m CAI, new, serviced, at the Col-Rean; goods ropeway from Masarè near Alleghe. Ascent to the hut 3¼ hours from Alleghe by the 'Ru Antersass' Path.
Starting Point At about 2150 m at the narrow rock-plinth jutting from the rubble in the cwm. You go up to the right of it (route hidden in the picture). One hour from the Tissi and 1¾ hours from the Coldai Hut to the start. Time for the climb, for a rope of two, 8–10 hours.
Descent Only down the East Flank along the Via Ferrata (II), mostly protected and marked, to the equally well-marked Tivan Path (1½ hours) and along it to the Coldai Hut.
First Ascent A. Andrich and E. Faè, 23/24.8.1934.
Guides/Maps CAI *Dolomiti Orientale*, vol. I, parts 1/2 (Italian). RR *Dolomiten-Kletterführer – Civetta* (GF series, German). AC *Dolomites East*. IGM 50M. Sh. 046 – Longarone (divisible into six 25M. sh.).
Plate The North-West Wall of the complete Civetta Chain from the Piccola Civetta (top right edge of the picture) across the main Civetta Summit, the Punta Tissi (top left below the main summit, with snow on its ridge), to the Punta Civetta (the sharper more heavily snow-tipped summit to the left centre of the picture), Pan di Zucchero (adjoining it to the left, to the right of the black gorge) and the Torre da Lago (to the left of the gorge).

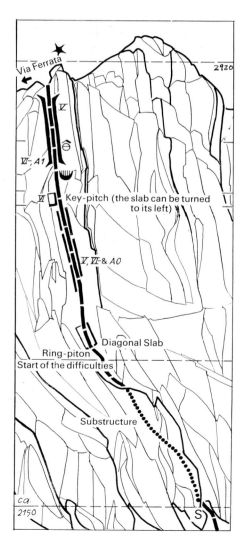

Dolomites (Civetta Group)
Torre di Valgrande 2715 m
North-West Face (Carlesso-Menti)
Grade VI−, A1/400 m

The Torre di Valgrande, that splendid rotund lump, belongs naturally to the majestic screen of the Civetta Wall. It is the third but last courtier in the North Ridge of the monarch which towers 500 m above it; none the less the route on its North-West Face takes its legitimate place among the exclusive elite of 'extreme' Dolomite climbs. Jürgen Winkler's photograph is a close-up of the tower. Joint study with the sketch allows immediate identification of all the decisive pitches: the substructure, the cracks leading to the cave, the overhang, the great 120-metre dièdre-crack, the grey one above it and the chimney leading out onto the ridge to the left below the summit. The tower can already be seen from Pieve di Livinalong, identifiable as a short, thick, rounded stump, to the right above the Torre Alleghe, and one gives thanks for the 'Carlesso-Menti Route'. This incredibly straight route up the cracks in an otherwise completely solid, vertical wall is without parallel for the logic of its line. After the first ascent in 1936 it was not long before the route had won the reputation of a first-class modern climb. Naturally it has lost some of that esteem during the last ten years, thanks to the modern 'piton-ladder' specialists: in 1958 it was still an engaging free-climb on which it was necessary to use one's 'Fifi' only once. Times change, fine climbs succumb to nails, valid prescriptions for excesses still hold sway. Of course we know that 'Extremists' set no store by muscle, not even on this 'Carlesso-Menti Route'. A good rope of two is kept busy on it for at least 5–7 hours, enjoying a good deal of clean, fresh air below, and thinking of the men who first climbed it: Raffaele Carlesso, that king among Dolomite climbers and his friend Mario Menti, who needed two days for the great 120-metre dièdre alone during their three-day ascent − on virgin rock, not yet a home for ironmongery. It was thirteen years before the next pair, Luigi Ghedina and Lino Lacedelli, climbed it; the third pair, Jean Couzy and Armando da Roit were two years later. In the following year Toni Hiebeler and Uli Wyss circumvented the roof of the cave, but their exploit aroused little notice . . .

This route is no 'training tour', nor a climb for a 'by-day'; at least nobody who has climbed it thinks so. It dries out quickly and is easy to get to, but just so long as it is not turned into an 'Iron Road', it remains a serious undertaking, for which only the best are fitted. The rock is superbly firm. Finally, another 'extreme' is a swim after the climb in the crystal-clear Lago d'Alleghe, cooled by the avalanche-debris. The hot day is soon forgotten, one's flayed skin tingles and the recovery is complete. Nor will the 'Rosso' which follows taste too bad.

Valley Resort Alleghe, 980 m (bus from Cortina d'Ampezzo and Agordo).
Bases Coldai (Sonino) Hut, 2135 m, CAI, serviced; 3 hours from Alleghe. Tissi Hut, 2281 m, CAI, serviced, on the Col Rean. Goods ropeway from Masarè near Alleghe: 1½ hours from the Coldai Hut. New motor road from the east as far as the Cas di Pioda. Jeep road above that.
Starting Point At 2350 m at the bottom end of the sharp, rocky spur between the two snow-gullies; 1½ hours from the Coldai Hut, 1 hour from the Tissi.
Descent Down the North-East Route, first down the 'Haupt-Lömpel Chimney' (II), reached from the summit cliffs and leading down into the cwm, at whose lower end one strikes the Tivan Path leading to the Coldai Hut. 2 hours from summit to hut.
First Ascent R. Carlesso and M. Menti, 15/17.7.1936.
Guides/Maps CAI *Dolomiti Orientale*, vol. I, parts 1/2 (Italian). RR *Dolomiten-Kletterführer – Civetta* (GF series, German). AC *Dolomites East.* IGM 50M. Sh. 046 – Longarone (divisible into six 25M. sh.).
Plate The Torre di Valgrande, 2715 m, with its North-West Face. To its left in the picture the Torre Alleghe. The photograph is so sharp that studying it with the sketch enables you to identify all the key-pitches.

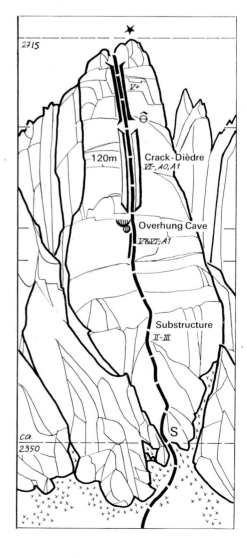

ITALY **78**

Dolomites (Pelmo Group)
Monte Pelmo 3168 m
North Face
Grade VI−, A0/850 m

Monte Pelmo, a solitary Dolomite monarch, rises gigantic like some huge rock-castle above the gentle slopes of green valleys. It was the first Dolomite summit ever to be climbed, when an Englishman, John Ball, made the first ascent in 1857; he did so by the long 'Ball Terrace', which slashes across the southern precipices and leads by a very exposed route into the main massif's big glacier-cwm. The North Face of this huge mountain, surging up with its two great gullies, was also the first great Dolomite wall attempted by climbers of the extreme persuasion. Our North Face Climb of 1924 is a classic. The boast of the first men to climb it, Roland Rossi and Felix Simon, is that they got up this 850-metre wall using only 8 pitons and only one bivouac. Free-climbing was naturally their trump-card and they were so delighted with it that these two experienced men rated the climb more highly than the South Face of the Schüsselkarspitze or the West Face of the Totenkirchl, at that time considered the greatest. Later climbers of course played down the understandable enthusiasm of the pioneers. However, the Pelmo has remained a Grade VI climb, VI− to be precise, and that is how it ought to stay. Anyone who comes to the Pelmo with legitimate Alpine rock-climbing ambitions, and not as an acrobat or an ironmonger, will enjoy on that enormous North Face a marvellous day's climbing, which he will never forget.

The comparison of our sketch with Jürgen Winkler's photograph will give all the necessary information. The Central Pillar, which splits the North Face, is well shown in the photograph but is actually much more prominent. It sets the character of the wall; our route touches it at several points from the halfway mark but only crosses it above the bivouac site. The ramp leading leftwards out of the steep snow-gully (to the right) was used by the second pair to make the ascent, Hans Steger and Paula Wiesinger, for getting onto the climb. The base below it was climbed by the Viennese pair, S. Brunhuber and H. Schwanda in a direct variant (avoiding

our hanging-traverse, chimney and sequence of cracks). As can be seen from the terraces of rubble in the picture, the lower part of the Pelmo is rather brittle, but it is not so further up. Atrun Meissner, who has climbed the route, says: 'A big climb, always to be taken very seriously. Often V+, with one or two definitely very difficult rope lengths. The rock is firm except in the zone of entry and halfway up. Splendid free-climbing almost all the way – we found only 15 to 20 pitons. The climb required ten to twelve hours.' An additional note from Heinz Steinkötter: 'The Rossi route is a V+. Several variants possible in the lower sector. A fine Alpine climb all the way.'

Valley Resorts Selva di Cadore, 1317 m, and Pescul, 1415 m, on the northern slope of the motorway over the Staulanza Saddle, 1773 m (Val Fiorentina-Val di Zoldo).
Bases Before: Malga Fiorentina, 1830 m, large Alp-dairy, overnight accommodation possible. After the descent: Refugio Venezia De Luca, 1947 m, CAI, serviced, at the Rutorto Pass on the east side of the Pelmo.
Starting Point At about 2300 m at the foot of the wall to the left of the snow-gully between the Pelmo and the Pelmetto. You climb the substructure, which is split by a horizontal band of rubble and at its deepest point pushes down into the terraced snowfield below, by its right-hand (western) side. There is usually a bergschrund to be crossed. A good bivouac-site is marked on the sketch. From the Alp to the start, 2 hours. Time for the climb, for a rope of two, fully 10 hours.
Descent By the normal descent on the South-Eastern Flank (the 'Ball Terrace', II−), taking about 2 hours from the summit. First down into the great cwm housing the Pelmo Glacier, then along the lengthy, very exposed 'Ball Terrace', horizontally, and by a narrow 'crawling pitch' from south to north.
First Ascent R. Rossi and F. Simon, 11/12.8.1924.
Guides/Maps CAI *Dolomiti Orientale*, vol. I, parts 1/2 (Italian). RR *Dolomiten*, vol. IIa (GF series, German). AC *Dolomites East*. TCI 50M. Sh. D54 – Cortina d'Ampezzo. IGM 50M. Sh. 029 – Cortina d'Ampezzo (divisible into six 25M. sh.).
Plate The broad North Face of Monte Pelmo, clearly showing the prominent Central Pillar. To its right, the ice-couloir separating the Pelmetto (out of the picture to the right) from the massif of the Pelmo itself.

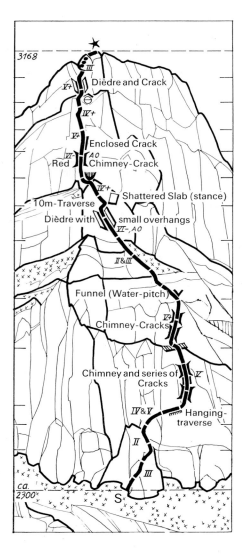

155

Dolomites of Ampezzo
Tofana di Rozes 3225 m
South-West Face (Pilastro)
Grade VI, A1/500 m

There are in the Alps so many 'hardest, longest, most dangerous and highest walls' the final choice has always been one of the pleasures of our love for the mountains. One thing is certain: the vast bulk of the Tofana di Rozes, towering above the Falzárego Pass Road, is admired by all as the richest of all in variety of colour. You only have to lie flat among the Cinque Torri and look across to the Tofana. More than a wall: surely a great chunk of primaeval architecture, weathered and worn to the ultimate limit, and glorying in every shade of red, grey and bright yellow. Here are three mighty pillars to the right and three to the left of the amphitheatre let deep into the middle of the wall, above it the vertical semi-circle of the summit-cliff, crowned by a true pyramid. That description will sound exaggerated only to an 'extreme' gymnast who, having 'done' his Pilastro, sits dog-tired on the Tofana's East Ridge and can't be bothered with the continuation to the summit. Who wants a view anyway? We know for certain that even such a 'Sexogradist, recently married, recently a parent, will cheerfully abrogate his 'extreme' tendencies and spend a day lying about at the foot of the Cinque Torri with his wife, or take her over the 'Baronessen-tour' on the South Face.

Even in black and white our photograph has a unique impact. A study of the sketch and the picture together reveals how knife-sharp it is: on it we can climb, in our mind's eye, with complete precision onto the smooth base, clutch the overhangs and push on up to the key-pitch, to the yellow masonry and out at the top. This Pilastro has become a fashionable climb for the 'Aces' and our VI −, A1 grading is no exaggeration. It is a highly impressive adventure on rock, testing morale and condition to the utmost. Exceedingly difficult slabs have to be climbed between relatively easy roofs. At places there are inset in the face astonishingly level ledges, most suitable for a breather or a snack. Then, the following chimneys, widely overhanging, exact almost brutal exertions. Higher up, it all becomes easier, and frequent rests enable

us to scan the familiar summits and faces – the massive shoulders of the Pelmo over yonder, the vast spread of the Civetta, the Antelao, Sorapis and Marmolada. Then up we go onto the summit, or head down from the East Ridge into the cwms, to the Cantore Hut or 'home' to the little Dibona. Here and there on the way one comes across ruined defences from the time of the First World War – the debris of hideous years of strife, debris of thousands of pitiable dead, debris of Europe's wretched history. Should anyone ask us what our attitude is to our achievements, there is an easy answer.

Valley Resort Cortina d'Ampezzo.

Base Angelo Dibona Hut, 2100 m, private, to the south-east below the Tofana's Face; by car along the Falzarego Pass road, 1 hour on foot from the road.

Starting Point At about 2500 at the base of the last-but-one (Eastern) Pillar of the South-East Face, in the middle between the two gullies bordering the pillars, about 1¼ hours from the hut. Time for the climb, for a two-man rope, 5–7 hours.

Descent After reaching the East Ridge the way down lies along the East branch to the Cantore Hut (Tofana Hut) and back southwards to the Dibona, in 2–2½ hours from the summit of the Pilastro.

First Ascent E. Costantini and L. Ghedina, 1946.

Guides/Maps CAI *Dolomiti Orientale*, vol. I, parts 1/2 (Italian). RR *Dolomiten*, vol. IIa (GF series, German). AC *Dolomites East*. TCI 50M. Sh. D54 – Cortina d'Ampezzo. IGM 50M. Sh. 029 – Cortina d'Ampezzo (divisible into six 25M. sh.).

Plate The Tofana di Rozes displaying its South and South-East Faces, photographed from the Cinque Torri opposite. At the top left we see part of the amphitheatre with the old 'classic' South Face climb (then the three splendid pillars adjoining it). The right-hand pillar, plumb centre of the picture, is our Pilastro. From its top we climb out on to the Tofana's East Ridge.

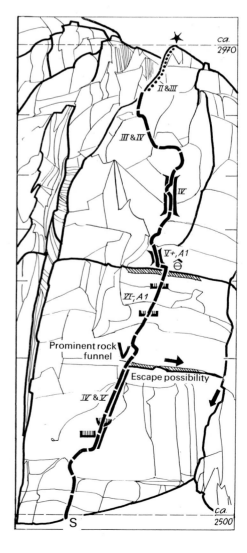

Dolomites of Ampezzo
Cima Scotoni 2874 m
South-West Face
Grade VI, A1/500 m

Close to the west of the Tofana's three summits and just to the north of the Falzárego Pass stands the Fanis Group – a wild upheaval of sharp Dolomite towers. The wise man will take the lift from the Pass to the Lagazuoi Saddle, from where he can see the whole assembly: the North, West, Central and Southern Fanis peaks, arrayed close behind each other. North-eastwards of the group's base stands the Scotoni Hut, on the edge of the Lagazuoi Alp. You can look down on it from our 'Cima Scotoni' which in German is called the Westliche Fanisspitze. Our interest is in its South-West Face: our recent Winkler photograph reveals that there is room between the Fanis Summits for a sizeable wall. This South-West Face – which remained unheard of in German-speaking lands for so long – a Grade VI, A1 wall of 500 metres, was not climbed till 1952. The second ascent was not made till the end of the 1960s. Further details became known and suddenly there was talk of the hardest route in the Dolomites – once the Quota IGM (Punta Tissi) had been duly provided with nails. The latest assessment (since the separation of free and artificial climbing) is VI, A1.

To go into the horrifying details: first, two pitches of the greatest difficulty, brittle and 'free'. These are followed by a dream of a pitch, then a ledge so overhung that you have to crawl along it flat on your stomach (as on the Barras). By contrast, you could ride a bicycle along the next terrace. In the middle section of this extreme climb which has achieved such sudden fame, there follow a few more difficult pitches of free-climbing, but after the second terrace, it becomes easier (III and IV). The approach is short: either from the Scotoni Hut, below the western precipice falling from the Fanis Ridge, or (more comfortably) by the ropeway from the Falzárego Pass to Piccolo Lagazuoi (2778 m), then climb down northwards to the foot of the wall. The descent from the summit is fairly easy. But beyond the ropeway lies solitude unimaginable: no hiker goes into that region to get himself lost. This climb is only really fine in a few of its

rope lengths, but grand and free all the way. The photograph is deceptive: the approach is harder than it appears.

Valley Resorts Cortina d'Ampezzo, 1210 m. San Cassiano in the valley of the same name, 1537 m.
Base Scotoni Hut, 2040 m, CAI, below the western precipices of the Fanis Range; approach from the Falzárego Pass road, San Cassiano (1 hour) or over the Forcella Lagazuoi, 1¼ hours. Better by ropeway to Piccolo Lagazuoi, then climb down northwards to the Hut.
Starting Point In the fall-line from the summit at about 2400 m, at the point where lighter-coloured rocks push up furthest into the yellow overhanging part of the wall (½ hour from the Hut, ¾ from the ropeway). Time for the climb, for a two-man rope, 8–10 hourrs.
Descent From the saddle at which you climb out, first eastwards, then to the left north-westwards and finally to the west down to the foot of the wall (walking-terrain). ¾ hour.
First Ascent L. Lacedelli, L. Ghedina and G. Lorenzi, 1952.
Guides/Maps CAI *Dolomiti Orientale*, vol. I, parts 1/2 (Italian). RR *Dolomiten*, vol. IIa (GF series, German). AC *Dolomites East*. TCI 50M. Sh. D54 – Cortina d'Ampezzo. IGM 50M. Sh. 029 – Cortina d'Ampezzo. (divisible into six 25M. sh.).
Plate The South-West Face of the Cima Scotoni with our route clearly distinguishable on it. At the extreme left-hand edge of the picture, the Forcella dal Lago.

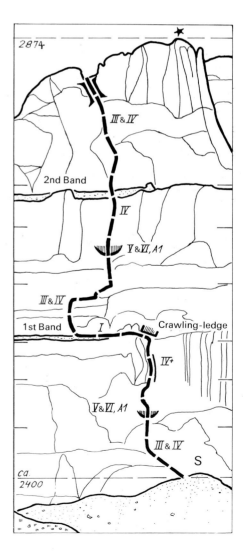

Dolomites of Ampezzo
Punta Fiames 2297 m
South-East Arête
Grade V/300 m

This slender arête of the Fiames in the otherwise small Pomagagnon Ridge does not appear to have much of a chance of making an impression in the neighbourhood of three Tofana castles, a Monte Cristallo, the Sorapis, Antelao and Pelmo. All the same, anyone sitting lazily on a hot summer afternoon outside one of Cortina's cafés, ladling ices into himself or whispering sweet nothings to a charming Anti-Alpinist, can suddenly find himself in love with that arête. It stands in the background, but is so unmistakably an 'edge' rising above the velvet carpet of the meadows that you suddenly know you must climb it. There are pleasant and nicely exposed 'pleasure-climbs' on it. But our direct South-East Route has its juicy Grade V pitch, and there is no way of avoiding it. As you drive up from Carbonin to Cortina you see the arête in profile, high above light-coloured larches. It is an ideal 'starter' and has the advantage of being snow-free early in the year. It is also a nice climb on a day in Cortina's late winter, though the traverse to the north on the way down to the Forcella Pomagagnon and the downward path might be something of a headache. We have marked the key-pitch (V) on our sketch: it consists of climbing a polished slab close to the edge, but a shallow crack makes the move easier. The key-pitch, a rope length earlier, is a crack with plenty of holds and made still easier by the presence of a few pitons, certainly no higher than IV in difficulty, but still a nice piece of climbing. The crack which follows, on the other hand, demands all your attention and exertions. Unfortunately the arête is only 300-metres high, but they are 300 beautifully exposed metres.

That most of the climbs described in this book are even more alarmingly exposed goes without saying but even 100 'extreme' routes have an upper and a lower limit in such respects, which does not take mere pleasure into account. The Fiames Arête lies at the lower limit of our offering of 'extreme' climbs, but it can afford the highest degree of pleasure. Let an unbeliever try it out for himself or ask Manfred Sturm, who has

climbed it three times, with or without his wife. Moreover, the little Cortina airfield lies close under the start of the climb, though naturally in the bottom of the valley. Some day in the future the dyed-in-the-wool 'Extremist' will be able to fly to the Fiames Arête and be back in Munich again in the evening downing his strong pint at the Nockherberg. Stranger prophecies in Old Moore have come true . . . Perhaps he could even combine it with a fabulous Marmolada trip – in May, June or even November!

Valley Resort Cortina d'Ampezzo, 1210 m.
Base None, unless hidden bivouac-sites in the woods.
Starting Point At about 2000 m below the dièdre carved into the left side of the gigantic gully falling between the Punta Fiames and the Punta della Croce. You reach it from the main motor-road, across grass, rubble and boulders to the very bottom of the arête in 2 hours.
Descent First to the saddle before the Punta Croce, then around the Punta to its north to the Forcella Pomagagnon (I); thence by marked path to Cortina, 2 hours. Or back to the foot of the wall from the highest point, to the right, southwards, till you climb down southwards again through a steep narrow cwm full of rubble, which enables you to traverse back to the foot of the face and so back to the road, 1¼ hours.
First Ascent Käthe Bröske and Francesco Iori, 1909. Direct variant from the foot of the arête: E. Castiglioni and C. Gilberti, 1930.
Guides/Maps CAI Dolomiti Orientale, vol. I, parts 1/2 (Italian). RR Dolomiten, vol. IIa (GF series, German). AC Dolomites East. TCI 50M. Sh. D54 – Cortina d'Ampezzo. IGM 50M. Sh. 029 – Cortina d'Ampezzo (divisible into six 25M. sh.).
Plate Top centre, the Punta Fiames (2297 m) and, adjoining it to the right, Punta della Croce in the Pomagagnon range near Cortina d'Ampezzo, seen from the South. Our South-East Arête forms the left-hand edge of the gully separating the two peaks, and is marked by several lateral bands rising gently from left to right.

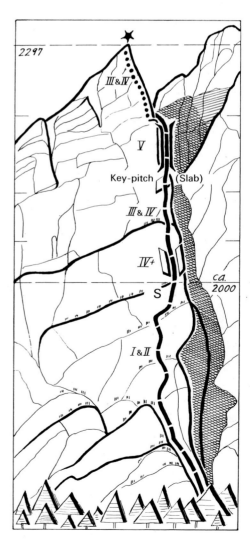

ITALY **82**

Dolomites (Bosconero Group)
Rocchetta Alta di Bosconero 2402 m
North Face
Grade VI−, A0/700 m

The great cathedral-like mass of the Rocchetta Alta stands in the South-Eastern Dolomites, equidistant from Civetta, Pelmo and Antelao, near Longarone in the Piave Valley, but easy to reach from the north over the Staulanza pass. Its North Face is vertical, as another photograph in *Alpinismus*, vol. 11, 1965 impressively confirms. The same issue carries an interesting account by the first man to do it, Milo Navasa, who, to the alarm of many 'Extremists', climbed the previously 'undiscovered' 700-metre face with two friends in a five-day undertaking, without bolts. At first there was talk of a 'new' Cima Ovest North Face. But Manfred Sturm put that right in *Jugend am Berg* (March 1969) saying that though the climb is extremely difficult and comparable with other highly regarded Dolomite routes, it was quite clear that the modern 'Extremists' had borrowed the Alpine 'Superlative' ready-made. The huge wall is still little-known and rarely visited; anyone coming from the reservoir near Forno di Zoldo eastwards along the grassy path to the Bivacco del Val Bosconero (also known as the Casera Bosconero) can see from the pitiable state of this tiny hut that it is hardly ever full to overflowing. Bosconero of course means 'Black Forest', as you can see on the way up to the hut through the woods. It is only half an hour from the hut to the start of the North Face, where at about 1600 metres the fine venture starts with a ramp going up from the left to right, which has been plentifully described. But let it at once be said that you should not start up this face when it is wet since, owing to the low altitude and its southern aspect, it is liable to have lichen growing on it.

Excellent and naturally inquisitive 'Sexogradists' like Manfred Sturm, Pit Schubert, Reinhold Obster, Klaus Werner, Karl Winkler, Michael Schneider have done the face in company, marching in three ropes, and arrived at the summit in ten hours, somewhat in need of a rest. There is no shortage of roofs (they turned them all) nor of bivouac-sites (see sketch). All the pitons are *in situ*, the doubled rope is as essential as the ten hours. There is an unexpected abundance of free-climbing. The long journey to the Rocchetta Alta can be made more rewarding still if you are aware that this splendid Dolomite mountain owns another very difficult climb on its North-West Arête, the 'Strobel', first climbed by the Cortina brothers Scialotti. Klaus Werner and Pit Schubert followed the 'tip' and have this to say: 'the "Strobel" is much the more difficult.' There is yet a third interesting route, opened up by Richard Goedecke and his friends. Whether this interesting wall remains 'unknown' probably depends on the number of editions of this book!

Valley Resorts Forno di Zoldo, 848 m (between Longarone and Alleghe reached from the north over the Staulanza saddle).
Base Bivacco di Val Bosconero (also Casera Bosconero), restored shepherd's-hut, 1520 m, 8 sleeping-places, 2¼ hours from the reservoir near the road to the east of Forno di Zoldo.
Starting Point At about 1600 m, a little right of the summit fall-line, at the start of a steep ramp running up from right to left. 1¾ hours from the Bivacco. Time for the climb, for a two-man rope, about 10 hours.
Descent From the first saddle in the summit-ridge you traverse downwards towards the east, then to the right, till you can find a way down over rubble terraces, scrub patches and short rocky steps. At the end, traverse northwards along a broad downhill terrace, up and down into a snow and debris couloir and so break to the bottom of the wall (I and II) about 1½ hours.
First Ascent Milo Navasa, Claudio dal Bosco and Franco Baschera, 22.7.1965 (of 120 pitons they left 55 and a few wooden wedges).
Guides/Maps CAI and RR guides under revision. AC *Dolomites East*. IGM 50M. Sh 046 – Longarone (divisible into six 25M. sh.).
Plate The North Face of the Rocchetta Alta, 2402 m, in the Bosconero Group between Longarone in the Piave Valley and Forno di Zoldo. The starting point is visible in the middle of the photograph.

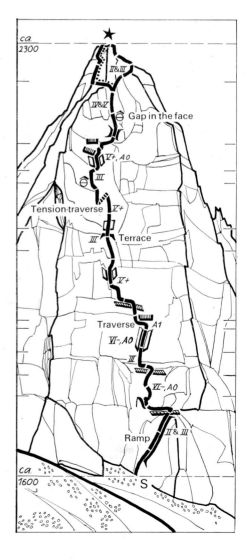

163

Eastern Dolomites (Sorapis Group)
Sorella di Mezzo 3011 m
North-West Face

Grade V+, A0/600 m

The Group of the Tre Sorelle ('Three Sisters') in the Sorapis group, between Lake Misurina, the Tre Croci Pass and the Valle di San Vito, falls north-eastwards with its greyish-black, sombre and shattered walls into the quiet, enchantingly lovely bowl around the little Sorapis Lake. Our route, the start of which can be easily and quickly reached from Cortina by way of the Luzzatti Hut, standing in the rocky cirque below the Sorapis Comb, goes up the North-West Face of the Central Sister, the Sorella di Mezzo. The height of this 600-metre wall is impressive, the climbing offers a colourful palette of possibilities on good rock, but on a North-West Face at relatively high altitude, cold and liable to be visited by snow. As our sketch shows when compared with the photograph, the route takes a somewhat complicated line up over moderate difficulties as far as the long series of chimneys which, in the picture, looks more like a sequence of cracks running up sunny slabs. It is marked as Grade V and is often damp or even wet. After five rope lengths up the roughly 150 metres of these cracks, there is a simple ramp and, after a chimney which succeeds it, comes the key-pitch – a vertical holdless slab (VI). There are pitons here . . . on the whole, this recondite, tough-looking wall may hardly match up to the demands of the modern 'Extremists', yet once on the way, as high-Alpinists, they seem for that reason to accept the somewhat twisty line taken by the route. Karl Lukan, who with his Viennese friends, Hans Hausner, Ernst Schuster and Hans Schwanda, formed the third party to make the ascent, declares concisely: 'This face is a free-climbing V and therefore harder than a VI.'

The history of the climb is interesting: Emilio Comici captured this route four years before he startled the world with his climb on the North Face of the Cima Grande. He started up on 26 August 1929 with G. Fabjan, but had to retreat. A second attempt next day proved successful, although accompanied by a blizzard, which soon led them into a catastrophic situation. Hardly had they reached the summit when they were

forced to risk an abseil straight down the ice-plastered North-West Face of the Terza Sorella and were reduced to dire straits by a bivouac on the face. But, as Comici himself remarked, he had done his first grade VI climb. Not far away, R. Cassin and F. Butti had in August 1947 completed the first ascent of the Prima Sorella's North-West Face (VI) by a great deal of free-climbing, 25 pitons and nine hours of climbing time. All in all, this ancient route, even if regarded by the moderns as a fossil from the first swift age of development, should still be interesting for today's technically experienced climber, even if only to enjoy the experience of pottering about on a Comici route.

Valley Resorts Cortina d'Ampezzo, 1210 m. S. Vito di Cadore, 1011 m (bus back to Cortina).
Base Vandelli Hut, 1928 m by the little Sorapis Lake. CAI, serviced, to the south of the Forcella Grande.
Starting Point At about 2400 m at the foot of the wall, above the small glacier, where a ramp, usually snow-covered, leads upwards (bottom centre of our picture). 1½ hours from the Hut. The start is over slabs to the right of the band beginning there, in the fall-line of the Central Sorella's summit. Time for the climb, for a rope of two, 7–9 hours.
Descent Only to the south (l) along a terrace with a gorge, then over grassy terraces to the Forella Grande, 2255 m, and southwards to the San Marco Hut on your way to San Vito di Cadore.
First Ascent E. Comici and G. B. Fabjan, 27.8.1929.
Guides/Maps CAI *Dolomiti Orientale*, vol. I, parts 1/2 (Italian). RR *Dolomiten*, vol. IIa (GF series, German). AC *Dolomites East*. TCI 50M. Sh. D54 – Cortina d'Ampezzo. IGM 50M. Sh. 029 – Cortina d'Ampezzo (divisible into six 25M. sh.).
Plate The North-West Faces of the Tre Sorelle in the Sorapis Group of the Ampezzo Dolomites, taken from the floor of the cwm above the little Sorapis Lake and the beautifully situated Vandelli Hut. Above, in the centre of the picture, the Sorella di Mezzo, up whose summit fall-line our route runs. Top right, the North-West Face of the Prima Sorella.

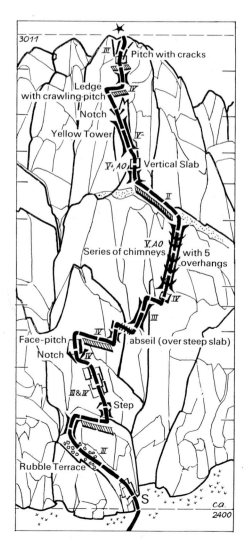

Tre Cime di Lavaredo Group (Sesto)
Cima Ovest 2973 m
North Face (Swiss Route and Cassin)
Grade A3, VI−/500 m

It took just thirty years to settle the fate of this 'unclimbable' North Face, this yellow-and-black 500-metre wall, whose fiercely jutting roofs constituted an unmistakable warning to keep away. Suddenly everything was changed and they became an uncanny attraction. In 1933 when Comici completed his hazardous first ascent of the North Face of the Cima Grande, Demuth, Lichtenegger and Peringer were already attempting the Cima Ovest. They only got as far as reconnaissances and first attempts. All the same, they won the consolation prize of success on the Northern Arête. Then Hans Hintermeier and Sepp Meindl arrived from Munich. In 1935 they made several attempts after thorough reconnaissances, pressing forward ever further and fixed on the famous 'endless traverse' the very pitons on which to everybody's surprise, in the presence of the Munich explorers, the mighty Riccardo Cassin and Vittorio Ratti pushed on and achieved the first ascent, in twenty-seven hours of climbing – a fateful but not exactly chivalrous push-forward. The 'Cassin', as it has for long been known, brought great glory to the Cima Ovest, neglected for such a long time. Not even the subsequent routes made by the later 'moderns', the French and Swiss Routes, could push the 'Cassin', with its fabulously airy traverse, into the background. The new climbs are almost entirely 'artificial', while the 'Cassin' (partly Hintermeier) remains, as a whole, a tremendous piece of 'free-climbing'. For that reason, it circumvents the overhang-zone which the Swiss Route penetrated by artificial means.

Once again we would like to quote a few comments from climbers of our time. They embody an actuality which lends a freshness to older values. Hans Hintermeier says: 'No ideal line, but a pleasant change from free-climbing and extreme piton-work. And a long, airy traverse thrown in. It is a pity that since the war no one has repeated Cassin's original start (see sketch) – the 100-metre dièdre with an overhang barring its exit. That is symptomatic of our development.' Hans Stutzig writes:

'What courage, that Hintermeier Meindl, Cassin and Ratti should even have thought of that perilous route!' Manfred Sturm's view: 'The combination of the Swiss and Cassin's Routes provides the ideal line. On the Swiss Route the greater part is piton-climbing, three of the pitches being definitely overhanging.' Dietmar Ohngemach says: 'The Cassin on the Cima Ovest is *the* Dolomite climb – airy, airy, airy, but firm and rich in holds. How was it that the great "Sexogradist" old-timers invested the "Ovest" with an aura of fearsome inviolability? One only has to read the reports by those famous men!'

Valley Resorts Sesto, 1316 m (bus from Innichen). Lake Misurina, 1755 m.
Bases Locatelli Hut, 2405 m, serviced, CAI, bus to the Val di Fiscalina, 2½ hours. Or Lavaredo Hut, 2344 m, private, serviced; bus; camping sites near Lavaredo Hut.
Starting Point At about 2500 m for the Swiss Route in the fall-line of the great overhanging roof; for the Cassin Route at the right-hand end of the base; reached by path from the Forcella Lavaredo, ½ hour. Time for the climb, for a two-man rope, 12–16 hours (usually with bivouac).
Descent On the South and West Flanks by the normal route (II) marked by cairns. 1½–2 hours from the summit.
Note: It goes without saying that these routes, representing the ultimate in 'extreme' rock climbing, can be undertaken only after studying all the available descriptions, even if from the very start the pitons blaze an unmistakable trail.
First Ascent R. Cassin and V. Ratti 28/30.8.1935. H. Weber and A. Schelbert, the Swiss Route, 1959.
Guides/Maps CAI *Dolomiti Orientale*, vol. I, parts 1/2 (Italian). RR *Dolomiten*, vol. IIa (GF series, German). AC *Dolomites East.* TCI 50M. Sh. D54 – Cortina d'Ampezzo. IGM 50M. Sh. 029 – Cortina d'Ampezzo (divisible into six 25M. sh.). IGM 50M. Sh. 016 – Dobbiaco (divisible into six 25M. sh.).
Plate The North Face of the Cima Ovest in the Tre Cime Group of the Dolomites. To the left the North-East (Demuth) Arête. The light and shade in the photograph reveal the unparalleled jutting of the famous yellow overhangs better than any words.

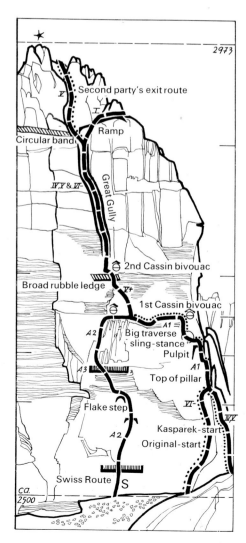

Tre Cime di Lavaredo Group (Sesto)
Cima Grande 2998 m
North Face Direct (Hasse-Brandler)
Grade A3, VI−/550 m

The development of modern climbing in the Alps suffered its sharpest interruptions on the Tre Cime and Mt Blanc's two Drus. In both areas the best of an astonishingly small élite in the end succeeded in pushing the limits of the 'extreme' higher than before. Their unbelievable courage, bordering on lunacy, was combined with careful planning and the highest degree of prudence, so they were able to refute the charge of 'madness' and legitimise their new style. It was not only the perfection of technical equipment which permitted that further step. The raging controversy about the classic conception of what could be done 'by fair means' led Alpinism to the brink of catastrophe. Climbing by artificial means is now accepted in the Alpine framework. The energy expended on this question of the 'utmost possible' was tough, damaging to many and quite extraordinary. At times it bordered on the comical, and punished excessive self-glorification with a whiff of the ludicrous. It is safe to say now that the total commitment of Dietrich Hasse and the superb skill of his three friends secured the ultimate standards. On the Cima Grande we see clearly marked, next to each other, the three steps in the march of modern climbing and of three generations of men: the 1909 'Dibona Arête' (IV), the 1933 Comici (VI), and the 1958 'Direct' of Dieter Hasse, Lothar Brandler, Jörg Lehne and Sigi Löw, at first severely criticised but eventually accepted. That 'Direct' is mainly the ascent of a wall, as dictated by the structure of that huge, completely vertical face. The sketch emphasises how little reliance on crack- or chimney-climbing there is on the upper half. Down below, the rule is almost entirely that of a piton-climb only made possible by the very last technical refinements.

None the less, there are sections on which free-climbing still holds the trump-card. The line taken is more logical than that of the 'Even more Direct' route between the Hasse-Brandler and the Comici, that 'Direttissima' climbed by the Saxons during the course of sixteen winter days. The famous, often terrifying overhangs,

beetling far out from the face (like something filched from a book of fairy-tales), were deftly mastered. All the necessary pitons are lodged there, and A3 tells the rest of the story. Broken pitons had to be replaced by new ones. The pioneers hammered in 180, plus 18 bolts, all of which they left on the face. Most of today's parties do the climb without a bivouac. Naturally, the highest degree of skill, courage, care and physical condition are demanded. Its pioneers brought to a conclusion the logical development which Hans Hintermeier and Riccardo Cassin had introduced on the Cima Ovest. The horrid smoke the Press made about this achievement has long since dissipated. Those who know best say that a man who gets over the first pitch in good shape is qualified for everything that follows. There is an escape-route, but only right at the top, along the great circular terrace.

Valley Resorts Sesto, 1316 m (bus from Innichen). Lake Misurina, 1755 m (bus from Carbonin and Cortina d'Ampezzo).
Bases Locatelli Hut, 2405 m, serviced, CAI, bus to Val di Fiscalina, then 2½ hours up on foot; or, Lavaredo Hut, 2344 m, private, serviced, below the Forcella Lavaredo, road to the Hut, bus, tent-sites.
Starting Point At 2450 m at the foot of the North Face, reached by path from the Forcella Lavaredo. The start is in the left-hand, yellow zone of the face, about 100 m to the left of the substructure of the Comici Route, near the broken-off shield with two steps in it. Time for the climb varies greatly, from 12 to 16 hours.
Descent Down the southern flank by the normal route (II) to the rubble couloir at the foot of the Cima Piccola. Plenty of cairns, 2 hours from the summit.
First Ascent D. Hasse, L. Brandler, J. Lehne and S. Löw, 6/11.7.1958.
Guides/Maps CAI *Dolomiti Orientale*, vol. I, parts 1/2 (Italian). RR *Dolomiten*, vol. IIa (GF series, German). AC *Dolomites East*. TCI 50M. Sh. D54 – Cortina d'Ampezzo. IGM 50M. Sh. 029 Cortina d'Ampezzo (divisible into six 25M. sh.). IGM 50M. Sh. 016 – Dobbiaco (divisible into six 25M. sh.).
Plate The North Faces of the Cima Piccola, Grande and Ovest.

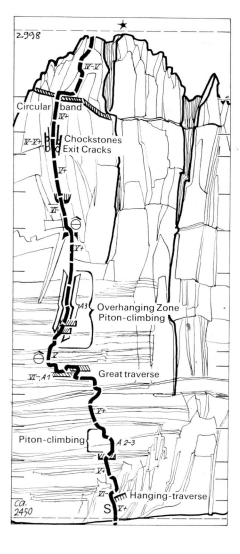

ITALY 86

Tre Cime di Lavaredo Group (Sesto)
Cima Piccola 2856 m
South Arête (Spigolo Giallo: The Yellow Edge)
Grade VI−, A1 (1 rope length)/350 m

The photograph and sketch will give an experienced climber all the information he needs about this famous South Arête. It is understandable that superlatives are needed at the very sight of it, not only those wrung from devoted mountain-hikers. So it is natural that the Alpine World was stunned when Emilio Comici, Mary Varale and Renato Zanutti first climbed this impossibly vertical column of rock as long ago as 1933. Its continual exposure on an apparently vertical sweep from bottom to top aroused a furore and ensured that climbers would always want to tackle it – even if the pundits all know now that only the first three rope lengths in the slightly brittle dièdre to the left of the bottom edge of the Arête, attract a VI−grading. The Arête has long been nailed, but that grading has never been reduced. Not even for the V, A1 key-pitch high up near the Arête before you actually return to its crest; yet that pitch is nowadays simply climbed by the use of étriers and a positive arsenal of pitons. Such excess spoils all the fun! . . . The exposure of this 'Yellow Edge' stamped it as the phenomen it is, even now that the 'Direct' on the Cima Grande has opened up a new dimension of exposure under and on its giant overhangs. Many of today's climbers grumble at the broken but at the same time incredibly exposed area after the first rope lengths, where the route leaves the actual Arête to its left. Here it is possible to go astray at several points and for once one has almost to rejoice that there are so many pitons to act as signposts. There are climbers who regard the Arête as a climb to occupy half of a 'by-day'; there have even been Alpine Supermen who have climbed it in 1½ hours or less, by the stop-watch. Even that has not downgraded the ratings.

It may be useful to quote the judgement of a few of today's climbers, some cool, some a little superior, but all confirming a point of view. Hermann Froidl contributes: 'The climber shudders when he has to compete at the start with a dozen other parties for the first few metres – for the start lies just above the motor-road. Besides scorching sun,

the Arête offers delectable free-climbing on finely-splintered rock with plenty of fresh air below your feet.' Manfred Sturm says: 'For its fame it has to thank its marvellous shape and Comici's name. The climbing is fine, but where has the Arête got to? For the expert this is a pleasant afternoon's stroll.' Harry Rost writes: 'The middle section is totally disappointing. The route runs mostly at the side of the Arête, the only really fine part is the section on the Arête itself, high up – and, of course, all the time, the view down into the valley.' Dietmar Ohngemach's opinion: 'An attraction you simply cannot resist.' Finally, Reinhold Messner: 'Its reputation is greater than its attractiveness – the show-piece of the perpendicular. A "Six"? Yes, twenty years ago, but today there are too many pitons.'

Valley Resorts Sesto, 1316 m (bus from Innichen). Lake Misurina, 1755 m (bus from Carbonin and Cortina d'Ampezzo).
Bases Locatelli Hut, 2405 m, CAI, serviced; bus to Val di Fiscalina, then 2½ hours up. Lavaredo Hut, 2344 m, private serviced, below the Forcella Lavaredo, road to the Hut, tent-sites.
Starting Point At about 2500 m at the foot of the Arête (15 minutes from Rifugio Lavaredo). Time for the climb, for a two-man rope, 4–6 hours.
Descent Down the normal Cima Piccola Route by the South-West Face (III) in the gorge between the Cima Grande and Cima Piccola (abseil pitons); 1½ hours from the summit.
First Ascent E. Comici, M. Varale and R. Zanutti, 8.9.1933.
Guides/Maps CAI *Dolomiti Orientale*, vol. I, parts 1/2 (Italian). RR *Dolomiten*, vol. IIa (GF series, German). AC *Dolomites East*. TCI 50M. Sh. D54 – Cortina d'Ampezzo. IGM 50M Sh. 029 – Cortina d'Ampezzo (divisible into six 25M. sh.) IGM 50M. Sh. 016 – Dobbiaco (divisible into six 25M. sh.)
Plate The Cima Piccola from the south with the 'Yellow Edge' clearly picked out by the sunlight.

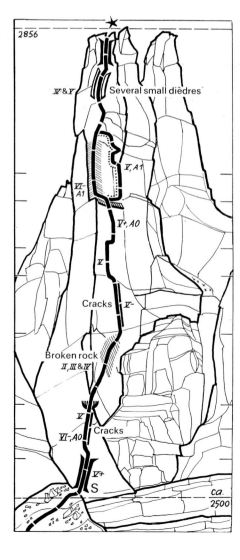

171

Dolomites/North Croda dei Toni Group (Sesto)
Cima Una 2696 m
North Face/Right-hand Super-Direct
Grade VI–, A0/800 m

All around the Locatelli Hut, the Tre Cime di Lavaredo steal the show. Correctly interpreted, this can quickly lead to the conclusion that there are quieter places elsewhere. For example, near the Cima Una, soaring from the heavenly Val di Fiscalina, which runs to the south from Sesto. You can see the Cima Una from the little tarn just below the Locatelli Hut. If you go nearer to it through the Val Sasso Vecchio, it reveals itself as a monster in a cold, stark Dolomite wall. The structure of these 800-metre-high massive walls, fashioned of pitch-black and sulphur-yellow slabs, on which the sun never shines, with shattered runnels, chimneys, cracks and gullies often filled with snow-debris, is fascinating simply for its size and inhospitable nakedness. It is a coarse great lump, which attracts the rock-climber more, the more closely he examines its structure. During forty years, eight interesting routes have been opened up on the Cima Una from Grade III to VI.

The one we have chosen is the 'Weg der Jugend' (Via della Giovinezza), straight up the North Arête to the summit. This pillar route was first climbed in 1928 by that competent and likeable pair Hans Steger and Paula Wiesinger. The details are like the mountain itself: even the start is hard to find, so you have to study the appropriate passages in the guidebooks carefully. And there is a good description in *Bergkamerad*, 15, 1960. You also need a good nose for route-finding. It is a fact that most of the bivouacs here have resulted from losing the way. The route, like the scenery, suffers from a serious and depressing drawback already mentioned: not a ray of sunshine dries the rock or comforts you while not actually climbing. Up you go, utterly lonely, looking for the route, finding a footmark or a piton, waiting till the leader reaches the next stance and looking down from your shadowed wall far, far down into the sunny Val di Fiscalina, where you can recognise hikers as tiny dots not guessing that someone up there is athirst for the sun or a drink of water from a mountain-stream. Surely charming Parisian ladies sometimes wander through

that Val di Fiscalina? . . . up on his stance a man has leisure, while he waits, to picture such things . . . till 'Up you come!' or an unscheduled shower of rain interrupts his dream.

It is always bad to lose your way, but on the Cima Una if the weather breaks it can lead to hard and dangerous consequences. In our picture the actual start from the western cone in the cwm is screened by the slabs masking it on the right; but you can recognise the edge of the ramp running up to the left with the sun on its top. The entry-gully runs up just behind that edge to the little crest in the sunlight and then on to the rubble-pitch. Up to the bivouac-site, marked on the sketch below the difficult crack, all four routes on the North Face are identical.

Valley Resorts Sesto, 1316 m (bus from Innichen) on the Monte Croce Pass motor-road.
Bases Hotel Dolomiten (Val di Fiscalina), 1540 m; bus from Innichen, camping sites. Locatelli Hut, 2405 m, CAI, serviced; 2½ hours from Val di Fiscalina.
Starting Point At 1900 m, to the right of the summit fall-line. Start from the most westerly of several debris-cones. Short cuts to the start 1 hour from the Locatelli Hut. Time for the climb of rope of two, 7–9 hours.
Descent Down the normal South Face Route (II) into the Una cwm (1 hour) then along the path to the Zsigmondy–Comici Hut; traverse above the cliff to the Alta Val di Fiscalina (3 hours from summit).
First Ascent H. Steger and P. Wiesinger, 10/11.9.1928.
Guides/Maps CAI *Dolomiti Orientale*, vol. I, parts 1/2 (Italian). RR *Dolomiten*, vol. IIa (GF series, German). AC *Dolomites East*. TCI 50M. Sh. D54 – Cortina d'Ampezzo. IGM 50M. Sh. 016 – Dobbiaco (divisible into six 25M. sh.). IGM 50M. Sh. 017 – M. Cavallino (divisible into six 25M. sh.).
Plate The North Face of the Cima Una in the North Croda dei Toni group. Left top, the main summit, with our pillar-arête and its 'Weg der Jugend Route' in its fall-line.

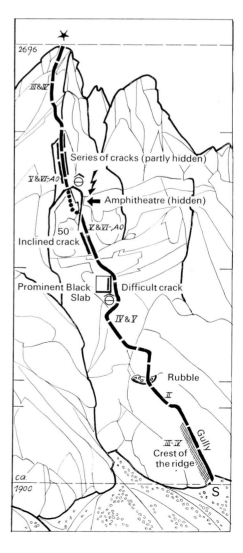

ITALY 88 Croda dei Toni 3094 m
North Arête
Grade VI−, A1/650 m

This is a big, serious climb of definitely high-Alpine proportions, with a great deal of free-climbing. The very early first-ascent in 1932 need not put anyone off any more than the relatively low rating of the difficulties on the enormous ramp of slabs leading to the 250-metre high crack-chimney, where the first Grade V climbing is met. It then gets still harder on the Arête itself up to the finish, where the angle is virtually perpendicular. Reinhold Messner gives his cool judgment: 'The rock is sound throughout though the start of the great chimney is sometimes brittle. This North Arête offers free-climbing in the classic style, but still ranks among the most magnificent rock-climbs in the Sesto Dolomites. It has till now been overshadowed by the faces of the Tre Cime because there are few pitons on it. Within a century they will be mining iron on those faces. I prophesy that the North Arête of the Croda dei Toni will then come into its own.'

In September 1931 two young Sesto guides, the Schranzhofers, had made an attempt, but had retreated after a bivouac. On 30 July 1932 they met with success, mastering the vertical pillar at the top. Four hours later Hans Steger and Paula Wiesinger also reached the summit – as 'also climbed'? There is yet another 'Direct' route on this North Face which combines parts of the Del Vecchio, the Happacher and, in its final quarter, the Schranzhofer routes. According to Messner it is straighter and even finer, but it is hardly ever climbed. It is easy to trace our Schranzhofer Route up to the 250-metre chimney by studying our sketch and photograph together. After that there are only a few places where you can take a breather. The route just follows the seemingly vertical pillar, well-defined by light and shade, high up in the plumb-line of the nearby summit. It then veers slightly to the right. An 'over-thirty Extremist', and married, would do well to do the classic Grade IV route on the Croda dei Toni – first climbed on 24 August 1899 by Pietro Dimai and Giovanni Siorpaes (both sons of famous fathers and fathers of famous sons): a great, almost un-

known, definitely high-Alpine climb on which one can dispose of 750 metres in seven hours (cf. route 66 in my book *Im Schweren Fels*). This pleasure-climb runs parallel to the left of our 'extreme' route and makes use of the huge gully in the North-East Face; this leads above the mountain's left-hand upper shoulder to the easy rock of the summit – and to an altitude of 3094 metres!

Valley Resorts Sesto, 1316 m, on the motor-road to the Monte Croce Pass.
Bases Zsigmondy-Comici Hut, 2224 m, CAI, serviced, at the head of the Fiscalina valley; 2½ hours from the Val di Fiscalina car-park.
Starting Point At 2450 m, close to an ice-cave at the foot of the face, about 100 m to the right of the great dark gully between the smallest Croda dei Toni and the base of the North-West Face. The same start as for the Dimai North-East Face climb. 1 hour from the hut. Time for the climb, for a two-man rope, 7–10 hours.
Descent Down the confusing normal route on the southern and south-western flanks (rock-path, II) danger from falling stones. This takes in part of the circular summit-terrace and a traverse over the narrow Forcella della Croda dei Toni, 2524 m saddle to the descending face. At least 2½ hours.
First Ascent A. and F. Schranzhofer, 30.7.1932.
Guides/Maps CAI *Dolomiti Orientale*, vol. I, parts 1/2 (Italian). RR *Dolomiten*, vol. IIa (GF series, German). AC *Dolomites East*. TCI 50M. Sh. D54 – Cortina d'Ampezzo. IGM 50M. Sh. 016 – Dobbiaco (divisible into six 25M. sh.). IGM 50M. Sh. 017 – M. Cavallino (divisible into six 25M. sh.).
Plate The Croda dei Toni, the classic Dolomite screen above the Val di Fiscalina. To the left, the Piccola Cima. Extreme top right, the western subsidiary summit of the main Croda dei Toni.

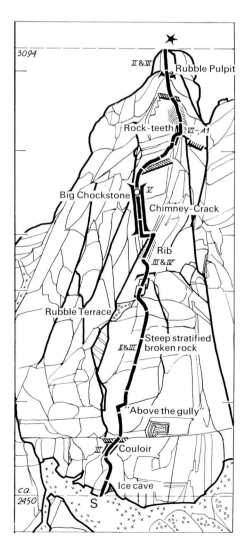

Dolomites of Lienz
Laserzwand 2614 m
North Face Direct
Grade V+, A0/600 m

Geographically and also as regards status and fame, the Dolomites of Lienz in the Eastern Tirol are far behind the classic Dolomite walls between the Tre Cime, the Catináccio and the Brenta Group in popularity. But anyone who looks carefully at our photograph and is also told that this vertical limestone of the Laserzwand Face has four remarkable routes running up it, can confidently immerse himself in the problem of our North Face Direct Climb, pioneered by Gustl Thaler and Gerald Leinweber. Here, above the steep, rubble-covered cwm of the Auerlinggraben between the North Ridge proper and the North-East Pillar, an impressive clean-cut and daunting wall unfolds its steep, wide screen: great abrupt bulges, black overhangs with water pouring over them, gaping gullies, chimneys – all these are here . . . Not till half way up it do we come to a massive flight of slabs, through which systems of cracks and chimneys force a way up to the exit-notch. Those who have done the climb assure us that not a metre of it is easy, and there is plenty of free-climbing.

Franz Unterasinger of Lienz, who has done it several times, gives full details: 'The start is near the small snow-patch or, in late summer, at the left-hand corner of the slabby hollow. Here, from the inmost corner, a slightly brittle crack runs up to the rubble-covered pedestal. Then follows the big 25-metre-high vertical gully with its obstacles. Later, at the start of the smooth 27-metre traverse out to the left – the key-pitch – there is a ring piton at about head-height. This is the one to use, not the later misleading ones (and there are plenty!). On reaching the broad terrace above, the route immediately goes to the left up the cracks and chimneys – very difficult at first, then becoming a little easier – of the wall, which is often wet. At the big chock-stone you have come up $5\frac{1}{2}$ rope lengths from the rubble-terrace and can take a breather. Then it is easier work to the snow-patch on the ramp and from there through the exit-cracks onto the notch in the summit-plateau which is the outlet from all these North Face routes.' A study of the photograph and

sketch shows that the start from the snow-field is directly below the vertical centre of the picture, above which stretches a second rather longer snow-field. On the summit of the Laserzwand, to which there is an AV-path from the nearby Karlsbader Hut, but is still not overcrowded, one can sit as if on some prehistoric bench of stone, high above the Drave Valley, with Lienz and its villages dotted about like toys, and can, at leisure, number the summits of the Hohe Tauern, whose broad snow-shields tower grandly beyond. The Hochgall and the Schober Group are also visible, but the great centrepiece in all its moving grandeur, filling the space between the green world of valleys and the serene empyrean dominates the scene. This Laserzwand in the Dolomites of Lienz, which are comparatively rarely visited, was once considered the end of the world – now it is easily reached by way of the splendid Felbertauern road-tunnel.

Valley Resorts Lienz, 678 m, in the Drave Valley in Eastern Tirol (reached from the north through the Felbertauern road-tunnel).
Bases Dolomiten Hut, 1620 m, private, serviced; bus from Lienz. Karlsbader Hut, 2260 m, DAV, at the Laserz Lake; 6 hours from Lienz or $4\frac{1}{2}$ hours from Tristacher Lake (bus), or $2\frac{1}{4}$ hours from the Dolomiten Hut (bus to the hut).
Starting Point At about 2000 m near a small snow-field below the huge (right-hand) dièdre in the summit's fall-line. Reached from the Dolomiten Hut in $1\frac{1}{2}$ hours over the Auerlingköpfl or from the Karlsbader Hut in $1\frac{1}{2}$ hours over the Hohe Törl. Time for the climb, for a rope of two, normally $5-6\frac{1}{2}$ hours.
Descent In $\frac{3}{4}$ hour by the easy AV-path to the Karlsbader Hut.
First Ascent G. Thaler and G. Leinweber, 5.8.1939.
Guides/Maps RR *Lienzer Dolomiten* (AV series, German). AV 25M. Sh. 56 Lienzer Dolomiten.
Plate The compact North Face of the Laserzwand in the Dolomites of Lienz, above the Auerlinggraben. Our route uses the shorter right-hand of the two huge dièdres falling from straight below the summit. At the top left-hand edge of the picture, the Rote Turm (Red Tower).

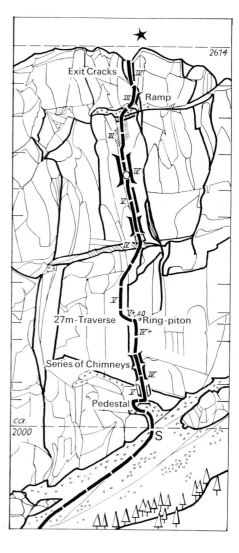

Western Julian Alps

ITALY 90 **Torre delle Madri dei Camosci 2503 m**

North Ridge (Spigolo Deye-Peters)

Grade V+, A0/700 m

In the Julian Alps, more blessed with floral beauties because of their southern location, the Jôf Fuart Group, adjoining the Montasio to its south-east, is of great importance. The mighty northern precipice of the entire range, which includes the Jôf Fuart, Cima di Riofreddo, Cima Piccola (Innominata), Torre delle Madri dei Camosci and Alta Madre dei Camosci, consists from base to summit of Dolomite rock and is similar to many another Dolomite group in its savage scenic contrasts between dramatically fractured rock structures and gentle valleys stretching in their lush green below. A joint study of the sketch and the picture shows a quite simple formula for the ascent of the North Ridge – an easy right-hand traverse to the sudden obstacles barring the way to the huge dièdre, whose lower end breaks off abruptly. The top end of the chimney in the dièdre becomes a kind of gully, after which follows the climb up to the 'Cengia degli Dei' ('Terrace of the Gods'), which cuts diagonally not only across our peak but the North-East Gully of the Jôf Fuart as well. Here the key-pitches begin, following which the less steep section of the Ridge leads to the exit-area below the summit.

For an appreciation of the difficulties on the decisive pitch before reaching the Terrace of the Gods one has to know the details of the first ascent by Adolf Deye and Rudolf Peters. When this pair had climbed the 200-metre dièdre on 16 August 1929, they hammered their first piton, but soon climbed down to the right into the North-East Gully of the Jôf Fuart, slept at the Pellarini Hut and returned next day to the attack. Using a rope-ladder, pitons, stirrups and a rope-ring, they spent four hours getting up the 10-metre overhang and found only a scanty stance. Then Peters had to defeat the last part of this key-pitch by an extremely exposed piece of free-climbing, which makes good reading in Deye's *Gefährten am Seil*, Leipzig, 1934. A tough, if less ambitious, piece of climbing, but still chancy and demanding high technical skill, is the entry into the 200-metre dièdre at the bottom of the climb, where

it breaks off into a black roof. Here in the first crack, two overhangs (V) have to be mastered in order to reach an exiguous stance 7 metres below the start of the chimney.

No doubt the present generation of 'Extremists', equipped with the most refined technical aids, would have overcome the key difficulties described above in cold blood and then equally cold-bloodedly downgraded them in all probability. That makes no difference. Much remains relative, and where free-climbing is possible or imperative Deye and Peters win back their ancient laurels. The two overhangs in the first crack below the breach under the dièdre are inside the 'Black Wall' seen in the sketch and the photograph – and represent a highly testing start.

Valley Resort Valbruna (Wolfsbach), 807 m, at the entrance to Seisera, on the north side of the Montasio–Jôf Fuart Range (railway line Tarvisio–Pontebba).
Base Luigi Pellarini Hut, 1500 m, in the Carnizza di Camporosso, below the north-east flank of the Jôf Fuart, simple service in summer, CAI, 3 hours from Valbruna. On the descent: Guido Corsi Hut, 1874 m (south flank of the Jôf Fuart), CAI, serviced. Thence over the Forcella di Riofreddo, 2180 m (Giorgio Cavalieri Path) back to the Pellarini Hut.
Starting Point At 1700 m from the left-hand snow-couloir to the right on to the band running up to the big dièdre. 1½ hours from the Hut. Total time required, 7 hours.
Descent Easily down southwards to the saddle before the Alta Madre dei Camosci and then again to the south down the gully to the Corsi Hut, 2 hours from the summit.
First Ascent A. Deye and R. Peters, 16/17.8.1929.
Guides/Maps CAI *Alpi Giulie* (Italian). WCP *Julian Alps* (note). IGM 50M. Sh. 033 – Tarvisio (divisible into six 25M. sh.). PZS 50M. Juiijske Alpe West.
Plate Shows the mighty North Face of the Torre delle Madri dei Camosci with its huge dièdre, overhung at the top. Far left, the North-East Arête of the Cima di Riofreddo. High up and close to it, the Innominata.

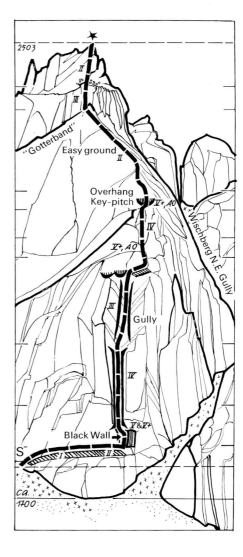

Eastern Julian Alps
Špik 2472 m
North Face Direct
Grade V+, A0/900 m

Seen from the Sava Dolinka Valley, Špik's northern wall forms a huge limestone pyramid rising 1700 metres above our viewpoint and fully 900 above the start on the 'Green Top'. That wall is dauntingly steep: with Triglav it lords it over the Julian Alps. It is seldom climbed, which cannot be blamed on Špik's being – at least as far as its North face is concerned – a 'Lady's Peak', for, way back in 1925, an outstanding woman-climber, Anna Escher, attempted it with the great Angelo Dibona – that same Dibona whose enthusiasm sent him ranging throughout the Alps from the Laliderer wall to the Cima Grande, from the Coste Rouge Ridge of the Ailefroide to this very Špik. But Dibona and his comely partner had no pitons and were forced off onto the North-West Face. The second lady was the young Alpinist Mira Marko Debelakova, who climbed alone to the 'Green Top' to reconnoitre. She then led a party up this extremely difficult face in a snowstorm, and with a grim bivouac, in thirty-one hours; the third man on the rope was taken ill halfway up and had to climb down alone. That was in 1926. Five years later, the third woman, Pavla Jesih, arrived and with Jože Lipovec found a new route up the North Face, the 'Skalaška Pillar' (V, one or two V+ pitches). Pavla opened up several other important routes in the Julians where she was on her home ground; but Miss Pibernik, who became famous after her marriage as Mrs Debelakova, died tragically in 1948 after a long and painful illness.

The Špik North Face Direct is a fine climb for anyone with a good route-finding sense and in the pink of condition. The 900 metres from the 'Green Top' to the summit can normally be climbed in eight to nine hours. There is the occasional menace of falling stones on the lower half. Up to the 'Dibona Ledge', striking up diagonally to the right, it is comparatively easy, but the route then becomes – as the guidebook indicates – a considerable proposition. At that point it aims full at the centre of the face where dièdres, cracks, traverses, small cliffs with equally small holds, and

chimneys bring it close to the sharp-edged Central Pillar, so well shown in the photograph, up which the 'Skalaška Route' actually runs. We now climb roughly parallel with that route, to the right till, above the pillar, we reach the prominent curving 80-metre dièdre (IV) and find our way by chimneys, cracks and traverses to the notch in the upper part of the North-West Ridge. The limestone of the Julians is mostly solid and lacking in fissures, but often splintery and brittle, so that it is only possible to fix precarious pitons.

Valley Resorts Gozd-Martuljek (Wald), 743 m, in the Sava Dolinka Valley (station). Descent to Kranjska Gora (Kronau), 810 m, in the Sava Dolinka Valley.
Bases The Valley resort or Koča v. Martuljeku (Martuljek Hut), 930 m, Slovene Climbers' Association, unserviced, door locked, ½ hour from Valley resort.
Starting Point At about 1500 m below the 'Green Top', reached from the hut up a hunters' path up the 'Pod Srcem' screes into the high cwm below the North Face. From the snowfield there, up a slabby couloir, to the 'Green Top'; about 2½ hours. Time for the climb for a rope of two, 8–9 hours.
Descent Easy debris track (boulders, I), then through the Kacji graben to Krnica, deep in the valley to the west and on to the Pišnica Bridge on the Vršič Pass road (marked, 4 hours from the summit).
First Ascent Mira Marko Debelakova and Stane Tominšek, 5/6.9.1926.
Guides/Maps CAI *Alpi Giulie* (Italian). WCP *Julian Alps* (note). IGM 50M. Sh. 034 – M. Forno (divisible into six 25M. sh.). PZS 50M. Julijske Alpe East.
Plate The mighty North Face of Špik above the Sava Dolinka Valley. Our route runs from the 'Green Top' (bottom right) to the Dibona Terrace, slanting diagonally up to the right and then to the right of the main dièdre, sharply defined by sun and shadow, in the fall-line from the summit ridge. In this main dièdre, i.e. parallel to the left of our route, is the course of the 'Skalaška-Pillar Route' pioneered in 1926 under the leadership of Pavla Jesih (V, some rope lengths V+).

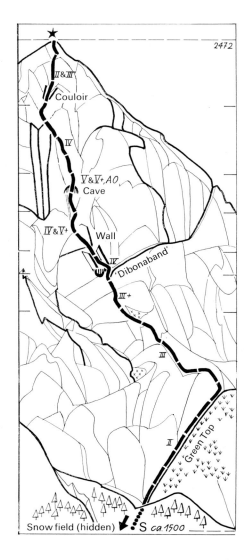

Dachstein Range
Torstein 2947 m
South Dièdre (Schinko-Bischofberger)
Grade VI−, A0/850 m

The Torstein, only the second highest but mightiest rock-structure in the Dachstein Massif, presents a face nearly 1000 metres high between the divided Windlücke in five pillar-like arêtes and East Ridge which leads up to the Lower Windlücke in five pillar-like arêtes and three marked indentations in the wall. High up in the left of our photograph we see the upper part of the Windlegergrat, above which to its right, is the South-East Ridge falling to the 'Torsteinwächte'. Below the summit can be seen three pillars and, a little to their right, three re-entrants – the west, central and east South Face cwms. Beware! there are falling stones here. The right-hand pillar, falling almost sheer from the summit and then overhanging in its sweep down to the Rauchkar, is the main pillar of the South Face and is also the site of our 'extreme' climb – the South Dièdre Route of Graz climbers Raimund Schinko and Adolf Bischofberger. It dates from 1934 and was a landmark in the great watershed between the permissible and the extreme. The use of pitons, lavish for those days, and the danger, it was said, downgraded it to a purely sporting climb.

Now everything looks different. Manfred Sturm says of it: 'A clearly defined dièdre, very homogeneous, which unintentionally spurs one on to an ever-quickening pace. Plenty of free-climbing, few pitons, yet every metre a joy, with no unpleasant surprises. Its only disadvantage: the last few hundred metres are merely broken rock before a very long descent.' Jürgen Winkler's photograph when studied with the sketch, shows us, with the help of strong sunlight, the whole of the route quite clearly. Down below, and in deep shadow, you can see the very steep ramp, then, after the cliff, the marked bivouac-site, the gigantic dièdre with its overhangs and the key-pitch at the end of the huge slab. The almost vertical pillar ends in slabs at the second bivouac-site, just where the relatively easy scree-arête starts up towards the summit, still some distance away. There you can do penance for many sins when the sun is strong. Should the weather break, one

should in no circumstances take refuge to right and left in the South Face re-entrant. The only way down from the summit leads to the Lower Windlücke and its 'Torsteinwächte' ('cornice') and then across the Gosau Glacier to the Adamek Hut – a very long descent not without its risks after so long a climb. There is another super-climb on this face, besides our 'parade' up the Torstein Gully – the South Face Direct (VI, A3) – 800 metres, 80 pitons, 2 wedges and eighteen to twenty hours – first made by Hoi and Stelzig, whose 'ideal line' has won much acclaim. We can follow part of this fabulously difficult route (in terms of yesterday), which comes out into the eastern of the South Face re-entrants, on the extreme right of our picture. The immediate future will pronounce a final judgment on that route.

Valley Resorts Ramsau Village, 1136 m (bus from Schladming in the Ennstal). Or Filzmoos, 1057 m.
Bases The Bachlalm Inn, 1496 m, serviced, to the south of the Windlegerkar–Rauchboden, 2½ hours from Ramsau, 2 from Filzmoos, motorable from Ramsau to below the hut The Dachstein South Face Hut, 1871 m, on the Schönbühel, private, serviced, 2½ hours from Ramsau. The Adamek Hut, 2196 m, ÖAV, below the Great Gosau Glacier, for use on the descent from the Torstein, otherwise you have a long way back to the Bachlalm (over the Windlegerscharte, 2½–3 hours).
Starting Point At about 2100 m, above the Rauchkarboden, 1½ hours from Bachlalm. Time for the climb, for a two-man rope, at least 6–9 hours.
Descent By the South-East Ridge (II) to the Lower Windlucke, necessitating the crossing of the 'Torsteinwächte'; 1 hour from the summit. Then down the glacier to the Adamek Hut, another 1½ hours, partly icy, crampons advisable for the final slope.
First Ascent R. Schinko and A. Bischofberger, 24/25.6.1934.
Guides/Maps RR *Dachsteingebirge* (AV series, German). AV 25M. Sh. 14 – Dachstein.
Plate The South Face of the Torstein, 2947 m, the most massive wall in the Dachstein Range. To the right in shadow, the South Pillar, on which the sun marks our great dièdre very clearly. To the left below the dièdre the very steep ramp up which the route starts. Above, on the right, the South Face's eastern cwm.

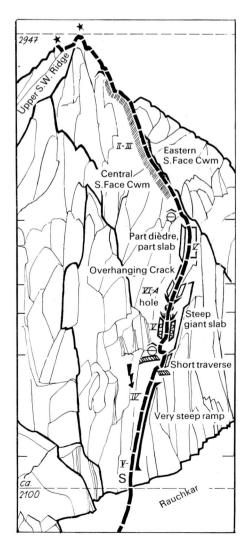

Dachstein Range

AUSTRIA 93 Südliches Dirndl 2829 m

South Arête (Maix Arête)

Grade V+, A0/650 m

The South Walls of the Dachstein, from the Hochkesselkopf and Torstein over the Mitterspitz and Hoher Dachstein to the Dirndls and the Koppenkarstein are the happy hunting-ground of the Viennese climbing élite. Except for a few gullies the Dachstein limestone is firm, rich in holds and comfortably structured: on the Hoher Dachstein itself closely and richly so, in picture-book fashion; on the Koppenkarstein split into a row of solid pillars; on the Hohes Dirndl broken up by diagonal ramps, but plunging to the Dirndlschlucht in walls of vertical slabs set on end. Our South Face of the Southern Dirndl, first climbed in 1929 by Kurt Maix and W. Höfler, deserves to be respected as the pattern of a 'classic' free-climbing route, not to be exposed to the ups and downs of freakish reassessments. The very splendid free-climbing on this imaginatively direct route is sufficient justification, besides which the belaying stances are safe and, in spite of the Arête's 650 metres, there is little danger from falling stones. Only breaks in the weather are to be feared, for they are especially liable to arrive on the southern front of the Dachstein like bombshells and have often led to tragedies, as the comprehensive literature records. Excessively dangerous as is the Dirndl Gully, which comes up below it, our Arête is relatively free from danger. It was six years before it was climbed a second time by climbers from Linz, but nowadays the 'Maix' is a favourite with 'extreme' climbers everywhere.

A study of the sketch and photograph together reveals that only the 100-metre series of cracks between the 40-metre traverse and that into the series of chimneys above (also 100 metres) can be rated as especially difficult. The two key-pitches in the narrow crack above the first (slightly grassy) cliff and at the truncated slab are certainly still worth their V+ rating. The traverse to the sequence of chimneys from a little pulpit can be effected diagonally to the right along a ledge with an uncomfortable breach in it (again V+). Usually, however, the climb from the pulpit to the start of the chimney is made by travers-

ing to the right without using the ledge, which is an easier and more pleasant way. The ledge above the last step in the chimney leads back to the Arête itself, above its unclimbable cliffs. The rest is broken rock till, on the steeper summit structure, there is a 60-metre exit-chimney (IV), then a short left-hand traverse to the summit-gully's splendid rock. Interesting points in the photograph are: high-up on the left, the sunlit diagonal (going up from left to right) of the classic Pfannl-Maischberger Route, and, to the right of our Maix Arête, the deep South Gully, menaced by stones. In the foreground stands the Dachstein South Face Hut, from which we started out.

Valley Resorts Ramsau Village, 1136 m (bus from Schladming in the Ennstal).
Bases Dachstein South Face Hut, 1871 m, private, serviced, 2½ hours from Ramsau (car toll-road to the Türlwand Hut, 1695 m, then only ¾ hour). Austria Hut, 1630 m, on the Brandriedl, ÖAV, serviced.
Starting Point At 2180 m at the bottom end of the Dirndlschlucht (gully), above the steep Hundsriese (frequently covered by hard snow). 1½ hours from the Hut. Total climbing time from the starting point, 5–6 hours.
Descent Ordinary way, on the northern flank of the West Ridge (II+) easy climbing, partly over snow, ½ hour to the Dachsteinwarte, thence to the Hünerscharte, 2602 m, 45 min, uncrevassed and mostly tracked. Then protected rock path (II+) into the Schwadringkar and to the Hut (1½ hours from the Hünerscharte). Warning: the Northern descent to the Simony Hut across the Hallstätter Glacier is usually only possible with crampons.
First Ascent K. Maix and W. Höfler, 9.9.1929.
Guides/Maps RR *Dachsteingebirge* (AV series, German). AV 25M. Sh. 14 – Dachstein.
Plate Southern aspect of the southern precipices of the Hoher Dirndl above the Hundsriese. Right centre, the deep Dirndlschlucht, to its left in the fall-line from the Southern Dirndl's summit, the South (Maix) Arête with its cliffy start below the snow-covered lower rock-ramp at the bottom of the South Gully.

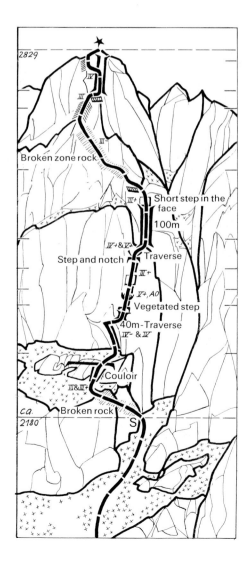

AUSTRIA 94

Grosser Koppenkarstein 2865 m

South-East Pillar Direct

Grade VI−, A1/400 m

The Grosser Koppenkarstein stands at the extreme south-east of the huge Dachstein plateau, with its three glacier shields. It marks the end of the long southern chain of the Dachstein complex, which starts at the Hochkesselkopf and the Torstein. Our polished South Pillar, which is only broken by cracks and chimneys in its central section, was captured in two separate eras of the technical development of climbing after the last war: in 1946 two Viennese climbers, Hubert Peterka and Fritz Proksch, climbed the Pillar in a hair-raising exhibition of free-climbing, though they made two concessions to contemporary 'fair-play' in Alpine sport by not starting the climb direct, circumventing the verticality from the left by a roof of sloping slabs – and they avoided the ultra-difficult cracks, with their overhangs, on the upper part of the Pillar by a wide and daring detour involving rope-traverses and a soaking wet dièdre. Higher up, they rejoined the arête and climbed the South-East Pillar in the same way as they had the South-West on the previous day. It was not till June 1963, after the universal sanctioning of all the modern technical aids, that two young climbers, Peter and Heinrich Perner with Klaus Walcher came and climbed the direct start; and again on 21 July Peter Perner and Walcher mastered together the long-neglected 'extreme' problems from the Small Crest (see sketch) to the top of the final difficult crack. In the meantime and again later, they, of course, climbed the Peterka–Proksch Route, but now they completed the route with the perfect line up the wall.

The South-East Pillar is strenuous; its key-pitches are at the bottom in the deep overhanging crack (V+, Ao) and, high up, at the hidden crack (see sketch) and the mastering of its overhanging cliffs (VI−, A1). If you subtract the last 100 metres of easier broken rock from the Pillar's total height, that leaves 300 metres. Of those 300, the central Peterka section, offering much fine free-climbing on magnificent rock, should not be underrated. Our photograph gives a true picture of the Pillar's steepness. The bases of all three pillars rise like the columns of a cathedral from the glacier at the bottom of the southern wall – a magnificent sight. Anyone doing this climb should allow himself the fun of exploring the old detour from the arête of the Pillar out into the vertical face to its left (following route 647 in the Rother guidebook), with its hazardous traverse, the abseil into the right-hand South Face cwm and then the way up sloping ledges back onto the arête. In truth a classic by-pass – or a little bow in deference to 'fair play'?

Valley Resorts Ramsau Village, 1136 m (bus from Schladming in the Ennstal).
Bases Austria Hut, 1630 m, ÖAV at the Brandriedl, serviced, 1½ hours from Ramsau; motorable to Dachsteinwirt, 1400 m, then 1 hour on foot.
Starting Point At about 2465 m close to the left of the Pillar's base. From the Austria Hut along the marked Edelgriess Path to the small Edelgriess Glacier, sharp right to the Edelgriesshöhe, 2505 m, and on to the South-East Pillar, 2½ hours from the hut, over rubble. Time for the climb, for a two-man rope, 3–5 hours; possible for a half-day.
Descent Down the ordinary West Ridge Route over the Koppenkarsteinfenster, 2796 m, and the Little Koppenkarstein to the Austriascharte or down the Lower South Face Terrace (II−) which starts between the Great and Little Koppenkarstein, into the Edelgriess Cwm. 2½ hours summit to hut in favourable conditions.
First Ascent Without the direct start and exit: H. Peterka and F. Proksch 16.9.1946. Direct start and exit: P. Perner, K. Walcher and H. Perner (lower part, 13.6.1963), P. Perner, K. Walcher (upper part, 21.7.1963).
Guides/Maps RR *Dachsteingebirge* (AV series, German). AV 25M. Sh. 14 – Dachstein.
Plate The three central pillars of the Grosser Koppenkarstein, the ice-roof marking the rim of the Schladminger Glacier. To the right, the South-East Pillar, at whose west point our route begins. At the very top left, the approach to the start of the descent by the Lower South Face Terrace.

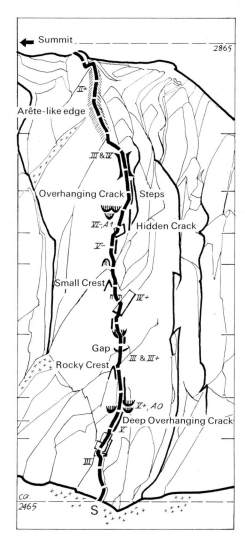

Dachstein Range (Gosau Chain)
Grosse Bischofsmütze 2455 m
North Face Direct
Grade VI−, A0/450 m

This route of Willi End's, the North Face Direct on the 'Great Mitre', the highest peak in the Gosau Chain, has been described as his greatest achievement, and the perpendicular wall-structure, with its water-bands showing up black in our photograph, lends credence to the extraordinary nature of this climb. The rock is sound, the line exciting. The history of the face, too, is extraordinary . . . In 1921 Karl Prusik and Julius Tschippan climbed this wall for the first time without a single piton, and up the prominent pillar leading to the Stuhlloch at that. Today their route is called the North Pillar Wall (still graded IV) to distinguish it from the North Pillar Arête, which Hubert Peterka and Hans Majer descended in 1927 by an abseil during their comprehensive traverse, including two abseils, of all the 'Mitres'. However, for twenty years after that, the North Face was considered unclimbable. Of course, the great 'divide' made itself felt here too. In 1941 the Salzburg climbers Franz Palaoro and Franz Spitzlburger abseiled back into the North Face after climbing up over abseil-pitons left by Ludwig Vörg and a companion during what Vörg described as Eiger-training in the autumn of 1937, and then mastered the great bulge to the left in the middle of the Face. Their further progress was then halted by heavy hail and thunderstorms. A fortnight later the same pair climbed straight up the Face on their own pitons, claiming to have overcome the horizontal overhang as well as the great bulge, continuing by a series of steep cracks to reach the summit-screes from the left. It looked as if the problem had been solved, but those who knew the terrain well had doubts about the claim and nobody succeeded in repeating the climb, nor did Palaoro give a precise route description. Then that likeable young cragsman, Hermann Buhl, repeated the Salzburgers' route and so refuted all the reservations. Ultra-difficult free-climbing was his verdict.

A short time before, two Badeners, Hans Dubowy and Willi End, had tried a traverse to the right out onto the Face, but found no traces of the Salzburgers

and then roped down it. Two days later Dubowy and Hans Bocek climbed straight as a die from the little re-entrant in the face, again looking for traces of the Salzburg climb, but were forced away to the left over onto the North-East Arête . . . The year 1948 brought a definite decision: Willi End and Dubowy made the direct route up the whole of the North Face, but found only a single piton with a rope-ring, left by predecessors. But by which of them? In the decisive dièdre after the little pillar-roof, which goes straight up to the summit, they found no traces of an earlier climb – maybe because the Salzburgers had used a series of cracks close to the 50-metre 'Moss-cushion' Dièdre. Willi End refuses to substantiate this. When the second pair to complete this route of End's, those splendid climbers Bruno Wintersteller and Erich Neubauer, did so on 11 September 1948, they threw doubts on precisely that possibility of the Palaoro climb.

Valley Resorts Filzmoos. 1057 m. Annaberg, 777 m (bus from Golling-Abtenau).
Bases Hofpürgl Hut. 1703 m, ÖAV, serviced; 2½ hours from Filzmoos or 1½ hours from Oberhofalm (end of motor toll-road). Theodor Körner Hut, 1462 m, on the Stuhlalm, ÖAV, serviced; 2 hours from Annaberg (motorable to Pommerbauer, then ¾ hour to the Hut).
Starting Point At about 1950 m in the narrow cwm lying to the left of the arête of the North Pillar which projects markedly directly in the summit fall-line. 2½ hours from the Hofpürgl Hut over the South Foot of the Mitres, down from there on to the Upper Stuhllochscharte, 2296 m, then steeply down over crags and rubble into the cwm. Also reached in 2 hours from the Körner Hut past the mouth of the Stuhlloch and up the big rubble-cwm. Time for the climb, for a two-man rope, 5–6 hours; a climb for a half-day.
Descent Down the South Gully (ordinary route II+), in 1½ hours to the Hofpürgl Hut.
First Ascent W. End and H. Dubowy, 3.8.1948.
Guides/Maps RR *Dachsteingebirge* (AV series, German). AV 25M. Sh. 14 – Dachstein.
Plate The North Face of the Grosse Bischofsmütze, 2455 m. at the south-east end of the Gosau Chain, whose highest summit it is. Our picture is cut off just above the cwm in which the start lies, but still shows the first rope lengths from the start to the first black cave.

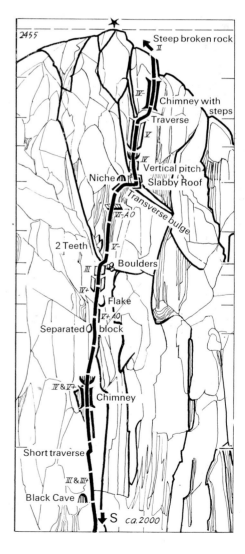

Dachstein Range (Gosau Chain)
Däumling (The Little Thumb) 2322 m
East Arête
Grade V+, A1/400 m

The Däumling ('Little Thumb') – high above the two Gosau Lakes dreaming below – is a misnomer. Regarded as the most difficult summit in the Gosau Chain, whose ordinary route is graded IV and can therefore be mentioned in the same breath as the Winklerturm and the Guglia di Brenta, is at the least a fully grown thumb. Its sharply soaring, smooth column of slabs offers a number of highly interesting routes; pure slab-climbing on the tower itself but on either side of its notch, the Däumlingscharte, delicate and rewarding chimney-work. Naturally, even this favourite Däumling lived through all the periods of the art of climbing, arguments, triumphs and all. The first to stand on its summit were a pair famous in Alpine history: Paul Preuss (who fell to his death on the Northern Manndlkogel hard-by) and Günther von Saar. That was in 1913; they were followed a year later by Adolf Deye, climbing solo. The magnificent South-East Chimneys succumbed in 1923, and the exploration seemed to finish there, for everything else was adjudged unclimbable. All the same, in 1929, Hubert Peterka made five further attempts, without success.

Who was to be the first to master the encircling bulge? In 1932 came those two youngest of the eternally young, Lichtenegger and Macherhammer, and built themselves a piton-ladder to success, but just below the bulge they traversed out onto the narrow northern side of the summit-structure, managing to reach the Deye Chimney – and had to climb down defeated. Success came on the following day. They climbed the Preuss Chimneys on the North Face and arrived on the summit by the South Arête, abseiling from it to the point below the bulge where they had had to turn back the day before. Only then did they succeed in climbing the crack in the bulge (V+, A1) to the summit. The second ascent was made in 1935 by the same pair, but this time finally climbing straight through. And it is now the fashionable route for 'Extremists' in the Gosau Chain! The modern technical expert now climbs, in happy exposure, up the 'Daumenballen' (base of the

thumb), traverses to the little tower, climbs out of its little notch to the right, to the first overhang in the rounded arête (below which there is a not too good piton-stance) . . . and so on and so forth.

Our sketch and photography (to some extent) and best of all the Rother guide-book, route 1809, give information about the character of this climb. Manfred Sturm, who has climbed it several times, writes: Not really an arête, rather a big, round, smooth, well-armoured tower. Delicate slab-climbing, only interrupted by the obstacle of the bulge. A jolly, vertical promenade for good Alpine track-athletes.' This opinion sounds a very youthful, splendidly superior present-day assessment. Equally belittling but a little cooler is the description by a climb-er from Reichenhall: 'A very airy but not too difficult slab-climb, the rock is very sound and firm. All the difficulties are concentrated into two rope lengths.'

Valley Resorts Filzmoos, 1057 m (bus from Eben/Pongau or Radstadt). Gosau, 779m.
Bases Hofpürgl Hut, 1703 m, ÖAV, serviced; 2½ hours from Filzmoos or 1½ hours from Oberhofalm (toll-road from Filzmoos). The Klausstube Inn, 933 m, at the second Gosau Lake (bus from Steeg and Gosau).
Starting Point At about 1870 m in the lower Armkar at the foot of the East Arête, at the base of the projecting Daumenballen (to the left in the picture). Time for the climb, for a rope of two, 3–5 hours.
Descent Down the South Arête (ordinary route, IV) short and steep to the Däumlingscharte between the Däumling and the Niedere Grosswandeck (also an abseil route); then down the South-East Chimneys into the Armkar. (IV and V). Here use of the abseil gully at the Schildüberhang is worth considering, 2–2½ hours.
First Ascent S. Lichtenegger and L. Macherhammer, 10/11.9.1932.
Guides/Maps RR *Dachsteingebirge* (AV series, German). AV 25M. Sh. 14 – Dachstein.
Plate The Däumling, which leans against the Niedere Grosswandeck, seen from the east. The picture shows the craggy 'Daumenballen', the sharp prominent 'little tower' (which the route leaves on its left) and, below the summit-block, the circular bulge which runs transversely round it.

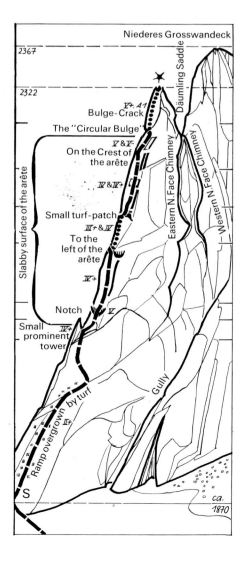

AUSTRIA 97
Rosskuppe 2154 m
North-West Arête
Grade V−, A0/500 m

Nobody should belittle this 'primaeval' Arête of the Rosskuppe, dating from 1925, before climbing it himself. This is an unusually airy and delicate free-climb on firm limestone; it is not for nothing that today it still remains a favourite among Gesäuse 'Extremists'. Until after the First World War Rosskuppe and Dachl were unknown minor features in the great ridge leading to the Hochtor. In 1925 Munich climbers were already familiar with Dülfer's piton-technique and rope-manoeuvres and used them to defeat key-pitches on difficult rock; but the Viennese 'Aces' were only allowed pure free-climbing by those Alpine Popes, Pichl and Jahn. Then the younger men unexpectedly changed horses, made friends with the modern Munich school (which meanwhile discovered the East Face of the Fleischbank) and experimented on this Rosskuppe Arête of ours. Fritz Hinterberger of Vienna and Karl Sixt of Munich started up it and at the key-pitch Sixt executed a rope-traverse in order to reach the vital crack. That was the first Dülfer traverse in Gesäuse rock. The Viennese climbers were stunned and went hay-wire. They even took a girl along on the repeat of the climb. Even so, Viennese parties unversed in the Dülfer technique turned back defeated.

Even the very strong rope of Peterka, Brocak, Majer and Hermann were on the point of giving up on the vertical cliff, where a rope-traverse was essential. The rather pleasing story goes that Hinterberger and Sixt, over on the North Face of the Dachl, shouted across to them: 'Do a Dülfer traverse!' ... But during the same summer Erwin Hein and Karl Schreiner, attempting the fourth ascent, by-passed the questionable 'Dülfer Traverse' by climbing, instead, an unusually difficult groove crack, the 'Hein Riss', which came to the rescue of the old Viennese principle of only free-climbing on rock of even the greatest difficulty. Not a word against the Viennese 'Extremists', however: in 1947 Leo Forstenlechner and Franz Miklas did the Direct Route on the Rosskuppe Arête to show how successful a technique of wooden wedges and rope-slings can be. In doing so they discovered a super-variant for the Arête, though it is seldom climbed. The 'Hein Riss' is the climb's great attraction; no crack deep into the rock, this, but a smooth, blunt-edged groove, demanding the utmost concentration and balance. It is an exhausting pitch, which has to be climbed in one move from the belaying-piton: not till you leave the crack is there a good stance for another belay. For the good 'Extremist' there are no difficulties after that. What follows is 'only' enjoyable free-climbing involving an interesting hanging-traverse and soon after it the edge of the Arête, just where the 'Direct' joins our route.

Valley Resort Gstatterboden, 580 m, in the Ennstal (station).
Bases Haindlkar Hut, 1135 m, ÖAV, serviced, in the Haindlkar. 1¾ hours from Gstatterboden.
Starting Point At about 1620 m, close before the start up the Peternpfad ('Peter's-path') in the top corner of the Eastern Kleines Haindlkar, near a niche by a block, 1½ hours from the Hut. Average time for the climb, including the Hein Crack, for a two-man rope, 4–5 hours.
Descent Down the Peternpfad (I+: no climber's-path, no protection, but old markings) mostly easy climbing, back into the cwm and to the Hut, 2–2½ hours from the Rosskuppe, from which a rock-step (II) and crags lead to the Peternscharte.
First Ascent F. Hinterberger and K. Sixt, 17.8.1925. Variant with the Hein Crack, E. Hein and K. Schreiner, 16.10.1926.
Guides/Maps RR *Gesäusegebirge, Nördl. Kalkalpen* (AV series, German). (Holzhausen) *Gesäusegebirge* (German). FE 100M. Sh. 6 – Ennstaler Alpen.
Plate Looking up from the bottom of the Kleines Haindlkar to the whole North-West Arête of the Rosskuppe (top, just left of the centre). To the left, the indentation of the Peternscharte, top right the summit of the Dachl, smooth as a wall. Between the Dachl and the Rosskuppe Arête, the once-feared 'Todesverschneidung' ('Death Dièdre') climbed by Schinko and Sikorowsky in 1936.

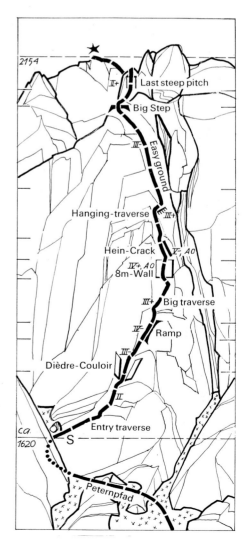

Gesäuse Range
Dachl 2204 m
North Face – Diagonal Crack
Grade VI, A1/350 m

The Diagonal Crack in the North Face of the Dachl ('Little Roof') was not climbed till 1955. It can be seen in our photograph as a very slender crack, for the most part running diagonally up to the left from the top of the subsidiary slabs to the plateau-like top of the Dachl. Unfortunately, Jürgen Winkler's photograph, taken from below, fails to reveal that it crosses not only vertical rock but a number of projecting roofs. There is a less good but more impressive photograph, taken by Werner Pongratz, the first to do the climb in winter, in *Bergkamerad*, vol. XV, 24th year, which shows the true inclination – the actual vertical. Only then can one credit that the difficulties, at least those of the 200 metres of the actual diagonal crack, are greater than those of the Cassin Route on the North Face of the Cima Ovest. That is a considerable claim. Of course, graded at VI, A1, it is a purely technical climb and if you should read anywhere that it is serious free-climbing, that is incorrect.

Before giving some interesting historical information, let us look at the brief route description easily followed on sketch and photograph, given in Werner Pongratz's notes: 'From the "Peternpfad" it takes just two hours to the starting point. One pitch of free-climbing over the upper cone of slabs straight up to a stance. Another pitch up to the left to a small cave, out of which you move to the left and then traverse to the right, above the cave, to pitons; then a few metres straight up followed by a difficult left-hand traverse to a stance. Up the overhang (H) which begins here and up a wide crack to a huge detached slab. The next two pitches pose the climb's chief difficulties. You go up the yellow crack (pitons) to a sling-stance, after which it is a little easier to the end of the crack; then, continually overhung, follow the pitons to a stance under a small roof. This is climbed free, slanting up to the right to an enormous slab overhung by big roofs (good bivouac-site). You keep to the left-hand edge of the roofs, crossing several small overhangs, to a ledge running up to the left, which you follow, then climb some rock steps to the clearly defined exit-cracks, which lead out onto the summit after some rope lengths of great difficulty.'

You see, it is all quite easy, 200 metres of a diagonal crack with piton-problems from start to finish, Grade IV pitches only on the cone, but a fine Grade VI free-climb as well, 350 metres from the actual start, 500 from the slabs at the bottom! This 'extreme' climb has become a great favourite. Even the 'Superlative', pioneered in 1963 by Klaus Hoi and Hugo Stelzig, with 150 pitons, 30 screw-pitons and 13 wooden wedges, between the Diagonal Crack and Death Dièdre – now called the Herman Buhl Memorial Route – does not surpass it. With the ascent of the Diagonal Crack the Dachl's North Face achieved the hall-mark of a super-climb of truly modern proportions. To qualify for the élite, you simply have to have climbed it!

Valley Resort Gstatterboden, 580 m, in the Ennstal (station).
Base Haindlkar Hut, 1135 m, ÖAV, serviced, in the Haindlkar, 1½ hours from Gstatterboden.
Starting Point At about 1850 m at the North Face's sub-structure, reached from the Hut by the Lower Peternpfad, not turning left before the Rosskuppe's precipices but climbing straight up; 1½ hours from the Hut. Time required for the whole climb, 6–8 hours.
Descent Down the ridge to the Rosskuppe, over it to the Peternscharte, then down the unprotected Peternpfad to the Hut; 2½–3 hours from the summit of the Dachl.
First Ascent L. Scheiblehner and K. Gollmeyer, 9/11.6.1955.
Guides/Maps RR *Gesäusegebirge, Nördl. Kalkalpen* (AV series, German). (Holzhausen) *Gesäusegebirge* (German). FB 100M. Sh. 6 – Ennstaler Alpen.
Plate The famous North Face of the Dachl above the Haindlkar. To the right, the massive pillar, further to the right the Prusik Gully in the North Face of the Hochtor. Bottom left, the cone of slabs, from whose top the Diagonal Crack runs leftwards up to the Dachl's summit plateau.

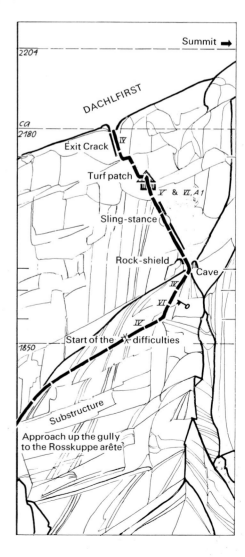

Hochschwab Group
Stangenwand – Nebengipfel (Subsidiary Summit)
South-East Face
2139 m

Grade VI−, A1/300 m

Here we offer one of the hardest climbs on the eastern rim of the Alps. It lies in the middle of the Hochschwab main chain, between the Trawiesalm and Rauchtalsattel, and the Bodenbauer Hotel is the base from which you start. This Secondary Summit of the somewhat loftier Stangenwand juts out from the southern rim of the great Hochschwab Range stark and smooth as the prow of a ship. The series of vertical dièdres to the left of the pillar look as daunting as the one hanging above them – sufficiently so as to remain untouched till 1938, when Raimund Schinko came from Graz, as great a master-cragsman of his time as were later Cassin, Niedermann, Werner, Buhl, Messner and the others – by whom I mean the last great climbers during the exploitation of Alpine glory.

Schinko's first attempt on that perpendicular wall got stuck after four rope lengths; bad weather having set in after he had climbed the first 50 metres in the starting-chimney; he tried an escape-route to the arête of the Pillar to his right and came down defeated. Three more attempts were equally unsuccessful. Schinko spoke despairingly of ten key-pitches and later confided to a friend: 'I came back each time, as worn out as if I had done a Civetta North-West Face and still stared up bewitched at that Medusa's countenance of a monstrous, repulsive wall. Finally he found the vital traverse to the left. At the fifth attempt on 25 June 1938, he and the two others took along with them a board which they nailed to the overhangs where they had been forced to turn back before. And so they achieved the first modern 'Bench-Bivouac', each man hanging from the face on three pitons, surviving an early-morning storm with thunder and lightning thrown in. Then they attacked the 30-metre problem. They used pitons galore, fixed a rope hand-rail, swung in the air; but they could not reach the little turfy patch – there were no cracks to take a piton. So: a second night's bivouac. Next day, wooden wedges, rope-stirrups and many pitons saw them up the 15-metre crack. They climbed the last over-hang in the chimney by lantern-light and reached the summit by midnight, half-starved and dehydrated.

Ten years later, the Viennese climbers Karl Lukan and Kozel improved the problematical left-hand traverse by a highly delicate abseil manoeuvre. And in 1941 E. Paulmichl and F. Duspiwa climbed the starkly overhanging, gigantic South-East Dièdre (hard to the right of the exact vertical centre of the photograph). People talked of VI+, A2 . . . That was then; now everything has grown easier with the proliferation of ironmongery. It was compared with the South-East Dièdre of the Fleischbank. That too was in the past. The latter remains the more difficult, because there is no possibility of making two of its VI pitches easier with pitons. Of course, they could apply bolts. But that would cause a revolution in the Kaisergebirge.

Valley Resorts St Ilgen, 731 m (bus from Thörl, 5·5 km from the Kapfenberg–Seewiesen road).
Base Alpen Hotel Bodenbauer, 877 m, at the head of the Ilgental, private, serviced; motorable to the house. On foot 1½ hours from St Ilgen.
Starting Point At about 1840 m at the foot of the wall, close to the left of the Pillar, which has a huge gully to its right, 40 m to the right of the summit fall-line a vertical series of chimney-slabs cuts up the middle of the face. Time from the hotel to the start, 1 hours. Average time for the whole climb (provided pitons are in place), 5–6 hours.
Descent Through the Rauchkar (1), rubble-track down from the summit then to the Trawiesalm and the hotel.
First Ascent R. Schinko, F. Sikorovsky and O. Pschenitsch-nik, 25/7.6.1938. Variant K. Lukan and L. Kozel 24/5.5.1947.
Guides/Maps RR *Hochschwab* (AV series, German). FB 100M. Sh. 4 – Hochschwab Mürztal.
Plate The Stangenwand's subsidiary South Face Summit, which juts out fiercely south-eastwards from the main summit (not visible in the picture). In the middle, the huge, partly overhanging, gigantic South-East Dièdre bordered on its left by the smooth slabs of the Pillar. At the left foot of the Pillar are the series of vertical cracks running upwards, and to the left above them the key-pitches, above which is the last gully, turning finally into a moss-grown chimney.

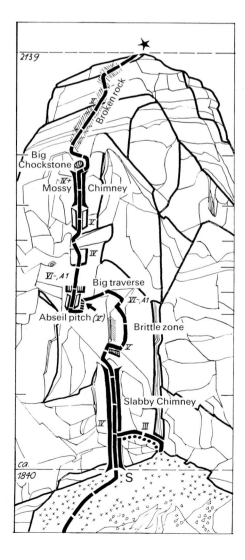

Hochschwab Group
Schartenspitze 1758 m
West Arête
Grade V, A0/250 m

To the south of the Voisthaler Hut and its Edelspitze, the western wall of the Mitteralpe, with the Winkelkogel Group at its centre-point, stands high above the broad floor of the Fölzalm. From that western wall the West Arête of the Schartenspitze juts out like a narrow wedge – the buttress of a 'foothill' not even 1800 metres high. Till thirty years ago this was a very unimportant sliver; today it is the favourite climbing-ground in the whole Hochschwab area and a kind of monument to modern climbing. Our route on the West Arête was climbed as long ago as 1932 and was classed as a fine, well-composed ridge-climb on exposed, particularly sound and reliable rock. All the belaying-pitons remain there, as usual. The direct start from the base has been done, but is not recommended. The grading usually given in guidebooks at V−, A1 for the key-pitch in the overhanging groove is probably a little high. Many recent climbers, on the other hand, assess the IV pitches as IV+. There is also the variant from the Köpfel to the left (on the left in the sketch and additionally marked with dots), which was made by K. Chibin and B. Hausegger in 1946, and carries a Grade V, A0 for surmounting a 10-metre groove with blunt wrinkles and a brittle overhang, followed by a short rope tension traverse down to the left, a crack, a cracked groove and a chimney already very prominent from below. To sum up, one can certainly say that, of a dozen respectable routes on the Schartenspitze, the one in our sketch and photograph is the most interesting.

This relatively small but famous mountain was an early victim of that genius from Graz, Raimund Schinko who, during the 1930s, rifled the Hochschwab of all its 'problems', using pitons even then. The North-West Pillar and North Dièdre of the Little Winkelkogel, our present West Arête of the Schartenspitze – till then held to be unclimbable – the North and South Faces into the bargain ... these were only part of the first ascents attempted, dared, and made by Schinko and his friend Bischofberger. He did this West Arête a second time with Heinrich Harrer. For the 'extreme' climber our Schinko-Bischofberger route is just a rewarding pleasure-excursion. Its little vexations are undoubtedly the overhanging groove (several pitons), with the overhang at its start and the ramp-like ledge finishing as a mere horizontal picture-rail, which can be seen clearly in our picture. We must admit that our photograph, of necessity taken from below, is somewhat misleading: the West Arête is in truth steeper and smoother than it looks on the opposite page.

Valley Resort Aflenz, 765 m (bus from Bruck/Mur or Kapfenberg).
Base The Fölzalm Huts (inns), 1472 m, private, serviced, on the Fölzalm; 3 hours from Aflenz, 1½ hours from the Schwabenbartl Inn, 804 m, in the Fölzgraben (motorable).
Starting Point At 1500 m on the north side of the Arête at the start of a broad, slightly downward-sloping band of slabs. 20 minutes from Fölzalm. Total time for the climb, 2½–3 hours.
Descent Down the ordinary route (II), first eastwards into the intervening saddle before the Little Winkelkogel (50 m, II−) then to the left down the North Face. Consult the guidebook, 1 hour from the summit.
First Ascent R. Schinko and A. Bischofberger, 10.9.1932.
Guides/Maps RR *Hochschwab* (AV series, German). FB 100M. Sh. 4 – Hochschwab Mürztal.
Plate The Schartenspitze shown as a prominent west buttress of the western precipices of the Winkelkogel above the Fölzalm, in close-up. Bottom right in the picture, the end of the ramp with the starting point. Top left, the deep notch before the Little Winkelkogel, from which the descent is made to the north. The descent route is easily identifiable.

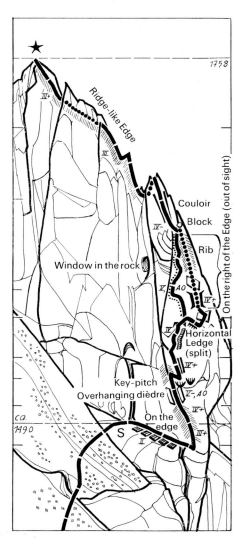

The Grading of Rock-Climbs

Gradings in Free climbing

I Easy.

Minimal difficulties. The simplest form of rock-climbing (but not easy walking-terrain). The hands are occasionally used for the preservation of balance and to further progress. Beginners should be roped. Progress facilitated by plentiful large foot- and hand-holds in well-broken rock-structures. Angle less steep and rock consequently well-fractured. Foot-sureness essential none the less.

II Moderately difficult.

Moderate difficulties. Hands essential for the preservation of balance and the furthering of progress. Genuine climbing on hand- and foot-holds (three-point balance). Practised climbers need not be roped, or can move together on a short rope. Less experienced climbers require belaying, especially on exposed or brittle pitches. If belaying for protection, the leader must belay himself positively.

III Fairly difficult.

Considerable difficulties. Hand- and foot-holds less frequent and smaller. Even practised climbers must belay themselves here, especially on exposed or brittle pitches. Here and there intermediate pitons on exposed passages in frequently-climbed routes. Vertical pitches with good holds demand a degree of application of strength. A safe knowledge of abseil technique necessary, since retreat and descent lines at times entail abseiling. This is the limit for 'occasional' climbers. Hammers, pitons, karabiners and rope-slings should always be carried. Perfect belaying of all concerned goes without saying. Simultaneous movement on the rope no longer advisable.

IV Very difficult.

Great difficulties. Climbing now becomes definitely stiffer. Only for experienced climbers in regular training. Sound technical skill essential. Longer exposed passages, requiring more intermediate belaying pitons. Stances occasionally exposed. Frequent exposed passages. Hammer, pitons, karabiners and rope slings indispensable. Such climbing on rock or on 'combined' ground demands an advanced degree of skill and endurance. On the descent, Grade IV passages are normally dealt with by abseiling.

V Exceptionally difficult.

Very great difficulties. Intermediate belaying pitons mandatory. Great strength and refined technique are demanded. Hand- and foot-holds very scarce and widely spaced. Almost always very exposed. Only for first-rate climbers with great stamina and experience. Complete knowledge of the use of all the usual belaying techniques (pitons, wedges, wooden or otherwise) all types of slings, etc, absolutely essential. Double-rope always handy. Long, high-Alpine routes, especially those involving 'combined' climbing, are of course serious undertakings, frequently involving passages of 'artificial' climbing, which are assessed separately according to the A-grading scale.

VI Extremely difficult.

Exceptional difficulties. Minute finger- and foot-holds demand unusual sense of balance and outstanding finger strength (intensive training on practice-ground essential). Continual great exposure, often allied to very small stances. Intermediate belaying at shorter intervals. Very exhausting and only recommended for exceptionally strong climbers with years of high-Alpine experience. Double rope essential. Normally combined with 'artificial' climbing falling in the A-grading scale, requiring increasing use of pitons, karabiners and étriers.

VI+ designates a pitch whose mastering entails a *near approach to the risk of a fall* even for the best rock-climbers in top form, in the most favourable conditions (dry rock), employing the utmost of his climbing capability (hand- and foot-holds, friction) and with the best of modern equipment (cut-out rubber soles). Usually confined to a few metres. Less frequently found on high mountain routes than on practice-grounds. A VI+ passage, by definition, is normally impossible in winter conditions without employing extra pitons to facilitate forward movement.

Gradings in Artificial climbing

Once regarded as an extension of Grade VI, today – thanks to the efforts of the UIAA – artificial climbing is regarded as a different form of rock-climbing and accordingly covered by different ratings. In artificial climbing, pitons, wedges, all types of rope-slings and other aids are used not only for belaying purposes but to further actual progress. This technique will, having regard to the length of time demanded by its application, only be employed where free-climbing, taking into account the best chances of survival, is impossible. By 'best chances of survival' we understand necessary precautions such as the avoidance of too much loss of time in searching for unaided progress, of the risk of too great or energetic a fall, and the need for rapid progress where a withdrawal is too risky or impossible.

The rating of artificial climbing is achieved by the use of the letter A (artificial) followed by the arabic numerals 0 to 4. This five-tier scale permits the assessment of artificial climbing from its simplest form (Ao) to its hardest (A4).

A short exposition of the separate grades is not usual or appropriate as in the case of free-climbing.

The following assessment of artificial climbing, in accordance with UIAA practice, does *not* distinguish between the use of artificial aids (pitons, etc) as means of progress and pure free-climbing while employing them.

A1

Pitons and other technical aids relatively easy to apply, and progress demands little strength, endurance or courage. The use of one étrier per member of the rope, frequently applied, is sufficient. A second is not mandatory.

A2–4

Greater difficulty in lodging pitons and applying other aids (solid rock, closed cracks, brittle and highly splintered rock) and/or greater bodily exertions in mastering the pitch (overhang, roof, greater distance between pitons) and/or greater exposure, demanding increasingly great capability on the climber's part. Two étriers essential.

On routes from Grade V upwards, free and artificial climbing interchange frequently. *Such climbs attract a dual rating of difficulties,* one set for the pitches climbable free and one for those only possible by artificial means. In such cases, in UIAA practice, the main consideration is which is to take first place, the free or the artificial. Two examples are appended:

Fleischbank (Wilder Kaiser) East Face, Schmuck chimney
Grading VI, A1: which indicates mainly free-climbing, greatest difficulties VI, partly (but less than half the climb) artificial in the A1 rating category.

Fleischbank (Wilder Kaiser) East Face, Scheffler–Siegert Route
Grading A2, VI: which indicates, largely artificial climbing in the A1 and 2 category, partly (but less than half the climb) free-climbing, the most difficult pitches being VI.

A0

The simplest form of artificial climbing. Pitons and other intermediate security aids (all types of wedges and rope-slings) have to be used on mainly free-climbing routes only as hand- and foot-holds. Étriers are nonetheless not requisite. However, when a climber uses a piton to lift himself, he is at that point abandoning free-climbing and moving into the artificial grade A0, even if he does not make use of étriers. Rope-traverses, rope-tension traverses and individual tension traverses fall within the A0 rating.

For this logically arranged and easily intelligible system of gradings of the difficulty of rock-climbs I am indebted to my mountaineering friend Pit Schubert – and his near classic book, *Moderne Felstechnik*. I have only used extracts from that brilliant store of Alpine knowledge. That book of instruction (published by the Bergverlag Rudolf Rother, Munich) should be read in its entirety – and with the same total commitment as if it were a love-story.

Explanation of Symbols, in accordance with UIAA usage

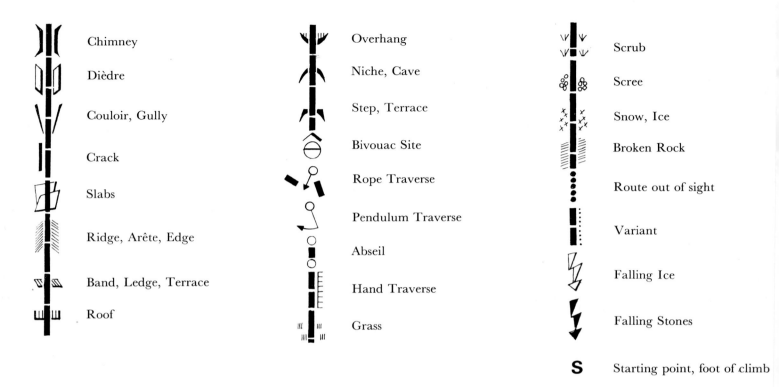

Chimney	Overhang
Dièdre	Niche, Cave
Couloir, Gully	Step, Terrace
Crack	Bivouac Site
Slabs	Rope Traverse
Ridge, Arête, Edge	Pendulum Traverse
Band, Ledge, Terrace	Abseil
Roof	Hand Traverse
	Grass

Scrub

Scree

Snow, Ice

Broken Rock

Route out of sight

Variant

Falling Ice

Falling Stones

S   Starting point, foot of climb

Abbreviations

— international geographical house codes for guidebook and map publishers and other symbols

AC	Alpine Club, London (produced by WCP)
AHD	Arthaud, Grenoble
ATP	Alpina Technica Productions, Reading
AV	Austro-German Alpine Clubs, Innsbruck and Munich
CAI	Italian Alpine Club, Milan
FB	Freytag-Berndt, Vienna
FB St G	Fehr'sche Buchhandlung, St Gallen
GF	Grosser Führer series of RR
IGM	Italian Military Map, Florence
IGN	French Ordnance Map, Paris

KF	Kümmerly & Frey, Bern
KK	Kompasskarten (Fleischmann), Innsbruck
LK	Swiss Federal Map, Wabern
M.	map scale, e.g. 25M. = 1/25,000. 50M. = 50,000, etc.
PZS	Slovene Mountain Association, Ljubljana
RR	Rudolf Rother, Munich
SAC	Swiss Alpine Club, Wallisellen
Sh.	map sheet number/title
T	tourist map series
TCI	Italian Touring Club, Milan
WCP	West Col Productions, Reading

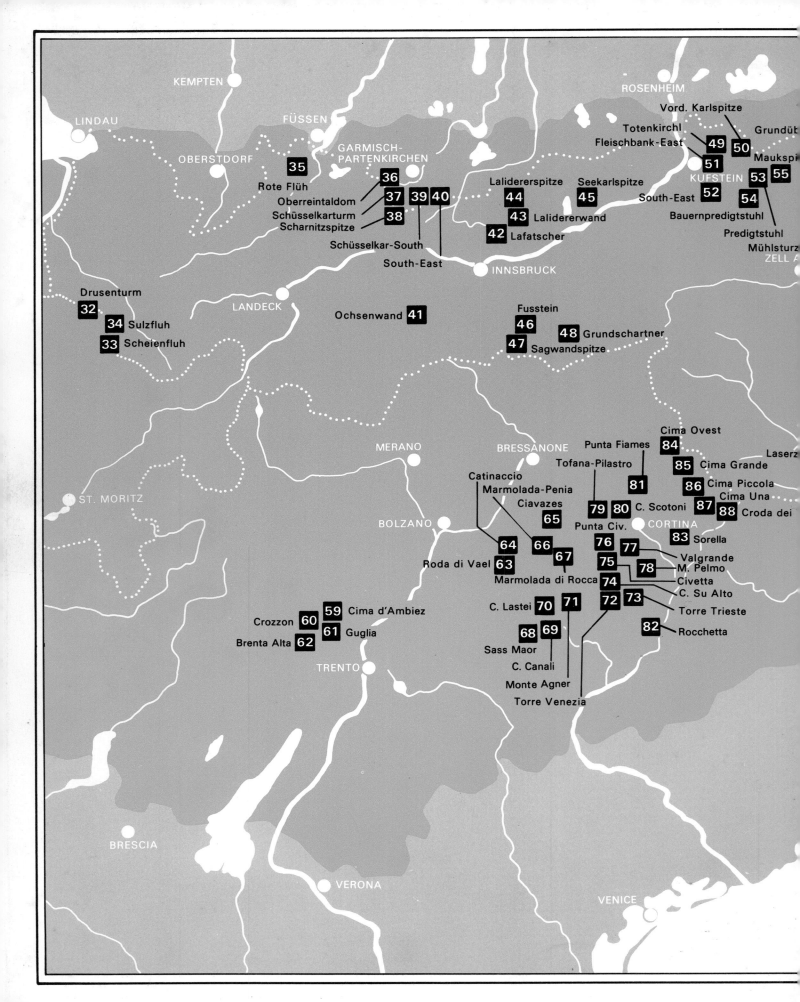